DATE DUE			
Dec 1 70			
May 24 '71			
Dec 7 '71			
Mar 8 '72			
Feb 24 '76			
Jan 28 '77			
Apr 22 77			
May 16 '77 P			
Dec 13 7 7 H			
Apr 15 '83			

GAYLORD M-2   PRINTED IN U.S.A.

Principles of Tragedy

Principles of Tragedy

*A Rational Examination of the Tragic Concept
in Life and Literature*

by

GEOFFREY BRERETON

UNIVERSITY OF MIAMI PRESS

Coral Gables, Florida

Second Printing, 1969

809. 916

B 75p

68685

February, 1970

Contents

Foreword

This book originated in a search for a definition either of tragedy or of the main tragic elements which would hold good on various planes and over a wide range of literature and drama. It seemed that if the term 'tragic' had any validity at all when used by a modern commentator it ought to include factors common at least to Sophocles, Shakespeare, Racine, and probably Ibsen and others, irrespective of the difference in their historical and ethical backgrounds. The simple conviction that this should be so runs into truly formidable objections, but the author eventually reached the conclusion that they are not insurmountable providing one confines oneself to essentials.

The first results of an inquiry of this kind are a number of negations. It quickly became apparent that the concept of tragedy has been over-extended by some commentators to include elements which do not belong to it necessarily or exclusively. If empirical and local, they fail when transposed to a different context. If 'universal', they can embrace too much and the concept becomes nebulous. An outstanding example, which can be attached to either category according to the angle of approach, is the nineteenth-century persuasion of the existence of a 'tragic' duality in human nature. Other interpretations appear on examination to be equally wide of the mark, not on the grounds of their general validity as explanations of the human condition, which the present writer claims no competence to assess, but on the narrower issue of their relevance to tragedy.

The wider issues cannot of course be ignored. Any general investigation of the nature of tragedy inevitably broaches questions belonging to theology or philosophy, or even (particularly when considering the *function* of tragedy) to sociology and psychology. Indeed the potential field of exploration is so wide that no one specialist could hope to cover it, while a symposium of specialists—if past experience is any guide—would fail to arrive at any agreed conclusions at all. It therefore seemed necessary, given the primary objective of progressing at least some way towards a clear definition, to conduct this inquiry along deliberately restricted lines. This involved, among other things, the deducing of first principles from individual works of literature, a labour which might well seem redundant or repetitive to the specialist in certain disciplines, but which proved in practice to be indispensable. It seemed unavoidable, for example, to re-examine the question of Pascal's tragic awareness in the writings of Pascal himself, even though much that emerges is already familiar to the *Pascalisant* and, on general lines, to the theologian, who can, no doubt, broadly identify Pascal's dominant assumptions with certain categories of Christian dogma. This, however, would not exhaust the subject for our purposes, which require a scrutiny of the work in the particular context of tragedy.

In much the same way, the problem of the Romantic dichotomy has been studied here in imaginative writers beginning with Blake, although it seems quite possible that an approach through the history of philosophy, with Hegel as a strongly indicated starting-point, would also yield fruitful results.

If the other approach has been adopted it is because the author is a literary historian and critic whose main interests lie in the ideological analysis of literature. This no doubt subjective reason may find a justification in the fact that the principal object of the inquiry *is* imaginative literature, especially drama, whose tragic quality or content is usually at the heart of any debate. In return, works of literature provide in general better illustrations of a contemporary ideology than the philosophically meditated work. They possess a greater immediacy, their ethical assumptions are often more significant because less consciously elaborated, and they respond rather more easily to a comparative analysis, whose results can of course be disputed but whose workings can be clearly shown. The main exploration in this book therefore bears on them. After a consideration of some of the major theories of tragedy, they are used as witnesses to attest the viability or otherwise of those theories. In writing as a literary critic, the author must accept the limitations as well as the advantages of such an approach. Not the least of them is the obligation to reach and state at least some firm conclusions while remaining aware that the whole history of criticism points to their not proving unassailable.

This book was begun several years ago, though for various reasons it was completed only recently. It was first contemplated in 1956, when the author had occasion to consider three newly published books, initially for reviewing purposes. These were Lucien Goldmann's *Le Dieu Caché*,[1] T. R. Henn's *The Harvest of Tragedy*, and H. D. F. Kitto's *Form and Meaning in Drama*. At about the same date the author was beginning a study on French classical drama, which brought the problem of finding a definition of tragedy more sharply into focus. Other activities, including the translating and editing of plays, university teaching, and papers for various societies, went on concurrently. While they delayed the appearance of this book they also provided new material for it, since several of them called for critical assessments involving the tragic concept. This lengthy gestation may therefore have served to give extra body to a work originally conceived as predominantly theoretical.

Meanwhile the seemingly inexhaustible debate on tragedy was continued in several studies, among them (in England) George Steiner's *Death of Tragedy* and Raymond William's *Modern Tragedy*—the second when this book was almost ready for the press. Numerous other studies, most of them earlier, might be listed. Many are not specifically concerned with tragedy, but contain criticism or comments on the various original works considered in the following chapters. Chiefly because of the vastness of the field and, in some cases, the tenuous relationship (as it would appear to the reader) of certain partial studies to the main subject, it was felt that a bibliography would be neither practicable nor particularly useful and it has therefore been dispensed with. Any work which is definitely referred to or discussed is of course mentioned in a footnote and appears again in the Index.

My debts to many writers and to others who in conversation and other ways have suggested ideas and counter-ideas to me are so various that it becomes impossible to specify them. I can, however, make one concrete interim acknowledgement: to the Trustees of the Leverhulme Research Awards who some time ago awarded me a fellowship for work on a kindred project which is not yet complete. This sprang out of that. I am equally grateful for their generosity and their tact in never pressing for immediate results.

G. B.

September 1967

---

[1] Published in England as *The Hidden God*, trans. P. Thody (Routledge & Kegan Paul, 1964).

I

Tragedy in Theory

1

The Notion of Tragedy

It would be a tragedy if, because of misunderstanding of the role of British investment overseas due partially to lack of information, Government policy resulted in a gradual but cumulative deterioration in the effective earning power of direct British investment abroad.
Lord Hampden, Chairman of Lazard Brothers & Company, Ltd, in letter to *The Times*, 17 March 1965

1

The prestige of tragedy as an intellectual and critical conception stands today in almost inverse ratio to its prestige on the stage. The commentaries published on the subject during the past fifty years have very easily outnumbered not merely new plays overtly entitled tragedies (if there have been any) but all new plays, however described, in which tragic elements as defined by any theory could be said to predominate. The twentieth century respects tragedy but does not produce it. If the analysis of it were presented as purely historical, the situation would be simple. This would be exegesis of a dead or disused genre of which we have lost the practice. Most writers on tragedy claim, however, with persuasive reasons, that tragedy expresses permanently valid truths about the human condition. They link it with psychology, with religion, or with social ideology, or with all three at once. They endow it with symbolic and moral meanings which far transcend the apparent limits of any one tragic drama or body of drama. Their mere existence points to at least one conclusion—that the 'tragic' is an element which persists and is recognisable independently of the dramatic works which are held to contain it.

3

Is there anything remarkable about this? Other words which originally described various kinds of literature and art, and nothing else, have outgrown their contexts and acquired wider and looser meanings. Adjectives such as 'epic', 'romantic', 'lyrical', 'poetic' and, of course, 'comic' and 'dramatic' itself are constantly used with no mental evocation of the types of artistic expression from which they derive. Can it be said that tragedy/tragic is a special case?

It appears to be so on two different grounds, both empirical. First, its prestige and its attraction for commentators not primarily interested in stage tragedy already point to the exceptional. Neither the epic, romance, or comedy are the subjects of far-reaching inquiries into their conceptual basis such as tragedy has inspired—although the psychological and sociological potentialities of such inquiries would be considerable. Is there not, for example, a fundamental divergence between societies and individuals which possess a 'comic sense' and those which do not? Even 'poetry'—a more general term than most of the others—which once provided a broader and seemingly more promising field than tragedy for explorations of the human mind is turned over to the professional and the specialist. While studies closely related to the work of particular poets and poetic movements are innumerable, nothing of much importance has been written on a general philosophy of poetry for some time. An exception might be made of the theoretical pronouncements of the surrealists, but apart from the fact that these concerned not only poetry but all art, they were rarely as wide-ranging as they appeared. Their chief interest was for artists, including poets, wrestling with problems of expression, i.e., how to render a new conception of human nature. Such an effort, if taken far enough, is more likely to produce an *ars poetica* than a philosophical elaboration.

In short, one could still today entitle a book *The Tragic Sense of Life* (as Unamuno did in 1913) and be expected to have something pertinent and important to say in it. But for 'tragic' substitute either 'epic', 'romantic', or 'comic', and the book becomes scarcely conceivable as a serious study. Neither is 'The Poetic Sense of Life', a likely title, in spite of the obvious richness of the material.

A second distinction between 'tragic' and the other generic adjectives is arrived at from a different angle. Ignoring the 'exact' meanings of these words and considering only their meanings in general usage, one is left with a list like this:

Dramatic: Startling; unexpected; exciting.
Epic: Vast and impressive; heroic.
Romantic: Sentimental; unphysical; impractical; non-functional;
quaint and attractive.
Comic: Laughable; grotesque.

These alternatives cover all the principal uses and abuses of the original words and one or other could normally be substituted for them with no sense of inappropriateness. It is very much harder to find substitutes for 'tragic'. Part of its meaning may sometimes be covered by 'distressing' or 'disastrous', but nine times out of ten these do not express all that the speaker intends. He will be reluctant to paraphrase what he does intend and if pressed will repeat 'tragedy' or 'tragic', thus showing that these belong to a small and select group of words which are 'felt' more easily than they are defined. When an abstract word is as irreplaceable as this in ordinary usage it is a sign that it is very much alive. Beneath it one would expect to find some deep-rooted concept which it would be mistaken to call vague. The fact that it cannot readily be expressed in different terms is a proof less of vagueness than of indispensability.

This persistence of an *idea* of tragedy in popular usage parallels on a different plane the mystique of tragedy in writings which can broadly be called philosophical, i.e., they have no specific connection with tragic drama and do not always imply a knowledge of it. Both postulate something called 'tragedy' which occurs in life, or the human reaction to life, without reference to its expression in artistic form. Both credit it with considerable importance.

Whether the tragic in 'life' is the same as the tragic in drama is a question which may be left in suspense provisionally. It would be logically satisfying to discover that the two are identical, to find that this is an instance of nature and art marching hand in hand shod with the same basic postulates. But it would be hazardous to make the assumption *a priori*. If we are to examine the significance of 'tragedy' in common acceptance, it will be better to ignore dramatic tragedy, together with the theories associated with it, until a later stage in the inquiry. All we can assume is the existence of a living concept which is potentially definable in its own field. The only guide to an understanding of it is current usage. No doubt this may seem a somewhat irresponsible guide, whose directions are sometimes debatable and need not always be followed literally. But such as they are, they are

5

all we have. If tragedy means anything outside the history of drama, this is where the meaning appears: in the usage of people of not less than average education and discrimination[1] but innocent, as far as possible, of any knowledge of philosophical or critical theory and free from the influence of previous definitions.

2

A 'tragedy' in ordinary usage always implies disaster, usually resulting in death. When death occurs in the natural course of things and cannot fairly be called disastrous it is hardly a 'tragedy'. To qualify as one it must take place in unexpected and striking cir cumstances. It must, at the least, be in some way remarkable.

Death is not an essential condition. One speaks of 'the tragic history of this family' (implying perhaps insanity or an inherited disease), of 'a tragic end to their hopes' (not invariably by death), of 'tragic frustration' (a waste of living rather than an end of life), of 'a tragic discovery' (normally of a dead body, but the phrase is also acceptable to qualify a betrayal, a sudden realisation of misfortune, or the revelation of an unsuspected weakness). And one can say that a person still alive has been 'tragically maimed'.

But these are still cases of disaster, whether or not they involve the death of the participants. The disaster is envisaged as final so far as those particular people or events are concerned. That is, no recovery is contemplated, there is no prospect of a 'happy ending'. The difference between a 'tragedy' which involves death and one which does not is merely a difference of emphasis. In the former, the finality of the disaster—the impossibility of recovery—is more obvious. It may well be, also, that the stress lies more strongly on the physical than the moral effects.

It is arguable that the word 'disaster' itself contains the idea of finality. On occasion it may do so, but not invariably. A disaster brings ruin and misery in various forms, but they need not be total. One speaks of 'the survivors of a disaster', of a group or an individual struck by 'a series of disasters', of a community 'recovering from a disaster', such as a cyclone or flood. One could hardly substitute 'tragedy' for 'disaster' in any of these phrases. This points to the

[1] This will exclude utterances of the blurb or public relations type in which the adjectives perform the function of deliberately unspecific superlatives. 'Tragic' has, however, suffered less from this kind of debasement by inflation than such words as *epic, dramatic, fabulous, and mythical*.

conclusion that a 'disaster' can sometimes be temporary or partial, while a 'tragedy' cannot.

There are minor exceptions even to this. 'Tragedy', like other words, is used metaphorically or with an exaggeration which, if it cannot properly be called humorous, is not wholly serious either. Sports-writers are the most fertile exponents of this type of the extension of language. The 'tragedy of a missed goal/catch/putt' is the kind of phrase which comes easily to the pen and is accepted easily by the reader. It will probably imply that in one particular contest the effect was calamitous. The chance of winning the game was lost without reprieve. A sporting tragedy might, indeed, go deeper if it spelt the end of a player's career on which he had set all his hopes and efforts. One could then comment that he was 'finished' as a first-class player and the status of his tragedy would depend upon the status which one attached to pre-eminence in sport. There is no theoretical reason why such a case should be in a different moral category from that of the artist, the soldier, or the statesman whose career was 'tragically cut short' by some cause other than death. On the whole, however, the missed shot or catch which spells defeat in one match cannot be analysed as far forward as this. It seems a tragedy to the journalist at the moment when it occurs, and is so described in the report made immediately afterwards and intended for reading the next morning at latest. If anyone ever re-reads it after a lapse of time, his probable comment will be, not that the player or the team 'recovered from the tragedy', but that 'it was not such a tragedy after all', i.e., that the word was too weighty for the event.

In another small class of phrases, the 'tragedies' may not, on re-flection, represent an irreparable state of affairs, yet at the point of time at which the word is used it does appear that a total breakdown has occurred. Such are: 'The tragedy of broken homes', 'the tragedy of a misspent youth' (a somewhat dated phrase today), 'a tragic waste of talent/effort', etc. It is a fair inference that the user of such phrases is not looking beyond the disastrous results of the broken home or the dissipated youth as they lie immediately before him. Like the sports-writer, he does not contemplate the recovery or the reform which, on a long-term view, would be a material possibility. At the time of utterance the notion of finality forms part of the notion of the tragic.

The same reasoning hardly applies to such phrases as 'the tragic plight of the refugees'. One can, in fact, without sounding non-sensical, say: 'Surely something can be done to *relieve* the tragic plight of the refugees.' Yet 'tragic' is the most fitting word in this context. One would not willingly replace it by 'miserable', 'terrible', or 'desperate', the other most usual adjectives to couple with 'plight'. It would seem that this is because the last two are too strong or too crude—they suggest over-directly that the refugees are nearing the ultimate in suffering or despair—and because the first, 'miserable', has a depreciatory flavour. 'Tragic' has the advantage of conferring a certain nobility upon whatever it qualifies and by the same process it removes us a step or two from the contemplation of harsh physical reality. It is used here as a status-word. One does not look down on people described as 'tragic'. This important point will be returned to later, but meanwhile it emerges that 'tragic' is a 'nobler' alternative to 'miserable' or 'wretched' and can be used in that sense with no necessary implication of finality. Sometimes it does little more than describe an appearance. 'She looked utterly tragic' is more impressive than 'utterly miserable'. 'A tragic figure' (e.g., a close relative at a funeral) is a phrase for which 'a sad figure' would seem an inadequate substitute. One uses it without always meaning that something which could properly be called a tragedy has really occurred, but merely as a descriptive epithet into which there enters a degree of respect.[2] These uses of the word stem plausibly from reminiscences of tragic drama—the image of some majestically woeful personage—or even from a vague mental picture of the tragic mask with its features fixed in stylised grief, in which case 'art' may be reacting upon 'life'.

The descriptive and ennobling function of 'tragic' must, in short, be admitted as an exception to what has already been said. It does not preclude an ultimate recovery. But apart from this usage, it is generally true that 'tragic' contains the notion of a disaster which cannot be remedied. This can reasonably be taken as a starting-point.

[2] E.g., from an account of Churchill's funeral by Alan Moorehead, a skilled and experienced writer: 'And now as the coffin advances, there is a moment of utter tragedy: Lady Churchill standing there with her son Randolph, and it is marvellous that she can go through with this . . .' *Sunday Times Colour Magazine*, 7 February 1965.

3

Not every final disaster is necessarily tragic. There are two sets of circumstances, almost directly opposed to each other, in which it is not. In the first, disaster is the direct result of deliberate action by an enemy, or is clearly seen from the beginning to be inevitable. If a powerful force defeats a considerably weaker one, or a battleship sinks a light cruiser in a classic naval engagement, the event in itself can hardly be described as tragic. The extent of destruction, suffering, and death makes no difference. One can test this by imagining the kind of comment which such occurrences most naturally call forth. To say: 'The odds were hopeless, but they sold their lives dearly. *It was tragic*', hardly rings true. Neither does: 'The odds were hopeless and they never made a fight of it. *It was tragic.*' In the first case the normal response to the situation would be: 'It was heroic', in the second, 'pitiful'.

The other kind of non-tragic disaster arises from circumstances which appear entirely fortuitous. This is the 'pure accident' or the 'natural calamity' which could not have been foreseen or prevented. Such events are admittedly rare, since the urge to discover a preventible cause and from there to allocate responsibility are strong in the human mind. But some deaths by accident and some disasters caused by factors such as storms and earthquakes evoke the familiar comment that 'it was just one of those things', to which it would seem incongruous to add: 'It was a tragedy.' The first phrase is a shrugging-off one, implying a refusal to look for a responsible cause. It denies by implication that any person or factor could have made things turn out differently from the way they did. In legal terms, the disaster was 'an act of God'. This phrase translates the attitude of lawyers when no one within the jurisdiction of the court can be held to blame. In civilised societies, God is not answerable in law, though primitive tribes have been known to punish their gods when things went wrong. Civilised law, however, recognises that the ways of God are inscrutable, at least by the judiciary. It is noteworthy that tragic drama, and perhaps the very notion of the tragic, excludes any such automatic recognition.

So the notion of tragedy attaches neither to a foreseen result due to a deliberate act, nor to the effects of pure chance; neither to the clearly expected nor to the totally unexpected. These two apparently incompatible types of disaster have common qualities. Both are

9

recognised, after they have occurred, as 'natural'. There is also a factor which they both exclude, the factor of failure. When the weak are defeated by the admittedly stronger, there may well be misery and destruction, but one cannot properly speak of a failure. To remark in such circumstances that the weak 'failed to win' is a form of words, possibly uttered in grim humour. It is in the same category as the comment that a stone 'failed to float'. Equally, if there is a seismic disturbance beneath the earth's crust and buildings collapse according to the law of gravity, there is no question of a true failure so long as this 'natural' explanation of the disaster is accepted. 'Only a miracle' would have preserved the buildings intact, caused the stone to float, or enabled the weak to triumph. Ruling out miracles, it is impossible to say in any of these cases that something has gone wrong which might have been expected to go right.[3]

But whenever an idea of failure can be introduced into these and comparable events, there is also scope for a tragic element. If the weaker army had had a chance of victory or even of escape, its 'failure' to make good that chance might well be called tragic. This would be even more true of the stronger side, if it was beaten when it appeared to have victory in its grasp.[4] In that case the failure would be more conspicuous. Something which had been confidently expected to go right would have gone very seriously wrong.

In the same way the natural disaster easily becomes tragic if it was believed at any point of time to have been avoidable. A community is wiped out by floods in spite of the dams which it has built to protect itself. The tragedy appears greater in proportion to the efforts and hopes which have gone into the building of the dams. It can therefore be said to be inversely proportionate to the margin of failure, which is not the same thing as the extent of the disaster. The second is

[3] Belief in the miraculous is belief in the possibility of supernatural intervention to influence the 'natural' course of things. People who held this belief strongly might see an earthquake as a tragedy if they felt that there had been a 'failure' of the supernatural to prevent it. It is, however, much more likely that they would interpret the calamity as a retribution and would seek explanations along those lines. The usual attitude to a miracle is that it is entirely gratuitous; it is the 'act of God' mentioned above. Its occurrence or non-occurrence is thus analogous to the incidence of 'pure chance'.

[4] Since 'tragic' is both a status word and a 'good' word, its use will be partly dependent on the sympathies of the user. He is more likely to call a defeat 'tragic' if he identifies himself with the losing side, whichever that is. This particular subjective factor is not taken into account in the above example, but is returned to below (pp. 18–19).

expressed by such phrases as 'more costly', 'more destructive', even
'more terrible'. The first is measured by the narrowness of the distance separating disaster from success, so ultimately by the height
of the fall. The fall may involve only a few individuals—in extreme
cases, only one—but this does not make it 'less tragic'. Tragedy is
qualitative, while disaster tends to be quantitative.

The failures associated with tragedy are of various kinds. They
range from some easily definable human mistake or weakness,
through more general miscalculations (as misdirected ambition,
love, attitude towards life), to a failure of the 'laws of probability'.
It will not always be possible to decide exactly where the failure lies,
but the feeling that there has been one somewhere is always present.

Macbeth

4

Can a 'tragedy' then be defined as a final disaster arising from an
unforeseen failure?

It will be recalled that the completely foreseen is non-tragic and
that its opposite, the 'pure accident', is equally non-tragic because,
though totally unforeseen, it excludes 'failure'. It would seem that
the notion of tragedy involves a combination of the two elements,
failure and unforeseeability. To the second of these is linked the
notion of probability, since what is clearly foreseen ranks as 'highly
probable', vaguely foreseen as 'less probable', and hardly foreseen
as 'improbable'. Three examples may be put forward to test and
illustrate these assumptions:

(*a*) An unskilled climber is killed on an ascent which is known to be
too difficult for him.

(*b*) A highly skilled climber is killed on an exceptionally difficult
ascent.

(*c*) A highly skilled climber is killed on an easy ascent.

Simply on the terms quoted, example (*a*) falls into the category of
the clearly foreseen or the highly probable. The climber's action is
a weak bid against formidable odds which 'naturally' meets with
disaster. It is perhaps sad but not tragic unless there are additional
features. Say that the unskilled climber has a family dependent upon
him, that his wife has tried to dissuade him from the attempt, and
so on. Then there might be something which could be called a
'failure' on the wife's part, or perhaps more generally in their whole
marital relationship, or more generally still in the feeling that it

was a 'wrong arrangement' for innocent people to be dependent on an irresponsible husband. But the introduction of such factors alters the whole case. The incidence of tragedy is now upon the family— 'It was a tragedy *for them*'—and it is the wife who becomes the principal tragic figure. The climber's death, considered in itself, is no more tragic *for him* than before.

Accepting this shift of emphasis, can it now be said that the disaster was in any degree 'unforeseen'? A detached observer, with a knowledge of the family, might remark after the event: 'I knew he was sure to kill himself one day.' But would he have said this before the event and—more important—would the climber's family? We may suppose that they lived in an atmosphere of general apprehension. Their fear was that disaster might overtake them any day. But they did not know which day, neither did they know what form the disaster might take. One supposes that the wife did not accept its inevitability, since she struggled to avert it. She may have hoped that when it occurred it would be a relatively minor disaster, from which recovery would be possible. All these uncertainties introduce an element of the unforeseen, a middle note between the highly probable and the highly improbable, which removes the case from the category of the stone which is sure to sink. The wife's situation can be described retrospectively as hopeless, but until the fatal accident occurred it was not seen to be so. Her case, therefore, which we spontaneously feel to be 'tragic', fulfils the conditions of failure and of a sufficient degree of unpredictibility. But the husband's, considered in isolation, fulfils neither. To find tragedy in this example, it is necessary (in terms of drama) to introduce new characters and create a new tragic hero.

In example (*b*) it must be supposed that, although the risk of failure was known to be considerable, the skilled climber had some hope of success. Disaster cannot be said to have been quite unforeseen but neither was it foreseen clearly. Like the wife's dilemma in (*a*), it falls acceptably into a middle realm of uncertainty. It was also a failure: the climber failed to make good an attempt which had, say, a fifty-fifty chance of success. In these circumstances his death ought to be 'tragic'. Yet one hesitates before using the word unequivocally. One feels that there may be factors which would modify it and one wishes to know more about them.

If we point up the case a little by assuming that the climb was one of unique difficulty, presenting a supreme challenge which the climber accepted with a clear knowledge of the risks, it would seem inappropriate to speak of 'a tragic failure'. An atmosphere of exaltation surrounds the attempt and spills over on to its result, so that the final impression might well be that this was not a failure at all but a moral victory. Once the notion of failure/defeat is eliminated, or at least overshadowed by the notion of success/victory, the protagonist ceases to be a tragic figure and earns the still higher status-word 'heroic'. So long then as the climber's death can be represented as no more than a *physical* failure, outweighed by a moral triumph, it does not easily qualify as tragic.

Normally, the skilled climber's death in (*b*) is felt to rise above tragedy, whereas the unskilled climber's falls below it. From another angle, relevant to both life and drama, climber B's act is heroic, climber A's act is foolish and contains potentially comic elements. It could be developed in a comic direction by disregarding the climber's family and emphasising the impossible nature of the undertaking and the climber's irrational obstinacy in attempting it. As long as it led to his death it would certainly be a 'cruel' comedy, but the category into which it fell would still be comic rather than tragic.

There remains (*c*), in which an experienced climber is killed on an easy climb. This is the plainest case of the three and is at once accepted as tragic. It contains a failure which is immediately apparent and which was not foreseen, while at the same time it cannot be classed as totally unforeseeable, like a 'pure accident'. One is always ready in such circumstances to admit a certain risk, however minimal, and the possibility of a disaster, however remote. This disaster is final and complete, with no uplifting features, no element of heroism. The only doubt about it would concern the circumstances. If these were so trivial, i.e., if the ascent was so easy that the merest novice should have succeeded, the status factor comes into play. The whole event seems in danger of being downclassed to the level of example (*a*), with the same scope for the intrusion of the comic. The difference is that the triviality of the event would normally be compensated by the standing of the climber—in dramatic terms, the 'hero'. His status is such that he will not be suspected of foolishly or wantonly courting disaster. This consideration (which is ultimately one of 'character') serves to retain the occurrence in the tragic field. In fact, the more trivial the cause of failure (provided it is not something completely ridiculous), the more 'tragic' this death will appear. All the skill,

13

knowledge and courage possessed by the climber have been 'thrown away' on an unworthy object.

The predominant impression is one of waste, as it was not in the other two cases. This notion of waste is frequent in the tragedies of 'life'. It is not so ubiquitous as to be a characteristic and it is, of course, only a consequence or a variation of the notion of failure. (Waste is a failure to make proper use of something.) Nevertheless, it is usually conspicuous in those cases which are most readily called tragic.

The second impression, hardly less strong, is that such disasters are 'ironical'. When an expert who has successfully carried out many hazardous ascents is killed on some simple climb, the word comes to mind almost unbidden. What is the force of this notion of irony?

5

Irony is often held to be an essential component of the tragic. As will be seen later, it is bound up with the concept of probability and also with the concept of destiny. It supposes, in its basic form, that a course of action is undertaken which has opposite consequences to those intended. In still more general terms, success is expected but disaster results. This will apply fully to the experienced climber just discussed, and one can add that the greater his confidence in success, the more ironical his failure will appear. But it will be noticed that the contrary case lends itself to irony just as well. If the unskilled and foolish climber succeeded in making the climb when failure was confidently expected, that would also be ironical. But it would not be tragic. The reversal of the conditions (disaster expected—success results) puts it instead in the comic field.

Irony may thus belong to either tragedy or comedy, without losing its essential quality. It is potentially present whenever there is a change of fortune from either good to bad or from bad to good, so long as it comes as a surprise. The surprise must, however, be relevant to the situation. Just any unexpected outcome, taken from an indefinite number of possibilities, will not do. To be charged with irony, it has to be the particular outcome which most pointedly belies expectation—a directly opposed alternative to the result envisaged.

All this is enough to awaken doubts. The fact that irony is not exclusively tragic need not rule it out, for neither is disaster or

14

clouded foresight. But the conditions in which it operates appear somewhat arbitrary. Is there not an air of neatness and even contrivance about them?

Irony is a favourite standby of the tragic dramatist because of the effectiveness with which it underlines the change of fortune. If a character merely muddles his way to disaster, the situation and its consequences do not necessarily cease to be tragic, but on the stage, where a coherent plot has to be developed in a limited time, there is an inevitable tendency towards sharper definition. The impact is stronger if a character can be shown moving towards disaster by his own acts, which at the same time contribute to the action of the play. If, again, he expresses his misplaced confidence in words, that also helps to define the developing situation. This legitimate and widespread use of irony in drama may well increase our awareness of irony in 'life', causing us to see it in places where we would not otherwise have looked for it. The search for it may easily become an obsession, comparable to the obsessional search for moral meanings corresponding to some preconceived pattern, which is also intensified by the influence of fiction. But it remains manifestly untrue, as a general proposition, that a perception of the tragic is dependent on a perception of the ironic. The second is a sophisticated concept demanding reflection of a more cultivated kind than a mere recognition of the tragic requires. The tragic exists whenever one can say: 'Once they were happy. Then something went wrong. Now they are (irreversibly) miserable.' The middle term ('Something went wrong') is realised or felt, but need not be developed. Irony, however, focuses the attention upon it.

It requires, as we have said, that expectation should be belied in a manner which gives point to the unexpected, with the consequent implication that if the signs had been read differently the outcome might have been foreseen. The tragic failure would have been realised at an earlier stage if 'we', as either protagonists or spectators, had not had our attention diverted elsewhere. We were not in a state of general uncertainty but were misled into following a particular false trail. When it is found, too late, to be false, the protagonist feels trapped and the spectators experience a shock of sophisticated surprise.

In drama, there is no mystery in this. The explanation is obvious and can be stated plainly without recourse to transcendental considerations. It is the dramatist who lays the false trail, his invented characters who fall into the trap, and the audience that relishes the irony of the operation.

When, however, this fictitious or artistic process is transposed to 'life'—of which, to be credible, it must to some extent be a mirror—the tragic characters and the audience can be supplied without difficulty from humanity, but the rôle of the dramatist can hardly be filled without the hypothesis of a supernatural power which manipulates events against the run of both probability (the normally expected) and pure chance. How exceedingly familiar, for instance, is the traditional interpretation of Greek tragedy as a mirror of Destiny toying with its human victims. Destiny can be personified as Fate, or one of the Fates, or else there is a god with fore-knowledge who, if he cannot influence Destiny, maintains the victim in ignorance as he goes down the path to destruction. However far one departs from this simple traditional conception, it is hard to avoid the notion of personification altogether. Even 'chance' may be personified, usually under the name of Fortune. There must always be a force possessed of sufficient 'personal' consciousness to be aware of the human individual's existence and to intervene in it. Beyond that, it is difficult not to assume that this force derives some degree of satisfaction from the victim's discomfiture. If not, its intervention would seem inexplicable. It is, however, possible to retain the notion of irony while adopting an agnostic attitude towards the reactions of the supernatural force. The force in that case manipulates events for reasons unknown and the experience of ironic contemplation is limited to the human spectators.

However this may be, there still remains the idea of manipulation, since the only alternative is blind chance. One can attenuate and depersonalise the assumption of a supernatural agent very considerably, but it seems impossible to discard it altogether. A man near the end of his financial resources works out a system for winning at roulette and, after passing fifty or a hundred turns, stakes everything on a chosen number. The bet fails and he is ruined. But on the immediately successive spin of the wheel the number which would have saved him turns up. If one can unreservedly believe that its incidence is fortuitous, there is no irony in the situation. But if one finds it ironical, there is no escaping the implication that the appearance of a particular number at a particular point has somehow been arranged. Not necessarily by a 'god', which is the most primitive hypothesis, but at least according to a 'law' which is outside human prevision. Yet a 'law' supposes a lawgiver[5] of some kind and it is at this concept that one eventually arrives. Providing one postulates a 'law' which can neither be foreknown nor altered by human means, the lawgiver cannot be other than a supernatural or extra-human agent.

An appreciation of the ironical in 'life' therefore rests ultimately on an admission of the existence of the supernatural. An appreciation of the tragic may well rest on the same assumption. In the majority of cases it probably does, which accounts both for the close relationship between tragedy and irony and for the common opinion that tragedy is 'numinous'. But the relationship is not essential, neither is tragedy inevitably 'numinous'. To return to the example of the gambler: a fully tragic situation existed as soon as he had made his calculated bet and failed. The appearance of the right number at the next spin of the wheel made the situation more poignant, more dramatic. It was an underlining, a refinement, but it did not create the tragedy. This already existed in a complete form when the stake was lost, based upon elements wholly contained within the limits of the gambler's psychology and his material circumstances.

6

The last tragic characteristic is status. This has already been touched on, but it bears further examination. We have noticed that tragedy is not easily associated with trivial personalities. In the older kinds of drama the principle was reflected in the practice of making kings and queens, or their equivalents in worldly position, the protagonists of tragedy. This may appear an artificial convention, consecrated by the stage practice of various countries, but it is a very convenient device which indicates *at once* the high standing of the characters and makes it unnecessary to establish the fact at length. What is required is moral stature, i.e., greatness of personality, and it is assumed that this will be found more readily in people of eminent position than elsewhere. Because of the authority and influence they wield, it can also be assumed that the issues at stake will be important rather than trivial. The future of Rome and Egypt was involved in the fate of Antony and Cleopatra.

[5] If not a lawgiver, at least a formulator. If one postulates a procedure forever outside the knowledge of any intelligence of whatever kind, one cannot term it a law.

On this plane there is no difficulty. Great people are engaged in great events, both appropriate to the noble genre of tragedy. But in more modern drama, as in the modern attitude to 'life', the characters can be scaled down considerably without becoming nontragic. How far they can be scaled down depends on the view which the spectators have of their own moral level. It is certain that the tragic character must not fall below this. If he is so diminished that he can be regarded with either laughter, contempt, or even excessive pity—that is, from an angle of superiority—he ceases to be tragic. He must clearly be some perceptible distance above the spectators' level. If his intrinsic personality is such that he can be described as a 'quite ordinary' man, he may still be raised to tragic stature by virtue of the situation in which he finds himself. According to one interpretation, he then sheds his individual ordinariness to become, through suffering and disaster, a representative of humanity or some part of it. In this capacity he acquires something of the moral status which would be accorded automatically to a national hero or leader. A convergent interpretation of the same phenomenon is that the seriousness of the events in itself raises the participants to the tragic level. Death, particularly in striking circumstances, commands awe, which may be defined as respect tinged with fear, and so tends to upgrade the merely average man. The events then compensate for the ordinariness of the participants, provided that the latter is not too marked. (An animal, a child, or a buffoon can hardly ever, on a normal view, be the principal figure in a tragedy even if the other tragic conditions are observed.) Conversely, it is possible for characters of high enough moral eminence to preserve a tragic climate in events which verge on the trivial, again with the provision that they do not descend squarely into it. (The death of a great man in an air-crash qualifies for tragedy unequivocally; if he is killed in a sports-car, the tragic quality becomes more dubious; if by falling off a bicycle, the whole conception is endangered.) Easily recognisable status there must be: ideally, in characters and events equally; but if not that, in one or the other, with neither of them falling so low that the disparity is unbridgeable.

But status, however arrived at, is not enough in isolation. If the upward angle of vision is too steep, the contact is broken between protagonists and spectators and the tragic is not felt. This is where the factor of sympathy enters in. Ridicule for what is below a notional level kills it, but so does admiration unqualified by pity for something which stands unattainably above it. With greater reason, the destruction of an enemy is not tragic, for here sympathy, requiring a partial identification with the protagonist, is obstructed not only by distance but by conscious aversion. The tragic element in the fates of historical characters depends on whether one is 'for' or 'against' them. Many years had to pass before the fall and exile of Napoleon could appear tragic to an Englishman. From the same national viewpoint, it would seem incongruous to describe Hitler's death in the Berlin bunker as 'tragic', though for a Nazi sympathiser it must be supremely so. Satan, leaving aside the somewhat equivocal treatment by Milton in *Paradise Lost*, could not be represented as a tragic figure until the Romantic Movement of the nineteenth century when a changed conception of evil made possible a measure of legitimate self-identification with the Prince of Darkness.

To stature, standing, or simply status, which evoke responses ranging from admiration to respect, we must therefore add sympathy as an attribute of the tragic character. If he does not command it, he may be detestable, comic or, on occasion, heroic, but he will not be tragic.[6]

7

It would be difficult to go further without borrowing heavily on the theory of dramatic tragedy, which we have assumed for the purposes of this chapter to be unfamiliar to intelligent people who use 'tragic' as part of their everyday vocabulary. For the same reasons we have not invoked the deeper theological and philosophical theories of causation and of good and evil, assuming that these do not influence the average person's reaction to a disastrous event. We have tried to confine ourselves to normal and spontaneous usage and to carry the analysis of what lies beneath it no further than any unspecialised mind can do after a little reflection. By this means we have discerned

[6] The qualities required in the protagonists of a tragedy must also be present in the events. Here the word 'sympathy' is inapplicable and some such term as 'credibility' or 'empathy' takes its place. Just as the onlooker must be able to identify himself with some aspect of the tragic hero, he must also be able to project himself, at least partially, into the hero's situation. When the events which make up the situation appear too horrific, too remote, or too 'far-fetched', the link is again broken by antipathy or distance and the tragic disperses.

what appear to be commonly accepted as the principal conditions of a 'tragic' happening. They can be summarised in a few lines:

A tragedy is a final and impressive disaster due to an unforeseen or unrealised failure involving people who command respect and sympathy. It often entails an ironical change of fortune and usually conveys a strong impression of waste. It is always accompanied by misery and emotional distress.   Macbeth

The last sentence is self-evident, and could be dispensed with for that reason. The middle sentence contains its own reservations, 'often' and 'usually'. The first sentence is basic, and is put forward as the essential definition.

2

The Legacy of Aristotle

1

Sooner or later any inquiry into tragedy must take account of the opinions of Aristotle. If Aristotle had not written on the subject there would still have been theories of tragedy and they might well have taken a different course. But his treatise and its influence have long been established facts and it is idle to pretend that any later commentator can ignore them. What, however, is desirable is to see them in some sort of historical and critical perspective.

The Greek philosopher is considered to have written his comments on tragedy, contained in the short work generally known as the *Poetics*, at some time between 335 and 323 B.C., and so during the last thirteen years of his life. At that time he was teaching at the school which he had set up in Athens, still the centre of a great intellectually advanced culture, if a little past the peak of its creative art. Greek tragic drama had appeared and reached its zenith in the previous century, in the hands of Aeschylus, Sophocles and Euripides. The last two had died only some twenty years before Aristotle's birth. The *Poetics*, to whose organisation we will return, are generally agreed to have been Aristotle's notes for his lectures.

So far as positive evidence goes, the *Poetics* virtually disappeared for many centuries. Traces of its influence have been seen, indirect rather than direct, in the *Ars Poetica* of the Latin poet Horace, in one or two Roman grammarians or literary exegetists, and as inconclusively elsewhere. But the analogies are nowhere close and there is no certainty that any writer whose works survive had a first-hand acquaintance with the *Poetics* either in the centuries of Rome's domination or in the whole of the Middle Ages of Western Europe, although the latter was the period when Aristotle's general influence on European thought was of paramount importance.

At the beginnings of the Renaissance the *Poetics* reappeared—or, as far as their influence on Western culture goes, appeared for the first time. Italian classical scholars evidently knew the work in the later years of the fifteenth century. Their knowledge was derived from manuscript versions and it is a reasonable hypothesis that these were based on some key manuscript brought westward by refugees from Byzantium after the fall of that city to the Turks in 1453. In 1498 the first printed version—in a Latin translation—was published in Venice. Ten years later a Greek text (but considered a 'bad' one) was printed, also in Venice. From then on numerous texts, commentaries and translations into various languages followed throughout the sixteenth century. Interest in the *Poetics* was intensified by the desire to recreate the genre of dramatic tragedy, which during the Middle Ages had remained neglected, and indeed unknown.

The most authoritative modern editions of the *Poetics* are all based on the earliest surviving Greek text, a manuscript (known as A^c) written in the eleventh century A.D. by a Byzantine scribe. This, although, of course, produced by some totally unknown hand over thirteen hundred years after Aristotle's death and brought into prominence more than two thousand years after it,[1] is accepted as a substantially accurate version of Aristotle's own thought and wording. It is confirmed at various points, and corrected on some others, by a slightly older tenth-century version in Arabic, brought to light late in the nineteenth century. This was a translation of a Syriac text (lost, except for a short fragment) of the sixth or seventh century, which in turn had been translated from some earlier Greek version. It therefore has a much older known ancestry than any other surviving text, but is so garbled after the two successive translations as to be almost incomprehensible. The Arabic translator had no understanding of the literary and other specialised terms which he was rendering. More important still, perhaps, he could have had no conception of what Aristotle meant by a tragedy, since tragic drama did not exist in his own age and culture. He was in much the same position as a modern translating machine which can transpose a

---

[1] The importance of A^c (or *Parisinus* 1741) was first established by the edition of the German scholar Bekker (1831).

word or phrase from one language to another, but cannot recast a sentence to make sense in a different idiom. But his stupidly literal rendering, though often nonsensical in itself, has proved all the more valuable as a word-for-word check on the accepted Greek text. It has helped, as has been said, to confirm a number of passages and to suggest variants of others.

Greek scholars now seem satisfied that they have in essentials what Aristotle wrote on the subject of tragedy. One might, however, say that from the point of view of dramatic theory—though not, perhaps, of Aristotelian studies as a whole—it would hardly matter if the text of the *Poetics* was authentic or not. What matters very much more is the deductions which have been drawn from it during the past four hundred years.

Some of them go a long way beyond the statements of the text. So far, in fact, as will appear presently, that they have overflowed the bounds of dramatic tragedy, which was Aristotle's subject, and have contributed to mould a conception of the tragic in 'life'. This extension of the influence of the *Poetics*, largely fortuitous as most seminal influences are, makes it desirable to consider the work at an early stage in this book.

The accepted text bears the appearance of the notes on which Aristotle based his lectures. It is more developed in some passages than others, has gaps which a speaker might fill in and, considered as a piece of reading-matter, is illogically arranged and badly co-ordinated. It contains obscurities and some at least partial contradictions. These may be due to the mistakes and interpolations of copyists, but they can be explained no less satisfactorily as the additions and second thoughts of a lecturer who gave the same course several times, developing and amending it over a period of perhaps several years.

Though the work as a whole had obviously not been tidied-up for publication, its central intention is quite plain. It is concerned with 'poetry' (i.e., imaginative writing) as a form of artistic expression, and particularly with what Aristotle considered to be the two highest types of 'poetry', tragedy and the epic. His investigation of these is carried out from what might be described in modern terms as the viewpoint of an intelligent and conscientious don, intent on examining their nature and the way they obtain their effects through the study of actual examples. Explicitly or implicitly, Aristotle always seems to be bearing particular works in mind and it is on them that his theories, whenever they broaden out into generalisations, are based. The examples he most admires are Homer's two epics, the *Odyssey* and the *Iliad*, which already enjoyed 'classical' standing in his time. He refers to tragedies by Sophocles, whose *Oedipus* he tends to consider as a model, by Aeschylus and by Euripides. He treats this drama of the preceding century as a still-living art and draws no distinction in kind between it and plays (now lost) by other dramatists whom he mentions, some of whom were probably contemporary with him. His comments are thus based on the chief works of Greek tragedy as they can still be read today, or on other apparently similar plays.

2

Aristotle's most consistent approach to his subject is aesthetic and technical. Thus, he devotes space to the discussion of different metres, to the uses of language, metaphor, and so on. Sometimes he is more general than this, but he never departs from the timeless attitude of the intelligent pedagogic critic, analytically taking to pieces the works before him and trying to deduce the principles which animate them, while avoiding speculation like the plague.

An example is provided by his remarks on the Unities, which were developed by Renaissance and post-Renaissance critics into a law for playwrights, particularly in France. According to them, the events of a play should occupy a limited stretch of time (at most, twenty-four hours), they should occur in one place (no changes of scene), and the plot or action should be a simple unity. Aristotle himself does not mention the unity of place. He is far from dogmatic on the unity of time. He merely says, in the course of an incidental comparison between epic poems and tragedies: 'They also differ in length, because tragedy tends as far as possible to keep within a single day and night or thereabouts, whereas the epic has no time-limit; though at first tragic poets followed the epic in this respect.'[2]

[2] *Poetics*, Ch. 5, p. 23, in *Aristotle on the Art of Fiction*, by L. J. Potts (Cambridge U.P., 2nd edn, 1959). The quotations from Aristotle in this chapter are taken for the most part textually from Mr Potts' excellent modern translation, to whose Introduction and notes I am also indebted. Comparison has been made for the more controversial passages with the translations of S. H. Butcher (*Aristotle's Theory of Poetry and Fine Art*, Macmillan, 3rd. edn, 1902), Ingram Bywater (*Aristotle on the Art of Poetry*, Oxford, 1909, and *Aristotle's Art of Poetry, with Introduction by*

This in itself is a perfectly sound and legitimate remark, based on observation of the practice of writers whom Aristotle had studied. It is not, and does not pretend to be, a rule. It may be connected by the reader (though Aristotle does not explicitly make the connection) with Aristotle's insistence on the *concentration* of tragedy—that is, its unity of interest, which in his eyes is one of its strongest points. The story of a tragedy, he says, must be a complete whole. It must have a beginning, a middle, and an end. 'A beginning is that which does not necessarily follow anything else, but which naturally leads to another event or development. An end is the opposite, that which itself naturally (either of necessity or most commonly) follows something else, but nothing else comes after it. And a middle is that which itself follows something else and is followed by another thing. So,' continues Aristotle, 'well-plotted stories[3] must not begin or end at haphazard, but must follow the pattern here described.'[4] Hence a tragedy, for Aristotle, is a self-sufficient whole. It is not a 'slice of life', it starts from its own data, it does not finish 'in the air'. He gives a further reason for this stipulation, a reason which has come to be looked on as typically Greek, and also 'classical'. It is that any beautiful object (he supposes that a work of art should be beautiful), must be properly proportioned within itself and be neither too large nor too small. In order to please, the work of art

---

W. Hamilton Fyfe, Oxford, 1940), J. Hardy (*Aristote: Poétique*, Les Belles Lettres, Paris, 1961), and the commentary of A. Rostagni (*La Poetica di Aristotele*, Biblioteca di Filologia Classica, Turin, 1934).

Apart from the fact that the present writer's Greek is much too rudimentary for him to attempt any variant translation of Aristotle's text which is not found or discussed in these recognised authorities, it must be said that the significance of the *Poetics*, for the purpose of this inquiry, lies in the meaning which can be given to it in a modern idiom and context. Were this an historical examination of varying concepts of tragic drama in different cultures, reliance on translations might be less desirable.

[3] Here and elsewhere I have substituted the word 'story' for 'fable' (Latin, *fabula*), which is the more usual translation of Aristotle's *mythos*. In the contexts quoted it will convey the meaning more directly to the modern reader. The 'story' of a play is distinct from the 'plot', which in the simplest analysis is the dramatist's way of presenting or recounting the 'story'. A 'story' (as usually with Aristotle's *mythos*) may already be well-known or traditional, e.g., Oedipus, Thomas à Becket, Cinderella. The main outline of such 'stories' is unchangeable, but different narratives or plays can be based upon them. The difference consists largely in the 'plotting', i.e., in the detailed handling of the material. See particularly *Poetics*, Ch. 17. Potts, pp. 40–1.

[4] *Poetics*, Ch. 7. Potts, p. 27.

obeys the same laws as the natural object and the living body. As the latter should have 'a size that can be kept in view', so 'there is a proper amplitude for stories—what can be kept well in one's mind'. The story of a tragedy must therefore have a clearly perceptible outline. It must not be obscured by the inclusion of diverse happenings unrelated by a logical connection, such as the various incidents which may befall a single character in the course of his life.[5] It must have unity, a conception which Aristotle illustrated in this way: 'Since the story is an imitation (i.e., here, a representation) of an action, that action must be a complete unit, and the events of which it is made up must be so plotted that if any of these elements is transposed or removed the whole is altered or upset. For when a thing can be included or not included without making any noticeable difference, that thing is no part of the whole.'[6]

From here Aristotle goes on, as any honest theorist must, to discuss what makes some incidents a necessary part of a unified story and other incidents not. The happenings in a properly proportioned story, he has already said, 'will make a chain of probability or necessity'. He now comes face to face in his argument with the notion of this 'probability, or necessity'. It may perhaps be remarked without disrespect to a great critic that he finds it as resistant to analysis as it appeared to us in the previous chapter; or at least, that in the surviving text of the *Poetics* it is not analysed. He makes no transcendent speculations, does not invoke the laws of chance or postulate anything whatever about cause and effect as a general rule of the cosmos. He treats entirely of what appears logically acceptable in a story or a play. He gives to this, implicitly, a subjective value, repeating the word 'probability' but not seriously attempting to justify it. He does, indeed, point out that some tragedies are concerned with 'real people'[7] and that therefore we accept the events in

[5] Works of the picaresque type, 'adventure' stories, soap opera and, of course, 'epic' drama, are therefore excluded from tragedy purely on structural grounds. By Aristotle's standards, all these unproportioned works are monstrous.

[6] *Poetics*, Ch. 8. Potts, pp. 28–9.

[7] The human characters of Greek mythology, such as the heroes of the *Iliad*, and such protagonists of tragedy as Oedipus, Orestes, and their families were looked on in this connection as 'real'. One hesitates to write 'historical' only because the line between the historical and the legendary character was less clearly defined than now. There was something of both in the heroes of Greek tragedy. For a parallel, it seems unlikely that Shakespeare's audiences clearly put Julius Caesar into one category and King Lear into another.

26

them because we know that they, or similar events, have really happened. But he does not seek to extend this partial explanation to the whole field of tragedy, recognising that some tragedies contain events and characters both of which are fictitious. All that he requires is that the personages should act 'in character' and that even when there are unexpected incidents and ironical surprises (as in the *Oedipus*) it is better for these to seem logical (on reflection) than caused by an arbitrary effect of chance.[8]

So Aristotle's 'probability' is no more than a built-in artistic element in a tragedy. We feel that it is fitting, he suggests, that event *b* should follow event *a* and should precede event *c*. But on why these events should have been selected as a coherent series he has no light to shed. The answer, apart from Aristotle, appears to be that their sequence must accord, or not too strongly disaccord, with common experience, leading to the formation of mental habits, and that the rest depends on the skill of the dramatist in so ordering his plot that he disposes us to find its developments plausible. This, of course, leaves unbroached any more fundamental explanation of which the need may or may not be felt.

Aristotle's treatment of probability and of the unity of action is typical of the *Poetics* as a whole. In every instance he is manifestly looking at tragedy from a deliberately restricted point of view and is constantly asking two questions. What makes tragedy superior to other art-forms?—for he finds it superior. How, when at its best, does it obtain its effects, which are to move us and give us pleasure? The explanations he finds and the points he discusses are of immediate relevance to the work of art and do not go beyond it. But deductions with wider implications which Aristotle did not draw, and evidently never intended to draw, are nevertheless latent in many of his remarks and have duly been drawn by others.

At this date we cannot ignore these developments. They have become woven, rightly or wrongly, into our general conception of tragedy. Far more than what Aristotle actually said, they constitute his legacy as it has been handed down to us. Its chief items are: the theory of catharsis; recognition; the tragic hero (neither wholly good nor wholly bad); the tragic error; action more important than character.

---

[8] His example: 'Even when events are accidental, the sensation is greater if they appear to have a purpose, as when the statue of Mitys at Argos killed the man who had caused his death, by falling on him at a public

Catharsis. One of the most debated passages in the *Poetics*, though not perhaps the most important, occurs in Aristotle's definition of tragedy:

> Tragedy, then, is an imitation of an action of high importance, complete and of some amplitude; in language enhanced by distinct and varying beauties; acted, not narrated; *by means of pity and fear effecting its purgation of these emotions.*[9]

Catharsis, the word translated as 'purgation' in the last sentence, is initially a Greek medical term. The extent to which Aristotle's use of it is metaphorical is debatable, but it can be taken metaphorically in a modern context (cp. 'He'll have to sweat it out'). The passage is now generally understood to mean that tragedy purges or relieves *an excess* of pity and fear (considered as burdensome emotions) in the spectators. It evidently does so by exciting those emotions and bringing them to the surface of the psyche whence they are discharged, on the analogy of a physical purge or an emetic. The spectator is finally left with a relaxed sensation of appeasement. There is no question of a 'purification' of *all* the passions, neither is any moral principle at issue. If there were, it might be argued that *pity*, as boundless as possible, is a necessary emotion in mankind and should not be removed or even diminished. A similar case might be made out for *fear*, though after considerably more psychological argument, since fear can be represented as necessary to self-preservation and its removal, with the consequent euphoria, as dangerous. But such considerations are not in Aristotle, whose interest, once again,

---

entertainment. Such things appear not to have happened blindly. Inevitably, therefore, plots of this sort are finer.' (*Poetics*, Ch. 9. Potts, p. 30.) This example was developed by Gustave Lanson (*Esquisse d'une histoire de la tragédie française*, Champion, Paris, 1926) to yield the following perhaps over-schematic definitions: 'A man is crushed by a falling statue: that is *pathetic*. He struggles a moment against the mass which is crushing him; there are a few seconds of alternate hope and fear: that is *dramatic*. The statue is the statue of Mitys; the victim is Mitys' murderer. If one admits that it is not pure chance, that is *tragic*.' (It will be noticed that in our view (pp. 14–17 above) it would be *ironic* rather than tragic.) Lanson concludes: '*The tragic* is the manifestation, in a case entailing suffering, of the limitations of the human condition and of the invisible force which dominates him, animated by either justice or caprice.' Yes, possibly. But it must be reiterated that there is no suggestion of an 'invisible force' in any passage of the *Poetics*.

[9] My italics. *Poetics*, Ch. 6. Potts, p. 24.

is in the 'pleasure' which the spectacle of tragedy gives. One can at least say, without entering on the debatable ground of the moral and psychological implications, that he believed that tragedy should *stimulate* the emotions of pity and fear—whatever happens afterwards—and that this part of the formula has proved generally acceptable.

Pity presents little difficulty. It is the emotion, which can be active and acute, which is felt for the victims of any disaster and, even more strongly, for the protagonists in a tragic disaster—the link of sympathy, discussed in the previous chapter, being postulated.

Fear is rather more complicated. Is the meaning that the spectators will fear for themselves, or will they fear for the protagonists in the tragedy? Why should they do the first, since they are seated at a safe notional distance from the disaster, with an invisible barrier between them and it? *Can* they do the second? Since they are watching the misfortunes of strangers, is 'fear' the appropriate word? Once again, the assumption of a bond of sympathy, and that alone, makes the answers plainly affirmative. We are so caught up in the spectacle that the notional barrier is temporarily abolished. We fear and even suffer with the actors because we identify ourselves with them.[10] In that case, to go back to *catharsis* and offer a very simple explanation of it which is not excluded in Aristotle, having exercised their emotions of pity and fear in the mimic disaster, the spectators return at the end of the play to real life and are 'relieved' to find that their distress was groundless. There is an analogy in the awakening from a nightmare.[11]

Another explanation of Aristotle's 'fear', which must be rather regretfully discarded, would equate it with the religious dread ex-

[10] That this was Aristotle's sense is confirmed by another passage in the *Poetics*: 'Pity is induced by undeserved misfortune, and fear by the misfortunes of normal people.' (Ch. 13. Potts, p. 33.) By 'normal people' is meant 'people on our own level'—although this runs counter to the 'status' condition of the tragic character. (If the two conflict, 'status' must evidently be subordinated to 'sympathy'.) Butcher translates: 'a man like ourselves', and Bywater, Hardy and Rostagni use wording equivalent to this. For fuller discussion of the catharsis of pity and fear, see Butcher, *op. cit.*, p. 242 *et seq.*, and Bywater, *op. cit.*, pp. 152–61.

[11] 'When my husband is away I cannot bear to watch a BBC thriller because there are no breaks to return me to reality. I enjoy ITV thrillers because the advertisement breaks—clothes going round in a washing machine, and fresh young teenagers popping sweets into their mouths— allow me to shake off the horror and return for another session.' Letter in *Daily Herald*, July 1961.

perienced collectively at an orgiastic occasion. This type of panic or infectious fear would be initiated by the actors in the tragic spectacle, functioning as the leaders of the rite, but would rapidly spread to the spectators, who would become equal participants in a mass outburst of hysteria. The notional barrier is completely obliterated—not, this time, by a temporary identification with the actors in their particular situation, but by a conviction that some inexplicable and supernatural force is directly threatening every individual present. All are caught up in an ecstasy of fear. All are maddened by a personal awareness—to use so-called Christian terms—that: 'It is a dreadful thing to fall into the hands of the living God.'

But although some germ of tragedy may have sprung from the Greek orgiastic religions, and although elsewhere (in the *Politics*) Aristotle writes of the cathartic effect of flute-music in an apparently orgiastic context (the flute brings 'enthusiasm', i.e., a pathological tendency to over-excitability, to the surface, leaving the sufferer normal and relaxed after the artificial stimulation), such powerfully primitive manifestations of religious terror would appear quite foreign to the nicely rational world of the *Poetics*. If we could transpose Aristotle's conception of tragedy to the world of the ancient Hebrews, we could make a simple correlation between his pity-and-fear and the 'wailing and gnashing of teeth' of the Old Testament. This would assimilate tragedy to an oriental funeral orgy with thunderstorm effects by the priests of Baal or Jehovah. Obviously, however, it would not conform to a modern conception of tragedy, nor, to all appearances, to Aristotle's.[12]

An important incidental feature of the theory of catharsis, which is not often stressed, is that it transfers attention from the work of art in itself to the effect which it produces on the spectators. In looking for 'tragedy' in a play or a situation, we are thus obliged to

---

[12] Yet the modern phenomenon of young adolescents driven into a temporary state of frenzy by performances of beat groups almost persuades one afresh that this was the Aristotelian *catharsis*. This would call for a fundamental revision of our conception of the Athenian *polis*, built up by generations of scholars who were perhaps over-civilised but were surely not that far astray? If they were, one could begin to compare a fifth-century B.C. performance of Sophoclean tragedy with the gladiatorial shows of Imperial Rome. The latter undoubtedly released a savage kind of *catharsis* in the Roman populace.

That the element of 'frenzy' was present in at least some Greek tragedy was demonstrated by the Greek Art Theatre's production in London of Aeschylus's *The Persians*, in April 1965.

take account of the reactions of non-participants. This apparently unexceptionable principle has far-reaching consequences. It must eventually lead to the conclusion that the significance of a work of art is dependent on the emotions which it generates. Developed logically, this destroys the possibility of establishing any absolute critical standards whatever and makes all assessments empirical. The empirical principle of the effective communication of emotion is highly defensible on one plane and need not be argued here, but if one adopts it one must be prepared to accept all its consequences, one of which is an ultimate subservience to spectator-reaction. What inspired pity and fear in the Greeks (and was tragic for them for that reason) may not arouse the same emotions in us, in which case it is no longer tragic. The evaluation of literature—the formation of judgments on the relative merits of different works—thus ceases to require a scrutiny of the inherent qualities of the individual work and demands instead an inquiry of the kind usually carried out under some branch of historical sociology. It is surprising that literary critics have not fought the Aristotelian theory of 'pity and fear' tooth-and-nail, since its implications could rapidly put them out of business. But fortunately both specialisation and human sloth have so far protected them. The sociologists, though no doubt aware of the relative nature of the historical bases of pity and fear have neither cared nor dared to look closely at the concept of tragedy from that angle. The literary specialists have taken for granted the stability of the tragic concept, have never seriously disputed that it includes the generation of pity and fear, and have almost totally neglected the historical relativity of those emotions. We must follow their example, since not to do so is to reject the possibility of reaching any definite general conclusions at all. Nevertheless, we are bound to recognise that the fear of offending a god or of committing incest would affect us less than a Greek of the Periclean age, and in short be a different fear. A dramatic situation based upon such hazards would not frighten us overmuch, though other hazards, of which the Greeks were unaware, do. The way round, which has become so familiar to the literary exegetist as to appear natural, is to reinterpret the original works so that they furnish new sources of pity and fear, either symbolically or by transposition. By recasting the primitive significance of the original (and here psychology is an invaluable instrument) we can preserve its classic status and at the same time evade the difficulty of having to reconstruct the reactions of a remote or alien society. A more respectable way of putting this, which is therefore preferred, is to say that the great work of art or literature carries within itself a multiplicity of possible meanings which become visible from different angles of perception. The inferior work, on the other hand, admits of only one approach and one interpretation.

Be that as it may, the arousing of fear—whatever its causes—has been felt from Aristotle onwards to be appropriate to tragedy. What is usually felt inappropriate is horror.

Here it becomes necessary, without troubling overmuch about etymology or the Greek and Latin connotations of similar terms, to define three words which form a kind of progression in modern English usage. Fear = strong apprehension. Terror = extreme fear, with a paralysing or panic effect. Horror = revulsion at the sight of something already accomplished, or in process of accomplishment. Normally, fear will come before the shock, terror during it or at the moment when it appears imminent, and horror when the consequences are apparent, which may be almost imperceptibly later. Fear, being anticipatory, has a forward attraction which cannot be removed until it has either been realised or proved groundless. Horror supposes repugnance. It creates an impulse to get rid of it, to escape from it by a positive effort. To linger upon or around it is considered 'unhealthy', no doubt because it is a sterile obsession —an acquiescence in the paralysing effects produced by a terror now past and a prolongation of them in the present—and because it is usually supposed possible to shake if off by an effort of will. Fear is considered clean, if painful, and in any case inevitable.[13] Horror is unclean, morbid, and can be represented as a perverse pleasure because one 'ought' to be repelled by it.

On this ground alone, horror will tend to be excluded from tragedy as a lower-caste emotion. In drama, the horror play, from *The Duchess of Malfi* to *grand guignol*, is of dubious tragic status. But some horror there must be, even in an indisputable tragedy. Horror is the fulfilment of fear, and if the fear proved empty the work would

[13] Only the heroic character can be described as 'without fear'. As has already been suggested, he is not tragic because his moral elevation severs the bond of sympathy. While it is true that the ordinary man can identify himself with the fearless hero, he can only do so during short periods of virtual intoxication which cannot be maintained as a condition of life. This would point to the conclusion that tragedy belongs to the realistic category of art, not to the idealistic or the 'sublime'.

not be tragic. In *King Lear*, the physical blinding of Gloucester before the audience is often felt to be 'too horrible' and its omission would hardly cripple the tragedy. But the mental horrors which overwhelm Lear at the end of the play are necessary and not 'too horrible'. If they are sometimes felt to be difficult to bear, it is because they are 'too harrowing'. What they may produce is an excess, not of aversion, but of pity, so that the purge, in terms of catharsis, becomes too drastic to be pleasurable. The spectator who feels this will tend to blame himself for being too weak to take the salutary medicine. For his shrinking from the blinding of Gloucester, however, he will blame the playwright or the production.

Horror, then, but in moderation and as unstressed physically as possible. Though it may be the culmination of a tragedy, it must not be allowed to dominate it either in anticipation or in contemplation. Two acts of build-up to a torture-scene and a third act for the actual torturing would not correspond to any idea of the tragic—and certainly not for a modern mind. If one had to give a reason, one could do worse than appeal back to Aristotle and argue that the emotions such a spectacle would excite would not be pity and fear so much as a sadistic delight in cruelty.[14]

There is some warrant for this in Aristotle's text, though perhaps hardly enough to establish that he drew a clear distinction between fear and horror in the sense that we have given to them. His objection bears primarily on the stimulation of spectator-reaction by material means rather than by the dramatist's mastery of composition and language. His main argument can be summed up by saying that he condemns crude theatrical effects and prefers the subtler (predominantly verbal) methods of the 'poet'. He certainly excludes the sensational horror, but hardly pronounces against a more refined type of psychological horror which for us would be distinct from 'fear':

[14] It is evident that *pity* cannot be coupled with *horror* in any psychological system which conceives such emotions as pure or separate states of feeling. Since the chief characteristic of pity is to attract us to its object, whereas horror repels us from it, the two things are mutually exclusive. A convenient illustration is provided by Jean-Jacques Rousseau, who conceived pity, in his theoretical writings, as the basic emotion which binds human beings together and distinguishes them from the animals. When however, in real life, Rousseau's companion collapsed in the street in an epileptic fit, he could not bring himself to stay and help but ran away from the, for him, horrible scene. Of the two 'natural' reactions, horror proved irresistibly stronger.

The pity and fear can be brought about by the *mise en scène*; but they can also come from the mere plotting of the incidents, which is preferable, and better poetry. For, without seeing anything, the story ought to have been so plotted that if one heard the bare facts, the chain of circumstances would make one shudder and pity. That would happen to anyone who heard the story of the *Oedipus*. To produce this effect by the *mise en scène* is less artistic and puts one at the mercy of the technician; *and these who use it not to frighten but merely to startle have lost touch with tragedy altogether* [my italics]. We should not try to get all sorts of pleasure from tragedy, but the particular tragic pleasure.[15]

In the Greek tragedy which Aristotle knew, horror (the contemplation of the terrible effects of an act or a disaster) was certainly not taboo. And while it can be said that the horrors shown were nearly always post-critical, static rather than violent, and nothing to what might have been shown, it is nevertheless apparent that the Greeks were not over-fastidious in this respect.[16]

[15] *Poetics*, Ch. 14. This passage is taken verbally from Potts's translation, pp. 34–5, except for my substitution of 'story' for 'fable' in lines 4 and 6. Other renderings of the sentence italicised give varying meanings. The French translator comes out plainly in the sense of our own general argument:

> *Quant à ceux qui suscitent par le spectacle non point la crainte mais seulement l'horreur, ils n'ont rien de commun avec la tragédie.* (Hardy, *op. cit.*, p. 48.)

Both Butcher and Bywater, however, render the *desirable* effects of tragedy, as described earlier in this passage, as 'horror and pity', and translate the italicised sentence thus:

> Those who employ spectacular means to create a sense not of the terrible but only of *the monstrous* are strangers to the purpose of tragedy. (Butcher, *op. cit.*, p. 49.)

> Those, however, who make use of the Spectacle to put before us that which is merely *monstrous* and not productive of fear, are wholly out of touch with tragedy. (Bywater, *op. cit.*, p. 39.)

Rostagni also uses the term *monstrous* and relates it to spectacular stage effects (*op. cit.*, p. 52).

For a confirmatory sidelight on the conception of dramatic 'horror', cp. the opinion of the actor Boris Karloff (William Henry Pratt), popularly typed as a film 'monster': 'Shock must come out of a good story line, not shock for the sake of shock. I believe in fear, excitement, terror, but not horror. I object to the term "horror films". Horror implies some sort of revulsion. They should never be revolting.' (Reported in *The Sunday Times*, 28 February 1965.)

[16] Prometheus being riveted to the rock (Aeschylus, *Prometheus Bound*); Oedipus with his eyes gouged out (Sophocles); the broken body of the dying Hippolytus carried in (Euripides, *Hippolytus*); the severed head of

Recognition. More than once in the *Poetics*[17] Aristotle refers to the principle of *recognition*, which Mr Potts translates as *disclosure*. It has close connections with the 'tragic error', but may be examined separately, as it is by Aristotle.

The characters in tragedy often act in ignorance of the nature of their deeds. Sometimes also—this may or may not embrace the same chain of events—they are ignorant of the true identity of the people with whom they are dealing. At a climactic point comes a recognition (disclosure, revelation) of the true nature of the deed and/or of the persons involved in it. The classic example which contains the two inextricably interconnected is of course the *Oedipus*. Here Oedipus 'recognises' that he has killed his own father and married his mother in ignorance. That was the deed. But he may also be said to have recognised the dead Laius as his father and Jocasta as his mother, although these are not physical recognitions which occur on the stage, as they do in certain other plays, and more particularly in comedy.

Aristotle himself is only interested in ignorance-and-recognition as a technical device used by the skilful dramatist to strengthen the effect of his plot. He does not explore the deeper implications which it possesses.

In Sophocles' play, Oedipus 'recognises' in the end not only all the persons in his life for what they are; he also 'recognises' himself for what he is. After this realisation, it only remains for him to put out his eyes in order no longer to see the world or himself as he now knows them to be. Similar 'recognitions' will be found in many plays classed as tragedies, though they are not often as telling as in the *Oedipus*.

'Recognition' in this sense is indistinguishable from what is commonly called 'the moment of truth'—the moment when the protagonist, open-eyed, comes face to face with a reality of which he was unaware or which he was seeking to avoid. In the circumstances, it must be a moment of horror. The nature and extent of the horror may vary, in proportion to the amount of imaginative

---

Pentheus carried in by his mother and, later, the mangled pieces of his body (Euripides, *The Bacchae*); Aegisthus uncovering the corpse of Clytemnestra (Sophocles, *Electra*); the dying screams of Clytemnestra (off-stage) and the corpses of Clytemnestra and Aegisthus revealed (Euripides, *Electra*); etc.

[17] In Chapters 11, 14 and 16.

preparation which has preceded it in the form of hope, fear, or cultivated illusion; also in proportion to the volume of self-reproach which
the subject experiences. Such things will perhaps deepen the horror,
but they will not transform it. The moment of recognition, or of
truth, is essentially the same for the rat which is about to drown as
it is for Othello standing over the body of his innocent wife.

One could never claim that this realisation, centred on horror
creating so strong a revulsion that the subject often kills himself or
goes mad, is foreign to tragedy. But at the same time, as has already
been suggested, it should not be dwelt upon too heavily. This is no
doubt because, while suffering is a necessary element in tragedy, the
spectacle of it quickly becomes sickening and demands strict control.
The greatest dramatists break this rule. Sophocles' Oedipus is in
mental torment before the audience for some time after his self-
blinding, and this follows a full narration of his mental and physical
agony by a messenger. The screw is turned further by the entry of
his weeping children. The recognition is developed in all its horror
and pathos. But where a great dramatist can succeed through sheer
skill, a lesser one will fail: even characters who remain on the
stage for only a few minutes lamenting their mistakes and describing
their sufferings can easily appear tedious. The moment of truth,
when there is one, is ruined by dilution. Ranting is always the pitfall.
This points to the conclusion that the motive for keeping the recognition[18] poignantly brief is largely an aesthetic one.

Finally, it may be asked whether tragedy is possible without
recognition. A full answer must await the examination of some of
the great dramatic tragedies in a subsequent chapter. But one can
anticipate to the extent of saying that in some established tragedies
the recognition is apparently dispensed with. More generally, in life
outside drama, it is quite possible to find an event tragic in which the
protagonists at least never realise their true plight. Circumstances
might lend tragedy to the victims of an unexpected disaster whose
deaths were instantaneous. There might still be a recognition, but
only by the 'spectators'. This of course leads back to the question,
which properly belongs to philosophy, of whether any event or situation has a significant existence unless it is apprehended by a human
mind. Birth, death, and so on are realities whether there is anyone
to witness or recognise them or not. Tragedy is not 'real' in the same

---

[18] The full recognition, by the protagonist. The dawning of it may be
very slow and occupy a considerable part of the play.

sense; it is 'only' a concept. But for the purpose of this inquiry we must postulate that it corresponds to some mental or emotional reality of which some elements are irreducible. We must assume that certain chains of events possess a certain quality even if they occur in independence of any conscious human reaction; that this quality can most appropriately be named tragic; and that it still exists whether it is perceived and named or not.

Meanwhile, it is clear that an event appears 'more tragic' when the participants realise they are doomed. (Cp. irony, above.) It is more tragic still when they understand the nature of their doom and its causes. These considerations would be obvious to a dramatist writing a tragedy of the *Oedipus* type—a tragedy of self-exploration leading to self-recognition. They would extend to any other tragedy, real or imagined, which depended on a revelation of personality and, often, of situation.[19] But they cannot be taken as indispensable.

5

The tragic protagonist. Aristotle makes two different observations on the characters in tragedy. The first is that they should be 'superior' people, like the characters of the Homeric epic. The word translated by Mr Potts as 'superior' (*spoudaiotes*) has been translated variously in different contexts. Other renderings are: 'of high value', 'important', 'serious', 'of merit', 'good'.[20] It is the same word used by Aristotle in his definition of tragedy quoted above (p. 28), and there translated as 'of high importance'. It is confined neither to moral excellence nor to worldly rank and can be taken in the present context as referring to people whom we regard as of some consequence, without examining the motive for our regard. Aristotle does not enlarge on this, and has no need to. His object is to define the characters proper to dramatic tragedy and he finds, comparing them to those of comedy, 'that comedy is inclined to imitate persons below the level of our world, tragedy persons above it'.[21] His approach

---

[19] Pure situation: a thirsty man struggles through the desert to reach a water-hole of which he knows. If he dies on the way, there is no necessary tragedy. If he reaches the water-hole and finds it has dried out, there is tragedy depending solely on the tragic recognition.

[20] '*Grave* and *great* are the two ideas contained in the word.' (Butcher, *op. cit.*, p. 241.) He suggests 'noble', but dismisses it as too 'moral' and opts for 'serious' instead.

[21] *Poetics*, Ch. 2. Potts, p. 19.

has already been made quite clear by his earlier comment that the characters in literature and art must be 'either above our norm, or below it, or normal'. This is in line with my own earlier observations on the *status* of tragedy and the tragic character.

Aristotle's second observation has proved more pregnant, though in its context it is also very clear and simple. Conceiving tragedy as a change from good fortune to misfortune, he is considering what kind of characters the spectators will be most ready to watch undergoing that change, bearing in mind that the desired effect is the stimulation of 'pity and fear'. He says this:

> ... first, decent people must not be shown passing from good fortune to misfortune (for that is not fearful or pitiful but disgusting). Again, vicious people must not be shown passing from misfortune to good fortune (for that is the most untragic situation possible—it has none of the requisites, it is neither humane, nor pitiful, nor fearful). Nor again should an utterly evil man fall from good fortune to misfortune (for though a plot of that kind would be humane, it would not induce pity or fear—pity is induced by undeserved misfortune and fear by the misfortunes of normal people, so that this situation would be neither pitiful nor fearful). So we are left with a man between these extremes: that is to say, the kind of man who neither is distinguished for excellence and virtue, nor comes to grief on account of baseness and vice, but on account of some error; a man of great reputation and prosperity, like Oedipus and Thyestes and conspicuous people of such families as theirs. So ... there must be no change from misfortune to good fortune, but only the opposite. ... The cause must not be vice, but a great error; and the man must be either of the type specified or better, rather than worse.[22]

Although it contains more, this passage can be partly summed up by saying that it is repugnant to see innocent people victimised (the stressing of suffering, with the appeal to sadism) and that it is untragic to watch the downfall of an utterly evil man, since this would evoke not pity but approval. Through stating these principles, Aristotle is drawn, perhaps over-logically, into describing the kind of man who is acceptable as a tragic victim. There the difficulties begin.

He must be a man between the two extremes of perfection and evil. He must not be faultless, yet his misfortune must be 'undeserved'.

[22] *Poetics*, Ch. 13. Potts, pp. 33–4.

38

To excite fear he must be on a 'normal' level, yet in some way he should be superior to us. If, for example, he is a 'man of great reputation and prosperity', so much the better.

The contradictions of these requirements are apparent, if they are considered purely in fixed terms of 'character'. Aristotle no doubt realised this, and he therefore quickly though tacitly abandons the attempt to reach a definition in such terms and throws the onus on to the 'error' which the character commits, using the same word twice in a few lines.

6

The tragic error. No one attaches a transcendent meaning to the 'errors' of comedy, much less of farce. Mistaken identities, mis-understandings about what some character said or meant, mistakes about bedroom doors—these help to complicate the plot and are all part of the fun. On the level of farce, Oedipus was mistaken about the identity of his parents, he misunderstood the true significance of what the oracle said, and he went into the wrong bedroom. In examining tragedy-as-drama by the analytical method, it was this class of error that Aristotle evidently had in mind. But the difference in tragedy is that the errors are fatal and that, although they can be dissipated at the end, their consequences cannot. One is therefore obliged to consider them more fully.

Aristotle's word is *hamartia*, an 'error' or 'false step'[23] which the tragic hero commits consciously, but without intending an evil result. It is virtually certain that that is all Aristotle meant here, but the word cannot be limited to a single English meaning in all con-texts. In the Greek New Testament, as Mr Potts reminds us, 'it is the regular word for sin'. In the course of a demonstration that the Greeks did not divide concepts into precisely the same categories as ourselves—that they did not, for example, make the same distinc-tions between the moral, the intellectual, the aesthetic and the practical, Professor Kitto writes:

> The word *hamartia* means 'error', 'fault', 'crime', or even 'sin'; literally, it means 'missing the mark', 'a bad shot'. We exclaim, 'How intellectuallist the Greeks were!' Sin is just 'missing the mark'; better luck next time! ... Our difficulty with ... *hamartia* is that we think more in departments. *Hamartia*, 'A bad shot', does

[23] 'Error or frailty' (Butcher). 'Error of judgment' (Bywater).

not mean 'Better luck next time'; it means rather that a mental error is as blameworthy, and may be as deadly, as a moral one.[24]

So going far beyond Aristotle to all the later accretions of tragic theory we are presented with the tragic error, or mistake, or fault, or defect, or flaw (but not crime). The choice between these terms and some of the consequent problems derives from the conviction that the suffering shown in tragedy is disproportionate to the human cause. This can be classed (primarily if not exclusively) as a moral conviction. It supposes an extra-human principle of equity which rewards right-doing and punishes wrong-doing, using each term in its broadest sense. According to this conviction, whose roots are of enormous depth, the disaster which ends a tragedy is retribution for something and the inevitable question is 'For what?'

When the mistake or false step is seen purely as a product of stupidity, one may still agree, though reluctantly, that a stupid choice deserves punishment. At least this is some explanation and it leaves intact the law of cause-and-effect. If the choice had to be made quite arbitrarily and so could not fairly be called 'stupid', it would still be possible to concede that the knowledge necessary to avoid it did exist somewhere, or potentially, and might be possessed by another man, or conceivably by some ideally postulated higher intelligence. Punishment in this case can still be swallowed, after some protest against the iron laws of nature, God, and so on.[25]

A 'fault' in one sense generally implies responsibility, not realised at the time but admitted afterwards. 'Yes, I can see that it was my fault. I ought to have been more careful,' sums it up. There is no pernicious intent, but rashness or laziness or lack of attention. This also may warrant punishment, though the degree of guilt can always be argued. But there is the second kind of fault, the 'fault in construction', which is the same as the defect or flaw. For this the decisions of the individual cannot be held responsible, yet it may lead to his destruction.

In this case it becomes inappropriate to speak of punishment or retribution. A different notion, for which there is no exact word,

[24] H. D. F. Kitto, *The Greeks* (Penguin Books, 1951), pp. 170–1.
[25] A car with faulty brakes is involved in an accident. All the degrees of 'error' can be read into this situation, according to the circumstances. The driver had been warned but thought he knew better; he suspected the brakes were faulty but did not bother; he knew they were faulty but for some reason *had* to take the car out; he should have known; he could have known; he did not know.

comes into play. A society—or, for that matter, a species—dies out on account of some defect which prevents it from adapting itself to changed conditions. A hereditary flaw or a defect of character (the commonest instances in tragedy) leads an individual to disaster. In such instances, since it is not possible to say that any particular law has been transgressed, the notion of a universal principle of equity is gravely weakened (and, if it has been conceived as divine equity, will be fiercely recriminated), but without removing the case from the domain of tragedy. The principle most likely to be invoked is 'the survival of the fittest', with its corollary, 'woe betide the weak'. This is not just, but neither is it unjust. The moral explanation, based on the concept of equity, has perforce been abandoned, but in its place is a scientific explanation, which is better than none at all.

At their wits' end before the apparent absence of *any* explanation in certain cases, some theorists who believe that a tragedy must incorporate a system of cause-and-effect have been driven to postulate a 'flaw in the universe'. The world possesses, so to speak, streaks of rottenness or evil which may crop out anywhere and destroy the wholly admirable and innocent. Distinct from this but comparable in its broad sweep is the theory of a built-in flaw in the whole human race, reflected in several mythologies (Noah's Flood; Zeus's intention to destroy mankind and start again with something better—see Aeschylus, *Prometheus Bound*). According to this second theory, *no* human being is essentially innocent, but is a tainted creature through the fact of being human (cp. the human attitude to 'vermin'). The Christian version of this is the doctrine of original sin, tempered however by the doctrines of redemption and grace. (It is interesting to note that the Hebrew myth in *Genesis* iii. attributes original sin to a conscious act—the Fall, begun with Eve's yielding to temptation—and so to a fault in the sense of an avoidable lapse, rather than to a flaw inherent in human nature. There was 'natural evil' in the Serpent, but not in the Woman, who had to be persuaded to perform an act she knew was forbidden. Perhaps, however, the whole explanation is that the myth's symbolism was easier to understand in this form.)

The concept of original sin, so important in a religious interpretation of tragedy, will be returned to in the next chapter. Meanwhile it is apparent that any 'tragic flaw' of that nature, however interpreted, is a very remote development of Aristotle's *hamartia*. It is distinct also from the mistaken decision for which the individual can, at least in some measure, be held responsible.

The 'mistake' and the 'flaw' will, however, be related if the view is held that personal qualities dictate our decisions; that, for example, 'character' determines acts. This, which is the mainspring of some of the most profound tragedies, leads to such judgments as: 'Being the man he was, he could hardly have acted otherwise.'

7

Being and Doing. Here again, Aristotle has set the ball rolling. 'Tragedy [i.e., tragic drama],' he says in a certain passage, 'is an imitation not of men but of doings, life, happiness;[26] unhappiness is located in doings, and our end is a certain kind of doing, not a personal quality. It is their characters that give men their quality, but their doings that make them happy or the opposite. So it is not the purpose of the actors to imitate character, but they include character as a factor in the doings. Thus it is the incidents (that is to say the 'story') that are the end for which tragedy exists; and the end is more important than anything else. Also, without an action there could not be a tragedy, but without Character there could be.'[27] /

This passage immediately follows an enumeration of the six elements which, for Aristotle, make up dramatic tragedy: the Story ('Fable'), Character, Language, Thought, the *mise en scène* (or 'staging'), Melody or Song (a reference to the sung choruses and other musical accompaniments of Greek tragedy). By Character he means something resembling what we mean by 'a good character' or 'a bad character'[28]—the stereotyped moral qualities attributed to the personages in the simpler kinds of fiction and which always foreshadow the way they will act—as the good Sheriff, the bold Buccaneer, gallant Sir Guy, prudent Penelope, resourceful Ulysses. That this is Aristotle's sense seems to be borne out by his remark in a different passage, in the course of his discussion of Probability, that: 'The universal [the "poetic" truth of fiction] occurs when a man says or does what is characteristic of his temperament, probably or

[26] In Aristotle's philosophy, 'happiness' (*eudaimonia*) is an activity, not a state; almost 'prosperity'—*doing well* rather than *well-being*.

[27] *Poetics*, Ch. 6. Potts, p. 25.

[28] Cp. modern idiomatic English: 'a bad type'. The tendency of these uses of 'character' or 'type' is always to subordinate individual distinctions, hence to flatten out the psychological contours.

necessarily, in the circumstances—*this is the point of the descriptive proper names in poetry* [my italics]; what Alcibiades [an "historical" personage] did or what happened to him is an aggregation of particulars.'[29]

Aristotle's argument is confined to the characterisation of dramatic tragedy. The personages, he holds, should act 'in character', but it is their acts and not their characters which make the tragedy. This is self-evident if one assumes that the opposite of what he had in mind would be a descriptive work, containing possibly a psychological analysis of the personages, but not showing them in action. Nothing would 'happen' to them. However, in a passage closely preceding that quoted above on p. 42 ('Tragedy is an imitation not of men but of doings') and so placed that it leads up to it, Aristotle appears to outline a conflicting theory. The relevant passage is:

> Again, since the object imitated is an action, and doings are done by persons whose individuality will be determined by their character and their thought[30] (for these are the factors which we

---

[29] *Poetics*, Ch. 9. Potts, p. 29. Butcher translates in a similar sense: 'By the universal I mean how a person of a certain type will on occasion speak or act, according to the law of probability or necessity; *and it is this universality at which poetry aims in the names she attaches to the personages.* . . . In comedy this is already apparent, for here the poet first constructs the plot on the lines of probability, and then inserts the characteristic names—unlike the lampooners who write about particular individuals.'
The other translators, however, render the text differently. E.g., Bywater: 'By a universal statement I mean a statement of what such or such a kind of man will probably or necessarily say or do—which is the aim of poetry, *though it affixes proper names to the characters* [my italics].' Similarly Hardy. Rostagni (*op. cit.*, p. 35) seeks to combine both interpretations: '. . . *ed è questo a cui mira la poesia, che i nomi li applica dopo* [*come epiteti*].' ('And this is the aim of poetry, in that it supplies the names afterwards—as descriptive adjectives.')

[30] By 'thought' Aristotle appears to mean the meditations, questionings, and observations expressed by a stage character (for it is hard to see how unexpressed thought could have dramatic existence), in later drama the typical material of the monologue. He would presumably have classed Hamlet's soliloquy, *To be or not to be*, as 'thought', though we do not separate it from character or potential action. Thus, schematically:

Character	Thought	Action
Irresolute Hamlet	What of the consequences?	Postponed
Jealous-and-impetuous Othello	My wife is unfaithful	Kills wife

To reduce the tragedies to such outlines makes it clear that, though the action may take place last (as a 'result' of the other factors), it must be planned first.

have in mind when we define the quality of their doings), it follows that there are two natural causes of these doings, Thought and Character; *and these causes determine the good or ill fortune of every one* (my italics).[31]

He then goes on to define his terms:

But the Story ['Fable'] is the imitation of the action—and by Story I mean the whole structure of the incidents. By Character I mean the factor that enables us to define the particular quality of the people involved in the doings; and Thought is shown by everything they say when they are demonstrating a fact or disclosing an opinion.[32]

Once again, it must be emphasised that Aristotle is examining only the different elements in a tragic drama. Within those limits, he is not inconsistent. There is no tragedy, he says, without action. The personages in the tragedy are so characterised (by the dramatist)

[31] *Poetics*, Ch. 6. Potts, p. 24. Bywater's translation agrees with this. Hardy and Butcher differ on an important point, e.g.:

. . . *il y a deux causes naturelles qui déterminent les actions, à savoir la pensée et le caractère, et* ce sont les actions *qui toujours nous font réussir ou échouer.* (Hardy, *op. cit.*, p. 37.)

Again, Tragedy is the imitation of an action; and an action implies personal agents, who necessarily possess certain distinctive qualities both of character and thought; for it is by these that we qualify actions themselves, and these—thought and character—are the two natural causes from which actions spring, and on actions again all success or failure depends. (Butcher, *op. cit.*, p. 25.)

The broad issue of action and character is well discussed in Butcher's commentary (*op. cit.*, p. 333 *et seq.*). Much of the difficulty, as he points out, rests on the interpretation of Aristotle's words *ethos* and *dianoia*, which do not exactly correspond to the modern 'character' and 'thought'. Yet these are the nearest equivalents available and the alternative to adopting them would be to admit that Aristotle's theory is not transposable to a modern context. At this point, Rostagni may be invoked for his observation that *ethos* and *dianoia* signify respectively moral and intellectual qualities ('*condizioni morali e intellettuali*') and for his further remark that these *condizioni* 'serve not only to qualify individuals, but also qualify actions; they are the two determining causes of the actions; and in the actions so determined all men find the good or bad fortune which is particularly important from a dramatic point of view.'

The detail of this argument is interesting, if not consistently of the first importance. But what cannot be got round is the fact that all the interpreters of this particular passage attribute to Aristotle the opinion that Thought and Character are the *cause* of success or failure, good fortune or bad—whether directly (as in Mr Potts's version) or at one remove through the actions which they 'determine'.

[32] *Poetics*, Ch. 6. Potts, p. 24.

that they must act in a certain way—the rash character rashly, the wise character prudently. In the circumstances of the story (which is the first thing for the dramatist to work out or 'plot'), they do indeed act in that way and end in good or ill fortune accordingly. And their fortune is realised in an act, to which they themselves have contributed, and to show which is the end or aim of tragedy.

This stops a long way short of claiming that, in life, a man with such-and-such a character will come to disaster in any circumstances, or that his character will shape circumstances so that they lead to disaster. The circumstances, for Aristotle, are shaped by the dramatist (the plotting of the Story) and the characters are either chosen or devised in order to fit them.

It would be only by assimilating real people to *dramatis personae* (and postulating also something resembling a superhuman dramatist to construct the 'real' Story) that we could credit Aristotle with any general theory on the logic of character.

Nevertheless, that theory is widely held. It connects a man with his acts in a relationship which is necessary if he is to be respected as a significant entity. Before he can be accorded the human status which will rank him as a tragic figure, he must act in consistency with his character, or his nature. (It does not matter that his acts are observed first and his character discerned afterwards.) If he does not, he is seen as either a hypocrite or an automaton. There are instances, with a high tragic potential, in which a man appears to act against his own nature or temperament (in describing such situations one tends to avoid both the word and the concept of 'character'). Superficially, these are struggles of the will to assert itself against a deeply-rooted impulse. But if one inquires for the source of the will, one can only conclude that it also proceeds from the man's nature. The impulse to go 'against nature' is as 'natural' as the impulse to go with it. Since the process of its emergence may be painful, it can best be compared to childbirth. A woman who gives birth to a personality distinct from her own is not for that reason a hypocrite. Neither is she unrelated to it, nor has she betrayed the integrity of her own personality as it was when she was still childless.[33]

On this analogy, decisions taken either with or without a conscious

[33] It is possible to argue, though on a somewhat theoretical plane, that the surrender of virginity *in any circumstances* entails a loss of personal integrity. The absolutist mind might well take this view.

45

assertion of the will may be said to be equally the products of character. The tragic significance which is attributed to them and, in general, the view taken of the relationship between being and doing, vary according to the historical period and the underlying philosophy. But it would be difficult at this date to deny that the relationship seems indissoluble. A tragic event seems incompletely tragic until one can assign to it a cause connected in some way with the personality of the participants.

8

Suffering and the unhappy ending. We have so far taken it for granted that suffering is inherent in tragedy and the fact requires little elaboration. Aristotle also takes it for granted, since his condition that tragedy should excite pity can be met only if there is suffering to arouse it. It would be something of a quibble to add that misfortune also excites pity, since the object of pity is still the suffering which misfortune brings. Suffering of some kind is essential, though if it is predominantly physical and is over-stressed it appears revolting and the 'horror' consideration comes into play. If it is too finely psychological it may escape our notice, or be condemned as illusory. Every sane man respects physical pain, but what constitutes mental or emotional suffering depends largely on a point of view.

What cannot be conceded is that the spectacle of suffering, as suffering, is the main point of tragedy. It is simply an inescapable accompaniment of a tragic situation.

Suffering is of necessity culminative in a tragedy with an 'unhappy ending'. We think that such an ending is inevitable in any general definition of the tragic, and we assumed it in speaking of the 'final disaster' and the principle of 'no recovery' in the previous chapter. Aristotle also advocates the unhappy ending for dramatic tragedy, while recognising that by no means all Greek tragedies have one. His position is implicit in his statement already quoted (p. 38) above, that 'there must be no change from misfortune to good fortune, but only the opposite, from good fortune to misfortune'. A few lines later in the same chapter, he makes the same point rather more explicitly:

> This [the plot containing 'terrible experiences or doings'] is the plot that will produce the technically finest tragedy. Those critics

are therefore wrong who censure Euripides on this very ground—
because he does this in his tragedies, and many of them end in
misfortune; for it is, as I have said, the right thing to do.[34]

Numerous dramatic works called tragedies, beside the Greek
examples which Aristotle knew, disregard his recommendation. They
end happily for the protagonists or for the 'good' characters—who
may or may not be the same. It would be too categorical at this
point to declare that they are never true tragedies and that 'neither
are their counterparts in real life. But when they occur it is worth
scrutinising them very carefully to determine the nature of the 'happy
ending'. It may be a matter of appearance only, bearing on a point
different from the central point of the tragedy, or affecting non-
central characters. It may, in the plainest case, be an offering of
consolation to the spectator to offset, at least superficially, a misery
too terrible to be contemplated.

9

Aristotle's formal definition of *dramatic* tragedy, quoted on p. 28
above, neither contradicts nor does much to confirm our own
general definition put forward on p. 20. But the latter is not invali-
dated by any of the propositions he advances and indeed it may be
said to run broadly along the same lines.

As has just been remarked, Aristotle believed that a tragedy
should involve a final disaster or 'misfortune'. His 'error' is com-
prehended in our 'unforeseen failure'—a term with wider implications, which we therefore prefer. Our 'people who command respect
and sympathy' will at least include Aristotle's 'superior people', if
they do not wholly coincide with them. Our 'ironical change of
fortune' is Aristotle's *peripeteia*, on which he insists, considering it
as basic and linking it with the notion of probability. 'Waste' he does
not mention, but our 'misery and emotional distress' is the 'suffering'
which has been discussed in the immediately preceding section.

It has always been a tricky matter to claim to be applying
Aristotle's theories with exactness. But at least it brings some reassurance not to be in flagrant contradiction with them.

[34] *Poetics*, Ch. 13. Potts, p. 34.

3

Tragedy and Religion

1

It is often claimed that there is a natural relationship between tragedy and religion; even that tragedy is an expression of the religious outlook. In one—the most easily definable—sense, this view is supported by a theory of the origin of drama. 'Tragedy', observed Aristotle, 'began with the leaders of the dithyramb [choric song in honour of Dionysus] and comedy with the leaders of the phallic performances which still survive as customary practices in many of our cities.'[1]

The theory is stated more explicitly by Aelius Donatus, a Roman grammarian of the fourth century A.D. whose grammatical treatises and commentaries on literature were widely used in medieval schools. 'Tragedy and comedy', wrote Donatus, 'had their beginnings in the religious observances with which the ancients performed their sacrifices in accomplishment of their vows made for their crops.'[2]

Plenty of evidence can be assembled in support of the theory. It is indeed highly probable that both the tragedy and the comedy of the Greeks developed ultimately from religious and para-religious rites, just as the medieval Mysteries and Miracles developed from the ritual and observances of the Christian Church. A religious origin—though not always a *ritual* origin—can be assigned with some confidence to all drama and, indeed, to all literature and art

---

[1] *Poetics*, Ch. 4. Potts, p. 22.
[2] Translation from H. W. Lawton, *Handbook of French Renaissance Dramatic Theory* (Manchester, 1949), which also quotes the original text.

and the myths on which these have drawn. Provided one goes back far enough, one reaches a point at which art and religion are inseparable—as in ancient Hebrew culture. But this would not justify the singling-out of tragedy from all other forms of artistic expression. To do that, a more specific theory is put forward.

What may conveniently be called the theory of the Corn King is already implied in the quotation from Donatus above. The King —to offer a generalised version of the primitive fertility rite as Frazerian anthropology reconstructed it—is appointed for a fixed term, during which he receives all the respect and honour due to his royal standing. At the end of the term he is taken out and ceremonially slaughtered and his blood is sprinkled on the fields as an offering to the mysterious powers which determine the quality of the crops. A new king is immediately chosen to reign for the next period, at the end of which he will be sacrificed in his turn.

In cultures which no longer live 'by bread alone', i.e., in which a successful agriculture is not the only vital element in their wellbeing, the fundamental principle of the propitiatory sacrifice remains the same, though its significance will be enlarged and spiritualised. The sacrifice will still be a 'King': he will incarnate the best that the community has to offer. He will represent that 'best' not merely as a physically vigorous individual, of high value for labour and war, but because he personifies the power and the aspirations of the community. In his sacrificial aspect, he becomes the hero who dies for his people, by whom he is offered as an outstanding specimen of the whole in the belief that this is a sufficient concession to satisfy the gods. If he suffers—no doubt, the more he suffers—the more acceptable the offering will seem to be. It will not only be a clearer token of the abasement of the highest in the community to a still higher power, but will also be intended to buy freedom from suffering for the community as a whole, on the principle of compensation.

It is somewhere here that the idea of atonement enters in. The sacrifice becomes something more than a buying-off of the demanding earth-gods with blood, humiliation, and pain—commodities which, to the primitive mind, they evidently value because they so often exact them. The idea now arises that the sufferings of the community, whether through famine, disease, or any other physical cause, may be 'deserved'. The gods are not merely greedy powers exacting tribute. They are also capable of being offended by the transgression of some embryonic moral law. (The gods also are now

49

necessarily credited with moral preoccupations, as they were not in the earlier phase.) With the birth of guilt goes the desire to be discharged from it. The transgressions of the community are transferred symbolically to the sacrificial King, who goes to his death loaded with both excellence and sin, with the shame of the community as well as its pride. The sacrifice has become expiatory as well as propitiatory.[3]

Thus the King, representing the 'best' qualities of the community, can at the same time be made responsible for its worst qualities, be at once hero and scapegoat. Is not this, it may be asked, the essence of the tragic ambivalence; a definition, in general terms, of the typical tragic hero? Further, is it not significant that so much dramatic tragedy treats of kings or their equivalents in exactly those terms—powerful yet fallible, admirable yet guilty—and do not most tragedies culminate in the ending of an order (the old Corn King's reign) and the inception of a new?

There is no doubt whatever that this is one of the great archetypal situations which have gone to mould and move human societies and which, in various but recognisable forms, still awakens a profound response in the modern world. Its relation to some fundamental principle in mass psychology is not in doubt. What is in question is its basic relationship to the concept of tragedy.

2

The focal point of Western religion is the Crucifixion, interpreted by orthodox Christians as a sacrifice of atonement for the sins, not just of one community or nation, but of the whole of humanity. Jesus incarnates all the finest moral qualities of mankind, raised to the level of divine attributes which make him the 'Son of God', in

[3] The foregoing is not put forward as an anthropologically exact account, if that were possible, but only as an analytically convenient break-down of a complex process still not fully understood. No doubt the most primitive being has some consciousness of guilt, created by a rebuke from its parent, if nothing else. But it is fair to assume that a moral law, requiring some *theory* of guilt, has not been indispensable to all human communities, any more than it appears to be to all gregarious animals. Provided that competition is not too intense, a certain level of communal material existence is possible without it and could still include the *propitiatory* worship of superior powers. A dog will try to propitiate its master without, as far as one knows, experiencing guilt. When human beings do the same —they 'crawl' but are not 'really sorry'—the *moral* sense is outraged. But we do it.

whatever sense this may be understood. In any case, he is a 'King'. 'Christ the King', 'The King of Men' and similar titles are accorded him. At the same time he 'takes upon himself the sins of the world' and expiates them on behalf of humanity with intense moral suffering (the 'agony at Gethsemane') and then physical suffering, leading to death.

This must be seen as the supreme development of the Corn King tradition; or conversely one could say that the Corn King tradition was a preparation for this supreme happening, making its significance familiarly clear when it came. With all this, it has never occurred to any orthodox Christian to call Jesus a tragic figure, or the Crucifixion a tragic event.

That is obviously because death was not the end of the matter. It was followed by the Resurrection and by a new hope for mankind in the doctrine of redemption through the sufferings of the 'King'. The same applied in a more restricted sense to the sacrifices of the primitive Corn Kings. Their communities were 'redeemed' for another year—if they were not, there would be no sense in 'expiation'. There may or may not have been a belief in their resurrection in the person of the succeeding King, but where there was not, the quality and office of kingship still continued. Morally, there was no death, but (through the association with fertility and the new crops) a fresh hope and a rebirth.

In any form in which it can be conceived, from the most primitive to the most sophisticated, the expiatory sacrifice of the King excludes all that we have so far seen of the tragic conditions. It is not, in any moral sense, 'final'. It is not a 'disaster', but a triumph. The suffering which it entails may engender pity—on an instinctive and unreflective level—but not fear when it is regarded as a labour necessary to obtain a certain reward. The same will apply to every example of Christian martyrdom, and indeed of martyrdom in any cause which is felt to have triumphed. The moment one envisages either a successful sacrifice of expiation or a reward beyond death one has moved away from the tragic, for these things can only imply, on some plane or another, a happy ending.

Any redemptive—and so ultimately optimistic—religion, like Christianity, assumes such an ending. The contrary would mean that death is final or that suffering (of the 'good') continues beyond it; also that the impulse to make expiation is futile. These are the negations associated with what are sometimes vaguely called the

Dark Gods and two of them lead in a direct line to a philosophy which the religious deplore as 'materialistic'.

There is only one assumption on which the Crucifixion, or any other sacrifice on the same model, could appear tragic. That is, if it were ineffectual. In that event, all the notions of failure and waste, with the unlooked-for and irreparable disaster and the horror of recognition, would automatically come into play. For the community which had committed themselves to the sacrifice, the tragedy would consist principally in the recognition that it would not save them and that they were now helpless before a danger against which they knew no defence. For the protagonist it would be typified by the exclamation of the dying Jesus as recorded in the first two Gospels: 'My God, why hast thou forsaken me?' For obvious reasons, these cannot be accepted literally as Jesus's last words, since they would destroy the basis of Christianity, and less damaging explanations have been found. If they were so accepted, it would mean that at the end Jesus realised the failure of the mission to which his life had been dedicated and he would become an authentically tragic figure. In the same way, other sacrificial heroes who doubted the efficacy of their sacrifice could become tragic. It may be assumed that, among the primitive Corn Kings, some were reluctant victims while others lost conviction at some point before their deaths. If it is further assumed that the community in general continued to believe in the efficacy of the sacrifice, theirs would be personal tragedies.

It follows that, in order to qualify as a tragic figure, the sacrificial King must be moving against the religious beliefs of the community. Whether he is impelled by 'honest doubt', fear, or intense suffering, he will—from the point of view of the accepted religion—become either a rebel or a renegade. The only other alternative is that his denial stems from weakness, in which case he has proved unworthy of being made a 'King'. It seems clear that none of the 'heroes' of Christianity, whatever the doubts and failures they experienced in the course of their lives, could ever in the final count be equated with the tragic hero.

3

The main point at which the tragic can enter is through the 'imperfect Christian'. This is the man who is aware of the religious virtues but is unable to practise them in living, or possibly the man who seeks to reinterpret them in an unorthodox way. The latter is uninteresting from the angle of this inquiry. Either he becomes an accepted reformer and, having triumphed, is not tragic; or his interpretation is not accepted and he remains a heretic and morally condemned.[4] But the first is the mirror in which a large part of humanity recognises its own image:

> Oh, wearisome condition of humanity
> Born under one law, to another bound,
> Vainly begot and yet forbidden vanity,
> Created sick, commanded to be sound.

This takes us back to the concept of original sin, the taint in human nature already touched on in the previous chapter. As expressed by the poet, the concept appears unequivocally tragic. It is the great dilemma which poses the impossible choice between nature and morality, being and doing, essence and existence. It places man, aware of a divine law (or any other) but unable to obey it, in the position of the fox which becomes aware of the human law according to which its activities are pernicious, and yet cannot live in any other way. Not merely 'nature' but necessity (though ultimately, no doubt, the two are the same) obliges it to kill game and poultry. What choice has the carnivorous fox? Either it can ignore the voice of its awakened conscience and continue as before—probably the healthiest solution if it can be achieved, and one which finds much support on the plane of modern psychology, but is neither 'moral' nor tragic. Or it continues as before but entertains a despairing awareness of its own sinfulness—this, as we have seen, is highly tragic. Or it may attempt to change its diet and, overcoming 'nature', to be vegetarian—this, the Stoic solution, is ultimately humanist and secular, though often incorporated in religious ethical teaching. It also has a tragic potential, high in ratio to the probability of backsliding. Or—the most desperate course, but certainly the most consistent with Christian doctrine—it can throw itself on the mercy of the farmer and hope to be adopted into his household.

[4] The mythical prototype of the unaccepted reformer is Satan, conceived as a Fallen Angel. If the myth has any meaning at all, his rebellion was motivated by the desire to run the universe better than the Almighty, for no one takes over a concern of which he is to be the head in order to ruin it. Because of his miscalculation and failure Satan can be presented as a tragic figure, and indeed has been. But this type of case is marginal and can be omitted from a general examination of the usual springs of tragedy. Apart from that, it is doubtfully 'religious'.

If the last course fails, it is again tragic. If it succeeds, there is a happy ending and no tragedy. It can only succeed if the farmer accepts the fox—a hazardous assumption for the fox to make beforehand—or, in a different set of circumstances, if it is picked up without its connivance and adopted.

Christianity would not regard the fox as incurably pernicious. But it holds that it cannot stop being pernicious by its own unaided efforts. It requires the farmer's help. This help, according to 'optimistic' Christianity, is given to any creature which sincerely desires it. But 'pessimistic' Christianity takes account of the uncertainty of the farmer's response, based on considerations which the fox may not understand, and it notes the apparently accidental circumstances in which some foxes are 'saved' without effort on their part.

The doctrine of grace in its most liberal form ignores these 'pessimistic' qualifications. But its less liberal refinements were evolved to meet them. They were attempts, of great subtlety, to rationalise a moral situation which had come to be recognised as irrational. They were typical of the main period of their origin, the seventeenth century. Their implications must be considered more fully in a later chapter.[5]

It is in this general area of dubiety that the tragedies of religion are most likely to occur. Grace need not be specifically mentioned or invoked, but the tragic element will be based on the uncertainty of human destiny and the unpredictability of the divine response. In this philosophy, the final disaster is not physical death but damnation—a permanent casting-out from life and happiness. To be tragic in the terms of our definition on p. 20 it must not only contain an element of the unpredictable but should involve 'people who command respect and sympathy'. It will not take in the 'hardened sinner', the 'villain' of drama whose destruction is felt to be deserved, inevitable, and indeed desirable. It will turn instead on the man who from the beginning appears to have a chance of salvation, but fails to make it good for whatever reason. The rest of our definition follows automatically: the frequent incidence of an ironical change of fortune, the feeling of waste, the emotional misery.

It must be emphasised that the theory of an ineradicable taint in human nature is not that either of orthodox Christianity or of tragedy.[6] The fox is not doomed from birth simply for being a fox. It,

[5] Chapter 8. See particularly p. 161 *et seq.*
[6] Not Christian because of the doctrine of redemption. Not tragic because disaster could be clearly predicted from the start.

too, always has a chance. To remain in this field of thinking, we have to modify a traditional phrase. The modification may wear the look of a rather pedantic verbal quibble, but in fact it is very much more. It becomes necessary to replace 'man's tragic destiny' by 'the tragic potentialities in man's destiny' and so to leave an escape-route open.

4

From what has been said it will appear that one Christian view of the human condition (the minority 'pessimistic' view) necessarily contains a tragic conception. The same would be true of any religion which postulated the weakness of man and the difficulty of understanding or obeying a divine law. But if tragedy is implicit in this kind of religion, is religion implicit in tragedy? The comprehensive answer must be *No*. The failure in the tragic hero and/or his acts and/or their pre-conditions can be transferred to quite a different context with no essential change. The 'law' which is misunderstood or transgressed may be political, social, or psychological.[7] The nation or the community may replace the 'god', and rejection by it will replace the damnation of the theologians. Disaster may even spring from neglect or unawareness of some purely material factor elevated to a 'law', such as the maximum stress-point of a metal or the alcohol-tolerance of the human body.

Viewed from a sufficient height some tragedies may appear relatively trivial, and it is of course true that those tragedies which touch deep moral issues (in general, these are the issues which religion also raises) will have the strongest impact and the widest resonance. But the others are tragedies, too. Although they may be placed lower in the scale, they possess qualities which on analysis prove to be the same. These cannot be refused the name of 'tragic', provided, to echo Aristotle, that their embodiment remains in some way or other above the level of the onlookers.

[7] This last word may seem to beg the question, but it is limited here to its more nearly technical meaning: acquired psychological knowledge based on experiment and research.

4

The Tragic Sense of Life

1

It is often argued that an awareness of the tragic varies, as a matter of social psychology, from period to period and from culture to culture. In some cultures it will be so highly developed as to typify their conception of life, in others it will be scarcely apparent. The same will apply—though here investigation is even more difficult—to individuals within the same culture.

In looking for this 'tragic sense of life' one need not demand a rigorous mustering of all the tragic elements tentatively deduced in the previous chapters, and certainly not a conscious mustering of them. The tragic sense may be allowed to exist in inchoate forms which never reach full development, though they should not appear to be incapable of it. It may be little more than a temperamental disposition, a propensity to regard existence and events in a certain way which never emerges in a clearly defined attitude. In the most general terms, it may be held to consist in a persistent awareness that human destiny is affected by uncontrollable factors and that its usual condition is unhappiness. That much would be expected as a minimum.

As a starting-point one cannot do better than turn to Miguel de Unamuno's book which in its day virtually launched the notion of the 'tragic sense'.[1] Like most of Unamuno's work, the book is a passionate yet exploratory statement of the author's own beliefs, which he relates to those of the Spanish people. In his profoundly

[1] *Del sentimiento trágico de la vida en los hombres y en los pueblos* (Madrid, 1913). Translated by J. E. Crawford Flitch as *The Tragic Sense of Life in Men and Peoples* (London, 1921).

personal reactions he claims to represent the 'soul' of his nation. He belonged to that generation of Spanish liberals which emerged at the end of the nineteenth century and who were shocked by the intellectual and material backwardness of their country in comparison with the rest of Europe. But some, like Unamuno, who had been reared in orthodox Catholicism, could not accept the apparent alternative of an abrupt transition to positivist materialism. Neither could they easily admit an inferiority in the national character which they tended, as Spaniards still tend, to identify very closely with their own individual characters. Against the evidence of a national decadence—the word was freely used—they placed the evidence of their personal vitality. The first might be deduced, but the second they could *feel*.

Broadly, Unamuno was tormented by a continuous conflict between feeling, conditioned by religious faith (though he rejected traditional orthodoxy, the legacy, as he put it, of the Inquisition) and reason. His preoccupation with the individual personality and hence with the problem of death and the immortality of the soul was at the root of what he called 'the tragic sense of life'. He placed this in opposition to the scientific spirit, to rationalism, and, at times, to intellectualism in general:

> There is something which, for lack of a better name, we will call the tragic sense of life, which carries with it a whole conception of life itself and of the universe, a whole philosophy more or less formulated, more or less conscious. And this sense may be possessed, and is possessed, not only by individual men but by whole peoples. [It] does not so much flow from ideas as determine them, even though afterwards, as is manifest, these ideas react upon it and confirm it. Sometimes it may originate in a chance illness—dyspepsia, for example, but at other times it is constitutional.

Here Unamuno realises that his 'tragic sense' might perhaps be classed as a diseased or morbid state, associated for the national society with the notion of decadence. He reacts against the implication:

> And it is useless to speak, as we shall see, of men who are healthy and men who are not healthy. Apart from the fact that there is no normal standard of health, nobody has proved that man is necessarily cheerful by nature. And further, man, by the mere fact of being man, of possessing consciousness, is, in

comparison with the ass or the crab, a diseased animal. Consciousness is a disease.

So far, this 'tragic sense' is nothing more definite than a melancholy disposition, intimately connected with a brooding on death and the destiny of the individual soul. It is not experienced by those without 'consciousness'.[2] It is not achieved by thought or reason. It is, for Unamuno, an essentially religious state of mind. He has previously said:

> What I think I know is that some individuals and peoples have not really thought about death and immortality, have not felt them, and that others have ceased to think about them, or rather ceased to feel them. And the fact that they have never passed through the religious period is not, I think, a matter for either men or peoples to boast about.

Elsewhere he quotes the Portuguese poet Antero de Quental who in his indignation at the British ultimatum of 1890,[3] had recalled Horace Walpole's remark that 'life is a tragedy for those who feel and a comedy for those who think', and had added: 'If we are destined to end tragically, we Portuguese, we who *feel*, we would far rather prefer this terrible but noble destiny to that which is reserved, and perhaps at no very remote future date, for England, the country that *thinks* and *calculates*, whose destiny it is to finish miserably and comically.'

Unamuno rejects these particular characterisations of the Portuguese and the English, but discovers a basis of truth in the general idea, 'namely, that some peoples, those who put thought above feeling, I should say, reason above faith, die comically, while those die tragically who put faith above reason.'

Turning to individuals, he gives a list of men whom he considers to have possessed the 'tragic sense of life'. He cites Marcus Aurelius, St Augustine, Pascal, Rousseau, 'René', 'Obermann', Thomson [author of *The City of Dreadful Night*], Leopardi, Vigny, Lenau,

---

[2] In Spanish, *conciencia*, which also means 'conscience'. This might be preferred as a rendering, but for the fact that the translation quoted was approved by Unamuno and must be assumed to have been checked by him. Cp. however Pascal's 'heart', pp. 167–8 below.

[3] Concerning the Portuguese attempt to annex the Shire Highlands, now part of Nyasaland, by military action. The ultimatum demanded the withdrawal of the Portuguese from that part of S.E. Africa. It caused deep resentment in Lisbon against the 'oldest ally' and, when complied with, led to the fall of the Portuguese Government.

Kleist, Amiel, Quental [the Portuguese poet just quoted], Kierkegaard, and describes them as 'men burdened with wisdom rather
than with knowledge'.

Including René and Obermann, fictitious characters who evidently
figure here as mouthpieces for their authors, Chateaubriand and
Senancour, the list is heavily slanted towards the 'dark' side of
European Romanticism. Most of the names are those of men
engaged in a losing battle with despair, sufferers from the *mal du
siècle, ennui, noia, tedium vitae, Weltschmerz, Angst*—the various
terms indicate the widespread nature of the 'disease of consciousness', as well as its varying forms. We will try to determine its more
radical causes in a later chapter. For the moment it is enough to
say that these were men more strongly motivated by 'feeling' than
by 'thought', and who shared a particularly negative view of human
destiny.

That view is typified in the 'epitaph' which Leopardi wrote in his
Memorable Sayings of Filippo Ottonieri—an alias for himself:

> Bones
> Of Filippo Ottonieri
> Born for Noble Deeds
> And for Glory
> Lived in Idleness and Futility
> And Died without Renown
> Not Unaware of his Nature
> And of his Fate[4]

This Romantic awareness, and the apathy and despair which
usually accompanied it, rested on a violent contrast between the
aspirations of the individual and his possibilities of fulfilling them.
The first were limitless (for reasons which, again, need not be
analysed at this point), and it became apparent at a fairly early age
that they were unattainable. Hence the lethargy, or world-weariness,
generally leading to a longing for death. Hardly any of Unamuno's
modern examples, with the debatable exception of Kierkegaard,
conceived their dilemma in a Christian context, or in that of any
other doctrinal religion, so that in order to reconcile the list with
Unamuno's contention that the tragic sense is religious, one has to
interpret that word very broadly. If one goes back before the nineteenth century to include the other names cited, one finds a preoccupation with Christian doctrine but not an easy submission to it.

[4] Quoted by Iris Origo, *Leopardi* (Hamish Hamilton, 1953), p. 260.

St Augustine and Pascal, as much as Rousseau, re-examine their faith in the light of the human condition as they themselves are experiencing it. The main motive force is still personal, though less excessively so than in the Romantics. Taking Unamuno's list as a whole, it is fair to say that it reveals a strong bias towards the subjective writer who is over-conscious of the distance separating his hopes from any possibility of fulfilment and who therefore feels doomed to a frustration felt as 'tragic'. Applied to peoples, the position is put more concretely, still through the medium of an individual example:

> The philosophy of the soul of my [the Spanish] people appears to me as the expression of an inward tragedy analogous to the tragedy of the soul of Don Quixote, as the expression of a conflict between what the world is as scientific reason shows it to be, and what we wish it might be, as our religious faith affirms it to be.

This interpretation of *Don Quixote* is debatable, to say the least, but Unamuno, a subjectivist to the limit, forestalls criticism:

> What does it matter to me what Cervantes intended or did not intend to put into it [*Don Quixote*] and what he actually did put into it? What is living in it is what I myself discover in it, whether Cervantes put it there or not, what I myself put into it and under and over it, and what we all put into it.

From a rich and rambling book, concerned with many other matters besides 'tragedy', one can retain the constant propositions that the 'tragic' sense is an acute awareness (1) of the unbridgeable gap between desire and achievement, and (2) of a conflict between the actual material order of the world and a preferred ideal order. In his interpretation and use of the Don Quixote theme, Unamuno might seem to imply that the longing for an ideal order is exclusively nostalgic. He parries this objection by remarking that 'everyone who fights for any ideal whatever, though his ideal may seem to lie in the past, is driving the world on to the future, and the only reactionaries are those who find themselves at home in the present. Every supposed restoration of the past is a creation of the future, and if the past which it is sought to restore is a dream, something imperfectly known, so much the better.'

This is the reservation of a mind at least partly progressive. It rejects the present as uncongenially materialistic but will not be chained to the past because it is obliged to recognise that the past is not only dead, but largely unknowable. What it seeks to do is to build the future on a 'dream' of the past.

2

The contradictions and inconsistencies in Unamuno's book are easy to find, but they by no means reduce its value as a piece of evidence. As a witness, the author was placed in a highly significant position. He belonged to a nation suspected of decadence and which in any case had declined steeply from the leading position it had once occupied. He belonged to a period in which it had suddenly become obvious that the old beliefs had lost their virtue as a basis of material well-being.[5] As an individual, he is conscious in his own person of the material realities of the present and of their irreconcilability with the culture in which he has grown up and which he is psychologically incapable of abandoning. He is an unfortunate link between the old and the new, a man placed at what should be the dividing-point of a whole society, but who cannot divide himself without being destroyed. The conflict is not properly in him, any more than it is in the rope used in the tug-of-war. What he feels is the strain set up in him by the two opposing forces. But he has the illusion that he can favour one side or the other, or else attempt to hold them together, and he sees his 'anguish' in those terms. Unlike both the last-ditch traditionalist and the radical progressive, he feels the tug both ways. His intimate awareness of it he describes as 'tragic'.

This situation can arise in any society which has fallen from prosperity, losing not only the material reality but the psychological *sense* of well-being. In the trivial but expressive phrase of the modern politician, it begins to feel the draught. The winds which blew at Troy and Jerusalem when those cities suddenly fell and the populations were at once exposed to slaughter or slavery were particularly violent and bitter, but sometimes the decline is so gradual as to be scarcely perceptible. If sudden it appears more 'dramatic', but not necessarily more tragic. It is tragic from the moment it is recognised

[5] The economic backwardness and the isolation of Spain delayed this realisation until the end of the nineteenth century, whereas in more highly industrialised countries it occurred nearer the beginning. The flash-point which illuminated the situation for Spain's liberal intellectuals was the war of 1898, as a result of which almost the last remains of Spain's overseas empire, including Cuba and the Philippines, were lost to the United States.

for what it is by the ailing community—which may occur long after the incidence of the historical cause. Whenever the miseries or short-comings of a particular way of life become sufficiently apparent to force a reassessment of an accepted philosophy of life, the way seems open for the 'tragic sense'.

That much can be deduced from Unamuno's study. It appears self-evident and capable of a wide application.

3

But the application of such a reasonable theory is more difficult than one would expect. There is no lack of potential examples—of peoples and societies which have experienced exile, subservience or decay. For long centuries until the foundation of the new state of Israel the destiny of the Jews appeared pre-eminently tragic. Another Semitic people, the Arabs, lived until recently in apparent decadence and apathy in some of the territories which they had once ruled as conquerors. Both peoples are religious, in the sense that their culture is intimately linked to their religion. Yet it could hardly be maintained that either possesses a 'tragic sense' more highly de-veloped than that of more consistently fortunate peoples. Nor can it be said that either has been indifferent to the material world or not at home in it when circumstances have permitted. What again of the Celtic communities, relegated throughout known history to the western fringes of Europe, to subsist on inferior soil or scratch a dangerous living from the sea, and still today, as in the Scottish Highlands, squeezed out like toothpaste from their traditional en-vironment by economic forces? If one finds a greater propensity to melancholy in these peoples than is usual further east—it is a big *if*—cannot it be as easily ascribed to climatic conditions as to innate sensitivity? Weeks and years of Atlantic rain might transform anyone's temperament. It is also noteworthy that the artistic ex-pression of the most vocal of the Celtic societies, the Irish, has proved, from Byron's contemporary Thomas Moore to Yeats, Synge, O'Casey and Brendan Behan, hardly less acceptable to the supposedly hard-headed English than to the nation which produced it. The young Yeats found some temperamental affinity with Maeter-linck, the Belgian Symbolist, a product of a very practical nation with its feet firmly planted in 'the world as scientific reason shows it to be'. For a long time the legends of Ireland, with their misty aura of disaster and decay, highly conducive to thinking 'about death and immortality', were as spiritually exportable as the Ossianic myths in Dr Johnson's day. And if the 'soul' of the Celtic peoples in general is revealed in the sadness not only of their poetry and drama but in some of their popular music—a fondness for the 'lament'—have they not also wildly gay music which sounds an almost orgiastic call to violent physical action?

What has happened to the Slav melancholy, considered as a widespread psychological characteristic not so long ago? Was it ever better founded than the melancholy of the Scandinavians, now thought of as a brisk, practical race, or of the Americans? The latter have often been held up as optimistic materialists *par excellence*, yet this image of them is at least partly modified by the proliferation of religious sects and the extensive demand for psychiatric treatment in the United States. Resorting again to music as a test, is there not a powerful element of nostalgic melancholy in jazz? And if this element, as can be convincingly argued, corresponded to the 'tragic sense' of African slaves in exile, why has it proved so congenial to the slaves' masters?

Questions such as these can be formulated in a few moments. A balanced answer to each could require the work of several years. Taken separately, they are probably all answerable, but it seems improbable that the sum of the answers would yield a general rule on the lines suggested in the earlier part of this chapter. One would like to say: 'Material prosperity brings satisfaction with the present, and with this a disinclination to look regretfully towards the past or with apprehension towards the future. Material misfortune condemns the present and throws the mind back and forward in an anxious "spiritual" search for causes and effects.' But, while this may be true of some societies, there are others of which it is patently untrue. The result of the widest investigation would in all probability be a jigsaw of exceptions and anomalies.

The modern social philosopher has grown dubious about the whole concept of national and racial character.[6] If this goes, the concepts

[6] See, e.g., Morris Ginsberg, 'National Character and National Sentiments'. The following passage has a particular relevance to Unamuno's theme:

> . . . Similar doubts are raised by the numerous attempts that have been made to link up racial characteristics with art forms. Professor McDougall, to take but one instance, has contrasted the art of the Nordic race with that of the Mediterranean. In the former the romantic

of national temperaments, of large collective tendencies towards optimism or pessimism, materialist or immaterial values, must go too or be seriously damaged. No doubt there are national or social *moods*, predominant ways of feeling induced by temporary states such as war or changed economic conditions. But it seems hazardous to maintain that these moods ever build up into something more permanent, profoundly affecting the outlook of a majority of the individuals in a particular national or ethnic group. This consideration must influence our readiness to attribute a 'tragic sense' to some peoples and withhold it from others.

One also becomes more wary of attributing it to the historical period. Certain generations, compared to their predecessors or their successors, may well appear to have more inclined to cynicism, emotionalism, intellectualism, or materialism. The images of these

---

qualities predominate, namely, a profusion of qualities, suggestion beyond what is actually portrayed, complexity of relations, indirectness of appeal, figurative and symbolic use of material, and a sense of mystery. The art of the Mediterranean peoples, on the other hand, is predominantly classic, characterised by clearness, formality, simplicity, directness of appeal, rationalism, and psychical distance. The difference is explained by a supposed difference in temperament and instinctive equipment racially determined. The Nordic is held to be constitutionally introvert, strong in the instinct of curiosity, the root of wonder, and weak in the herd instinct, the root of sociality. In the Mediterranean race the reverse holds good: it is extrovert, weak in curiosity, strong in sociability. This hypothesis is presented by Professor McDougall with his usual skill and persuasiveness, but its precariousness is made manifest when we find on turning to Jung and Seligman that precisely the opposite relations are asserted, introversion being connected by them with the classical qualities and extraversion with the romantic. (In *On the Diversity of Morals*, Paperback edn, Heinemann, 1962, pp. 249–50.)

Further:

No doubt there is some truth in such statements as that, on the average, Dutchmen are more 'stolid' than Italians, or Scotchmen cooler than Irishmen, or that while the Germans are 'heavy' and slow to react, the French are vivacious and mobile. But when we are told that the whole Mongolian division of mankind is 'reserved, sullen, apathetic . . . nearly all reckless gamblers' (Keane), or when a formula such as 'hypocrisy/practical common sense' sums up the Englishman and corresponding pairs of characteristics are assigned to other peoples, for example, 'clearness/licentiousness' to the Frenchman, 'thoroughness/clumsiness' to the German, 'dignity/cruelty' to the Spaniard, 'vulgarity/vitality' to the American (Madariaga), we begin to realise that the interest of these generalisations lies not so much in the truth they may contain as in the light they may throw on the growth of public opinion, and especially of the opinion that members of different nations have of each other. (*Op. cit.*, pp. 251–2.)

generations, as set up by historians of various kinds, provide a convenient ready-reckoner for any account of civilisation. For that purpose they are probably indispensable. They also contain a large element of truth, but like every image, on the analogy of the portrait, they exaggerate some elements and minimise or exclude others.

4

For any assessment of the climate of thought in the past, we are almost entirely dependent on literature, using that word in its widest sense. Something can be deduced from the visual arts,[7] while institutions, whether secular or religious, preserve traces of earlier mental and moral attitudes in the form of records, traditions, ceremonies, and ritual. But beside these the evidence of the creative written word is so much fuller and more articulate that it is inevitably given by far the greatest weight. Perhaps that weight is disproportionate, but it is not unreasonable to take the writer, whether he is a moralist, a poet, a dramatist, or a novelist, as broadly representative of a climate of culture.

One must avoid the mistake of assuming that cultures which have no tragic drama are deficient in the 'tragic sense'. This—if it is what Unamuno maintained it to be—can obviously be expressed in other media and in any case a flowering of tragic drama is impossible where there is no theatre of a suitable character to 'realise' it. But in those places where tragic drama has prospered, one would expect —though not exclusively—to find a correspondingly strong 'tragic sense' in the society which supported it; provided that there is any significant correlation at all between the 'tragic sense' and dramatic tragedy. This is where a further difficulty arises.

Three historical periods have produced unquestionably 'great' dramatic tragedy which was also materially successful and clearly not out of harmony with the age. Yet Athens of the fifth century B.C., Elizabethan-Jacobean England, and seventeenth-century France were each in a phase of confidence and expansion when they produced their most typical and highest kinds of tragedy. It is possible to object that at the end of the Periclean Age, when the later

---

[7] But not too much should be. One questions, while admiring, D. H. Lawrence's reconstruction of a smiling, hedonistic Etruscan civilisation based on the sole evidence of tomb-paintings. Cp. also psychological interpretations of the baroque style.

tragedies of Sophocles and those of Euripides were written, a certain war-weariness and self-questioning were detectable in the Athenian mind. One might also observe with about equal justice that the full force of the Elizabethan drive exhausted itself with the Queen's reign and that the later plays of Shakespeare and his successors reflect a certain loss of moral or artistic confidence, or of both. But there can be no doubt that in both societies the tragic drama peculiar to them was *formed* in a period of national growth, when the main trend was upward, creative and exhilarating. Nor should one exaggerate the importance of the later phase of either drama as a reflection of a change in social temper. It has much more the appearance of a development within the art of dramatic tragedy, seeking to renew itself by a fuller exploitation of ingenuity or sensation. It was more plausibly a variation of an established genre of tragedy than a sign of the awakening of some tragic sense which had lain dormant during the decades of optimism. It was those decades which created the distinctive tragedy of the two cultures, a fact which it seems impossible to reconcile with any theory of decline-regret-apprehension.

In France, the important period runs from the sixteen-thirties to the sixteen-seventies. During it the social trend was almost continuously upward. From the time of Corneille's first tragedies to Racine's last,[8] France was, and felt herself to be, in the ascendant. Much of her growth in power was achieved at the expense of her neighbour and rival, Spain, then in manifest decline. But declining Spain, though possessed of a flourishing and active theatre, developed no true tragic drama. And if, for France, doubt were to be thrown on the 'tragic' quality of Corneille's drama, it must be remarked that Racine, whose tragic quality is less questionable, was formed and wrote during the period of greater national confidence, when French society was at last united and aggressive under the still youthful Louis XIV.

On Racine, however, an interesting theory has been put forward by a Marxist critic which has general implications going well beyond the one particular case. M. Lucien Goldmann[9] derived Racine's 'tragic vision' directly from his Jansenism, and related this religious creed in turn to the discontent of a particular social class. This was

[8] I.e., *Phèdre* (1677). His two biblical tragedies, written around 1690 in fulfilment of a Court order, are a different matter.
[9] *Le Dieu Caché* (Gallimard, 1955).

the *noblesse de robe*, the higher ranks of the legal profession which (he argued) saw its powers and prerogatives curtailed by the development of a centralised bureaucracy directly responsible to the Crown. Whence came, not open opposition, but a half-conscious 'attitude of reserve towards the life of society and the State'.[10]

In his analysis of the tragic, M. Goldmann sets up three concepts or terms: God, the World, Man. When the middle term is out of harmony with the other two or, to put the proposition in another way, when God, though not absent from the World, is 'silent' in it, the man who is conscious of this possesses a tragic awareness. He rejects the World because it does not satisfy him—as occurs, according to M. Goldmann, in Jansenist theology and in Racine's tragedies when their basic significance is correctly analysed. In their implicit condemnation of the World—equated with the dominant values of contemporary society—these tragedies are, in fact, ideologically subversive.

On biographical and historical grounds, the case of Racine, stated very baldly here, is far from made out in M. Goldmann's book. It is equally possible to interpret Racine's dramatic career as the reaction against his Jansenist teachers which it ostensibly seemed to be and to trace an artistic and moral progression (with no reversal) from his first plays, composed around the date of his break with Port-Royal and his eager acceptance of the World, to his last (*Phèdre*). Alternatively it is easier to characterise the attitude towards the World of the Jansenist divines and their influential lay supporters as one of pugnacity, arrogance and aspiring leadership than as one of 'reserve'. But it would be as impractical in a few pages to attempt to refute M. Goldmann's thesis on the grounds of social history as it would be to summarise all the detailed and interesting arguments marshalled in its support, and it is perhaps unnecessary. The significant general point which emerges is that the 'tragic vision' is the mark of a man at odds with his material environment, and it would seem to follow that the same condition must apply to other great tragic dramatists besides Racine: to Shakespeare and to, say, Sophocles. We must then suppose that, when a whole society was flocking to the theatre to see plays which in some way corresponded to their confident and forward-looking mood, their greatest dramatists were in fact offering them the doubts and disapproval of a dissenting minority. They were not, by a long way, the only con-

[10] *Op. cit.*, p. 157.

temporary writers of 'tragedies', but they were the only practitioners of the genre whose work was truly tragic.

The theory is attractive and not necessarily self-dismissive. Historically, it might perhaps be possible to find at least indications of a link between some frustrated minority and every writer possessed of an authentic 'tragic vision'. Shakespeare can be attached to the recusants, the undercover Papists in a Protestant State. Something similar might be found for Euripides and even Sophocles. But the evidence, as with Racine, is far from being established, and the difficulties of proof are formidable. Proof, moreover, or at least a reasonable presumption, would have to be found not only for a few great writers, but universally. For this sociological explanation of the tragic is bound up with a definition of the tragic which does not allow of other explanations. The two are interdependent—more than that, they are the same thing. Reduced to essentials, they can be stated in this way: 'Dissatisfaction with environment produces the tragic vision. The tragic vision *is* dissatisfaction with environment.' One may go on, of course, to the consequences of this dissatisfaction, to the vain attempt to reconcile ultimate good with environment (reconcile 'God' with the 'World'), or to impose it upon it, and so on. But this, which is recognisably the so-called tragic conflict, is only possible if the tragic vision exists first. The latter is a type of awareness which precedes, and exists independently of, the acts it stimulates and the solutions it seeks. It must also be said that in the consciousness of most of its possessors it ranges far beyond the *social* environment and takes in the whole 'universe'. But it does not seem to be a misrepresentation of M. Goldmann or of the Marxist position in general to say that in his analysis the ultimate origin of dissatisfaction is a social one.

5

It will hardly have escaped notice that M. Goldmann's 'tragic vision' is the same thing as Unamuno's 'tragic sense of life' and that the conditions to which it is attributed are also basically similar. The superficial difference is that Unamuno's contentions led us towards a theory of the dying society which we found hard to substantiate in any field and which, if extended to the great periods of tragic drama, simply does not hold water. The greater merit of M. Goldmann's version is that it transfers the tragic sense from societies as a whole (thus avoiding the disputed notion of national characteristics) to sections or classes within societies. These may be sick or mal-adjusted though the majority body is healthy. But although, as we have said, this version is harder to disprove, it does not alter the identity of the two conceptions of the tragic nor of the diagnostic, which is simply applied by M. Goldmann on an intranational scale. The similarities between M. Goldmann's views and those expressed or implied by Unamuno are so striking that they deserve further comment, though there are no traces of a direct influence.

Like the liberal Spanish individualist, the objective Marxist in-vestigator finds the tragic vision to be incompatible with both rationalism and empiricism. He finds it to be, in the widest sense, 'religious'. His description of the position of a so-called 'tragic' thinker of the mid-seventeenth century—Pascal—strongly recalls the self-described position of the Spaniard at the beginning of the twentieth. Pascal, he maintains, rejected both the rationalistic philosophy of Descartes and the scientific mechanicalism which stemmed from the discoveries of Galileo. (The two combined are equivalent, in their historical context, to the 'scientific reason' which Unamuno rejected in his comment on Don Quixote.)[11] A new system had just been elaborated which seemed, philosophically and mathematically, to explain the physical universe far more satis-factorily than the old systems, yet it could never satisfy a mind such as Pascal's:

> The tragic consciousness at that period can be characterised as a rigorously exact understanding of the new world created by ration-alist individualism, with all its positive and valuable achievements and, above all, its definitive conquests in the field of human thought and consciousness, but at the same time a radical refusal to accept that world as the sole lot and prospect of mankind.
> Reason is an important factor in human life, of which man is justly proud and which henceforward he can never relinquish, but *it is not the whole of man*, and, more particularly, *it must not and cannot be a sufficient condition for human life*. It is insufficient in every domain, including that of scientific research and truth, to which it seems to be especially appropriate.
> For these reasons the tragic vision is a return, after the amoral and a-religious period of empiricism and rationalism, to *ethics* and

[11] See above, p. 60.

religion, taking the last word in its widest sense of *faith* in a body of values *which transcend the individual.*[12]

In a later chapter M. Goldmann expands his statement that reason is 'not the whole of man' and cannot suffice him. His conclusions would serve as a model explanation of Unamuno's passionately 'felt' desire for personal immortality, associating it with a longing for oneness or totality in the state of conflict which divides him:

What is this demand which 'tragic man' can never satisfy in the world and which obliges him to place himself entirely in God's hands? What does he expect from this silent and hidden God? His demand ... is a demand for unity, for a synthesis of conflicting elements, a demand for completeness. Hence in [Pascal's] *Mystère de Jésus,* the divine promise takes the form of a promise to overcome a fundamental duality—for the Christian thinker in general and, in the seventeenth century, for almost all thinkers—and here becomes a symbol of all the other dualities and alternatives which make up the life of man in the world: the union of the soul and the body in immortality.

Nothing which exists on earth can escape the death of all that belongs to the world and the body—there is no appeal from it. For that reason 'tragic man' can never accept existence in the world, since he can accept neither perishable values nor partial values—such as the soul separated from the body. His life only has meaning insofar as it is entirely dedicated to an attempt to realise *total* and *eternal* values. In its pursuit of these—and in no other way—his soul 'transcends man' to become immortal here and now. But the immortality of the soul exists only on the condition that it is truly human, that it transcends man in a search for completeness, and that implies *an immortal body.* The tragic soul is great and immortal to the extent that it seeks and desires the immortality of the body, tragic reason to the extent that it seeks a union with passion, and so on. Tragic faith is primarily faith in a God who will one day produce the complete man, possessing both an immortal soul and an immortal body.[13]

This is an interesting and extreme statement of a position similar to Unamuno's and expressed in religious terms. The point which M. Goldmann makes, here and elsewhere, is that the 'tragically

[12] Goldmann, *op. cit.,* p. 43. My translation, as throughout. The italics are in the original.
[13] Goldmann, *op. cit.,* pp. 91–2.

conscious' man, while rejecting the world as it is, does not abandon it entirely to seek refuge with a God who exists only outside it. That is the course taken by the *mystic*, and does not qualify as 'tragic'. The 'tragic man' seeks completeness. He must have the World *and* God, the body *and* the soul, in order to satisfy his craving for unity.

We need hardly say that we dissent totally from M. Goldmann's interpretation of Pascal, on ideological grounds which will be examined in a later chapter.[14] We believe that his thesis is anachronistic if applied to Christian thought in the seventeenth century. It rests on conceptions and attitudes which did not emerge until the late eighteenth century, as we will also try to show later (Chapters 8 and 9). Hence its relevance to the position of Unamuno, a tardy (by general European standards) renewer of Romantic ideology, but its inaptness to throw light on earlier tragedy and conceptions of the tragic.

Must we then discard altogether these concepts of the tragic sense and the tragic vision as erroneous? Or can we adopt them as valid from the beginning of the nineteenth century, but not much earlier —in that case being eventually forced to abandon a uniform conception of the tragic? It would be premature to attempt a definite judgment before considering some examples of the tragic concept in practice, i.e. in the works of some of the great tragic dramatists. But two points can at least be made.

One is that the external symptom of the 'tragic sense' (Unamuno), a melancholy disposition characterised by a brooding on 'death and immortality', is not in itself tragic, though it is quite likely to enter into tragedy and, as it were, set the tone of it. But it can find even more adequate expression in such forms as the funeral lament, the elegy, or the woeful narrative tale, all of which correspond to classic states of human emotion which are sorrowful rather than tragic. Usually it will have a religious context, since death and transcendence have immemorially been the province of religion, and if only the symptom were in question one could call this simply 'the religious sense'—which, so far, would satisfy both Unamuno and M. Goldmann.

Secondly, however, in relating the symptom to a deep-seated duality conflict, both authors conceive it as not only religious, but as *essentially* tragic. Here we hesitate to follow them, for it may prove

[14] See below, Chapter 8.

to be only incidentally so. On the grounds of social history alone, it seems improbable that it can be more than that.

6

Even if M. Goldmann's theory of the dissenting minority is not accepted *in toto*, there remains a further question to be considered. Is the 'tragic vision' perhaps necessarily a 'subversive' vision, possessed by the individual independently of any connection which can be established between him and a discontented social group? Does he question the accepted ideology as a condition of his 'tragic' insight?

As with many problems, this one is best approached by the simplest route. It is clear that the most direct intentional challenges to existing society or sections of it are made through satire and comedy (Rabelais, Molière, Swift, Voltaire, Beaumarchais, Shaw). If one is simply looking for subversive voices, this is the richest field to explore. Tragedy, on this count, can claim no special relationship with the subversive view. It might, however, be said that the comic genres stop short at the more superficial aspects of society, while only tragedy is equipped to challenge the values behind it—in short, its gods. It is doubtful if such a challenge can be made without both a spirit and *an appearance* of 'high seriousness', the element with which tragedy is normally associated and which it reinforces by throwing in the highest stakes, human happiness and human lives. But if this is admitted, it merely makes the tragic *more deeply* subversive than other modes, not uniquely so. The conclusion does not contribute much to a demarcation of the tragic field.

So far as writers are concerned, any one with sufficient stature to be found important will also be original. Originality lies in a modification of accepted values, whether intentional or not, fundamental or partial. This will of course embrace the great tragic dramatists and 'tragic' thinkers, but also many others. Every good writer and thinker is comparable to the primitive artist setting out to carve a replica of the tribal god. What he produces is not an exact copy but a new face, with features which may contain anything from a just perceptible innovation to a revolutionary reinterpretation. If this process is held to carry intimations of a 'tragic vision', in however varying degrees, one might as well conclude that all art is tragic and throw one's hand in.

As for the great periods of dramatic tragedy, it seems quite uncertain how they can be related to certain stages of social ideology. They do not correspond to the theory of the dying society[15] and hardly to that of the sick minority. Their greatest dramatists, one would incline to say, were conformists in intention—that is, they thought of themselves as solidary with the aspirations of the majority. If they modified the image, it was in virtue of their artistic insight and almost accidentally. And one can hardly neglect the evidence that their work was acceptable to society.

Hypothesis for hypothesis, we would put forward a different one. It is that a confident society can afford to tolerate subversion when presented to it in established art-forms. It comes expressed in a familiar language by one of its members speaking, as it were, from inside. Tragedy then serves, to borrow Aristotle's invaluable theory of catharsis, as a purge for its fears of real subversion—which must always be present. It expends its tragic heroes as insurance premiums,[16] and goes home relieved and fortified by the spectacle of dreadful happenings which it feels secure enough to contemplate. Why otherwise should Aristotle, and Racine after him, speak of the *pleasure* peculiar to tragedy? It would be an odd word if the tragedy of their periods spoke intimately to audiences of the frustrated misery inseparable from their condition. It is much easier to assume that a healthy society uses the tragic, in drama and on occasion in other literature, as an outlet for its misgivings and anxieties. On the other hand, a precarious society will not dare to ask questions for fear of the possible answers (we have already said that tragedy is more than a simple lament).

On this hypothesis, the historical incidence of tragic drama falls

[15] In this chapter we have not discussed the tragic literature of the nineteenth century in its relationship to both expansionist and declining societies beyond the point necessary to explain Unamuno's position. The subject will be returned to later in a wider context. Meanwhile a single example, that of Chekhov, goes to support our argument. Confidently held up by post-Revolution Marxists as the interpreter of a sick society (which was passing through much the same phase as Unamuno's Spain at much the same date), Chekhov wrote, not tragedy, but plays which he insisted were comedies. (See below, p. 214.) The case of the Russian novelists, notably Dostoievsky, is however more complex and would require further analysis.

[16] Not quite the scapegoat principle, which operates in its pure form when disaster is actually present or imminent. The analogy is more with the wise investment against possible future reverses undertaken from strength.

more logically into place. It accords more naturally with the upward curve or the plateau than with the downward drift. Great tragedy is always bold in its conceptions and the speculations which it opens up. Declining cultures are afraid of being hurt and are inclined to take refuge in petty repetitions and unadventurous didacticism.

II

Tragedy in Practice

Some Classic Tragedies :
'Oedipus', 'Hamlet', 'Macbeth', 'Phèdre'

1

Oedipus, the young Prince of Corinth, learns from an oracle that he is destined to kill his father and marry his mother. Horrified by the prediction and determined if possible to prevent its fulfilment, he abandons his home, leaving the King and Queen whom he believes to be his parents. In the course of his wanderings he meets an old man riding in a chariot who roughly orders him out of the way and strikes him as he goes past. Oedipus strikes back and kills him, killing also or routing his attendants. Travelling on, he approaches the city of Thebes, whose inhabitants are being terrorised by a ferocious monster, the Sphinx. Oedipus succeeds in guessing the riddle which the Sphinx sets its intended victims, and so destroys its power. He is welcomed by Thebes as its deliverer and elected King in succession to the old King Laius, who has met his death obscurely while on a journey. Oedipus marries the widowed Queen, Jocasta, has children by her, and enjoys some fifteen years of happy and prosperous rule.

At the end of that time plague and famine break out in Thebes. Jocasta's brother, Creon, is sent to consult the oracle of Apollo and brings back word that the cause of the disaster is the presence of 'an unclean thing' in Thebes. This 'unclean thing', concludes Creon, must be the undetected killer of King Laius, whose death so long ago has never been cleared up or avenged. Oedipus swears to discover the criminal and punish him, and from that point the whole truth is gradually made clear.

His own inquiries ultimately lead Oedipus to realise that it was he who killed Laius. He learns from Jocasta that a prophecy was made to Laius that he would be killed by his own child, and therefore when a son was born to them it was taken out to the mountain to perish there. He finally learns that the shepherd who was ordered to abandon the child took pity on it instead and handed it to another shepherd belonging to the King of Corinth. This man carried it to his master, who adopted it as his own son. The child was without doubt Oedipus himself.

Jocasta perceives the truth a little before Oedipus. She goes into the house and hangs herself. Oedipus follows, cuts down the body, and blinds himself with one of her brooches. So he will no longer see his shame, nor their children 'whom he should never have seen'. The royal authority has already passed to Creon, to whom Oedipus submissively leaves the decision whether he should be put to death or banished.

This story, as dramatised by Sophocles, is rich in tragic implications. According to which of them is stressed its significance changes, or appears to change. For the modern mind, though less certainly perhaps for the Greeks, its deepest significance is extracted by treating it as a study of a single but representative human destiny. Oedipus, the individual hero, carries within him the germ of his own destruction. He is warned of the danger and attempts to avert it by a practical act, but all his efforts only lead him more surely towards it. His destiny proves to be inescapable.

This is almost self-evident, but it leads to a further implication, involving the identity of the individual. Oedipus is guilty of these crimes because he is the man he is. The same acts performed by a different person would have lost most of their horror. (There would have been no question of parricide and incest, only of a man's marriage to a woman whose first husband he had unwittingly killed.) Oedipus believed himself to be a different person, a prince of Corinth, and performed well and even meritoriously in that part, supposing it to be his true one. But then everything shifted. The things on which he had based his life were not the things which belonged to him, the things which he loathed were. No wonder that, like other tragic heroes, he realised that he had no place in the scheme of things and blinded himself to see nothing more. Of the different views one may take of the nature of the human personality, this is the most desolate and may fairly be called the most tragic. What we do and what we are are inseparable; we have no control over what we are and usually no true knowledge of it; it is ourself in the most intimate sense, yet its nature is decided by an outside agency—God, the gods, fate, social forces, or a fortuitous combination of genes. There is nothing whatever we can do about it.

Seen and felt in this light, the destiny of the individual is tragic almost by definition. Seen in another light it may be comic, which implies acquiescence in a kind of defiant helplessness. A religious view would be that the individual destiny can be influenced by help from outside; according to an heroic interpretation it could be affected by an effort from within (the act of will). The religious and the heroic can of course be associated. But the tragic interpretation, as found in *Oedipus*, excludes both. The act of will proved futile and there was no divine reprieve. What we have here, pre-eminently, is a conception of destiny embodied in personality, or—to vary the terms —a refusal to draw a distinction between destiny and personality.

—A simpler and more usual interpretation is to see Oedipus purely as a victim of Fate. Fate is a generalised name for some cosmic force which decides the particular destiny of the individual. This destiny is still inescapable but it is distinct from the personality. The latter thus possesses some independent essence of its own. Theoretically it could even have an independent existence. One might perhaps use the metaphor of the plant trained up a stake. It must follow the line of the stake, but it is not the same thing as the stake and it could perfectly well be conceived as existing without it. When instead of a plant there is a conscious individual, he may well have the illusion of doing just that. In mind, if not in act, he can 'rise superior to his destiny'. He can shout defiance at the external thing before it forces him back into line. Some essential part of him— expressed as his personality, or his soul, or his spirit, or his will— remains unbroken. The objection against reading this conception into Sophocles' play is that, if it were there, Oedipus ought to have gone down with his flag flying. He should—and it would have been perfectly in character—have been 'heroic'. But, instead of condemning Nemesis for the filthy tricks she plays on mankind, he fully accepts his guilt. From the moment when the truth dawns upon him, he does not offer a word of self-exculpation. He takes the full horror of responsibility upon himself.

We may now ask why Oedipus was guilty. The Aristotelian theory of *hamartia* is hardly adequate, for where did Oedipus go wrong? One obvious but hardly tenable explanation is that his acts and the consequences of them derived from his character, taking this word in its Aristotelian sense. Oedipus' 'fault' was his over-confidence, his *hubris*. Having heard the dreadful prophecy in his youth, he tried to falsify it and came to believe that he had succeeded by his own initiative. In the play his self-confidence is at first evident, giving the dramatist ample opportunities for irony and increasing the steepness of the eventual fall. But dramatically effective though this may be, it does not contain the *cause* of the hero's destruction. One could not re-title the play: 'The Pretentions of Oedipus, or the Boaster Deflated' without travestying its nature.[1] Alternately, perhaps, the error of Oedipus was an error of judgment. He misunderstood the original prophecy and went out to meet disaster instead of staying safely where he was. But if the oracle was a true one—and there is no suggestion that it was not—it must have been fulfilled in one way or another. Nothing that Oedipus did or omitted to do would have made any difference.

We are left with only two alternatives. Either the gods, having decided to destroy Oedipus in any case, amused themselves by playing with him first. This, besides being a doubtful interpretation of the Greek fifth-century conception of the superhuman powers, would not account for Oedipus' overwhelming personal feeling of guilt, as we have already suggested. Secondly, we are brought back to the only tenable hypothesis: the built-in flaw in the individual, which goes much deeper than 'character'. Once again, Oedipus fails because he is the man he is. He himself is the failure.

Certainly this does not square with Aristotle's stipulation, based though it is on such tragedies as this one, that the tragic hero should be 'the kind of man who neither is distinguished for excellence and virtue, nor comes to grief on account of baseness and vice, but on account of some error'.[2] Either Aristotle was wrong in this instance, or our moral focus has changed so radically that we no longer comprehend his conception of *hamartia*.

---

[1] It would be diminished to the level of a trite little morality, in which Oedipus is punished for his perkiness. Though of course the notion of *hubris* exists in Greek literature and though Sophocles makes some discreet use of it here, it seems to us that the general theme of the *Oedipus* is immeasurably bigger. Whatever the irritation-value of *hubris* for the gods of the Homeric age, its true dramatic place is in homely comedy, where the clown trips over the obstacle because he is too conceited to look at his feet.

[2] See above, p. 38 *et seq.*

2

The Oedipus legend and Sophocles' dramatisation of it can be approached from another direction. The play opens in Thebes when Oedipus is at the height of his power. (The events leading up to this are recalled as the play proceeds.) Thebes is in a calamitous state, beset by pestilence and struck by sterility in its crops and its women. That is almost the whole, strongly stressed, situation in the opening scenes. It carries the interest directly to the return of Creon from his visit to Apollo's oracle, to his message that what is amiss with Thebes is the presence of the evil thing in the community, and to the quickly drawn conclusion that this thing is the killer of Laius, whose blood cries for vengeance. The evil is finally proved to lie in the King himself, the honoured head of the community and once its saviour from the Sphinx, who is now marked down as a necessary sacrifice.

It is impossible not to recognise in this some of the main features of the Corn King tradition—the offering of a victim prominent enough to satisfy the gods and upon whose head all the disease or sin of the community can be heaped. And no doubt somewhere in the genesis of the Oedipus legend this element was dominant, no doubt also its influence persists in the tragedy which Sophocles wrote, as it does in numerous other tragedies. But it is not the main theme. To begin with, it disappears from the play as soon as the possibility of the personal guilt of Oedipus takes shape. It is not mentioned again and, although it can be assumed that the self-punishment of the King and Queen has the effect of delivering Thebes from its misfortunes, Sophocles never troubles to say so. The Chorus of Theban elders who close the play speak only of the miserable fall of Oedipus the individual and draw from it a moral for other individual men. It may be added that the sin of Oedipus is never envisaged as representative or symbolical of a collective sin. The entire disease is in one man or, at the most, in one family. When it is stamped out there, the whole place is clean again. Thus, while the Corn King element hangs vaguely round the periphery, the tragic centre consists of a working-out of individual destinies, whose correlations are not with the tribe but with humanity in general.

It might indeed be argued that Sophocles—and at least some of his contemporaries—had no belief in the Corn King principle and did not really associate the 'evil' in Oedipus with the pestilence at Thebes. It was sufficient for the Thebans in the play to believe in it, in order to set in motion the inquiry which led to the destruction of the individual hero. This would explain why the notion of communal expiation through a scapegoat gets lost as the tragedy gathers round the person of Oedipus.

3

On reflection, it is odd that a story which seems to go to the roots of the human condition should have to be so artificial. The plot is full of contrivances. In his flight from Corinth, the man whom Oedipus runs into and kills is Laius. The city he reaches is his birthplace, Thebes, whose King has died in mysterious circumstances at some past date left unspecified, but which cannot have been so long before. Succeeding Laius as King, Oedipus takes no interest in his predecessor's fate and is not even told what happened to him. During the long years of his marriage to Jocasta, Oedipus never speaks of the fight at the crossroads, nor—which is perhaps more important—does he mention the reason for his departure from Corinth. Nothing, therefore, awakens memories in Jocasta of her own 'guilty secret', the disposal of the newborn child following the prophecy of parricide. Neither Jocasta nor Oedipus associate any of their past actions or their past knowledge with their present happy-seeming situation, and this blindness extends even to the physical stigmata which Oedipus bears. When he was exposed on the mountain as a child, his ankles were bound together and a nail was driven through them, as Jocasta knows. The marks are still there in the grown man and the very name of Oedipus (meaning 'swollen foot') advertises the deformity. A comparatively minor coincidence is the fact that the messenger who arrives from Corinth with the news of the death of Oedipus' adoptive father is the same man who once carried the child off the mountain and took him to the king. He reveals now what he has known all the time, that Oedipus was not a son of Corinth. The final and perhaps greatest contrivance is to allow fifteen years to elapse between the death of Laius and the consequent visitation of the gods' anger upon Thebes. But the plot or the story visibly requires some such interval. There must be time for Oedipus to be prosperously and 'securely' established as King and for children to grow up from his union with Jocasta.

These objections on the plane of realism do not diminish the tragedy of Sophocles, who sees and provides for some of them in the dialogue and makes most of the rest appear irrelevant. No doubt they are, but the question is bound to arise why so profound a story should require so much willing suspension of disbelief before it can exist at all. We recognise and respond to the great issues raised in the *Oedipus Tyrannus*, but once we are away from its spell we have to admit that they arise from a most unlikely conjunction of circumstances. It is not a question of the supernatural elements—the oracles, the Sphinx, and perhaps the plague—for these should be conceded anyway, but of the human and factual elements without which Oedipus and Jocasta would not have married, the pair would not have continued in such unreflecting ignorance of each other's identity, and so on. If, merely as an exercise, one tries to construct another story, with a modern or any other setting, to incorporate the universal truths which the *Oedipus* undoubtedly contains, one arrives at a hotchpotch of melodramatic implausibilities which even Hollywood would reject in its most lunatic moments.

It is not merely the incompatibility of poetic truth and realism. Most great legends, like most fairy tales and even animal tales, are logically consistent within themselves and can be transposed to another milieu without losing their moral-cum-psychological impact. The Oedipus story only *appears* consistent and, as we have suggested, could only be transposed by extremely ingenious contortions which it would be almost impossible to conceal. To return to Aristotle's terms, it possesses poetic or artistic truth (though by a bare margin) but rejects historical or realistic truth, as is legitimate. But we demand from it another kind of truth, psychological truth, which is a new requirement since Aristotle's day. Or more exactly, it is a new category which he saw no necessity to distinguish from 'poetic' truth. We cannot entirely divorce psychological truth from factual truth. That is, we have difficulty in associating it with events which probably never occurred and could hardly be imagined as occurring again in a different context.

Yet, as a matter of experience, we do accept the psychological truth of the implausible Oedipus story. This is incidentally a tribute to the skill of the dramatist.[3] But, which is more important, it is a reminder that tragic drama, at its most moving and profound, may

[3] See Aristotle's remarks on unity and probability, discussed above pp. 25–7.

be a highly artificial creation. It may be far removed from the 'tragic' of everyday life, a thing almost instinctively apprehended by anyone with a heart to feel. Dramatic tragedy has to touch that everyday cord, but the means by which it does so is hardly by the simple process of heart speaking to heart.

4

The story of Oedipus lends itself particularly well to the exploitation of certain tragic devices in the hands of the dramatist. It yields a dramatic tragedy in which the 'recognition' is of supreme importance. Everything that precedes those terrible moments when first Jocasta, then Oedipus, realise the true nature of their relationship is a leading-up to the recognition. When it comes to Jocasta, she delays only in a last brief attempt to save Oedipus from it, then, seeing that that is futile, disappears as rapidly and finally as though she had fallen through a trap-door—as, morally, she has. Oedipus returns after he has put out his eyes to demonstrate to the audience—and also to prolong for himself—the full agony of the realisation. This is so well prepared, so stunning when it arrives, and so powerful when it is contemplated, that one is led to believe that the recognition *is* the tragedy.

In this case it seems justifiable to conclude that it is. In many tragedies the recognition is the culminating point. Nearly always it gives a touch of completeness and finality to a drama which would otherwise be a less clear-cut emotional experience. But it is not often that the tragic situation only exists in virtue of it, as it does in Sophocles' play and would do in any dramatisation of the story presented in a similar way, which appears to be the only effective way. As long as Oedipus is ignorant of the truth, he is happy and there is no tragedy. As soon as he knows the truth he becomes the complete tragic figure. The transformation is effected solely by the dispersal of his ignorance.

This tragedy of recognition is full of opportunities for irony, which the dramatist takes up. If one assumed an audience ignorant, like the hero, of the dénouement, most of this irony would be lost. But if, as is far more probable, the audience knows how the tragedy will end, the irony is constantly in evidence. It is present from the first moment when the people of Thebes come humbly and trustingly to Oedipus to ask him to deliver them from the pestilence. It becomes

more open when Oedipus puts his ban on the unknown killer of
Laius:

> No matter who he may be, he is forbidden
> Shelter or intercourse with any man
> In this country over which I rule.
> ... Nor do I exempt myself from the imprecation:
> If, with my knowledge, house or hearth of mine
> Receive the guilty man, upon my head
> Lie all the curses I have laid on others.[4]

As the revelation grows nearer, so the speeches of Oedipus become
unconsciously more double-edged. Even when Jocasta has perceived
the truth, Oedipus is still blind enough to believe that her horror is
caused by the fear that he, her husband, was a slave's son. So that
was the secret of his birth?

OEDIPUS: I must pursue this trail to the end,
> Till I have unravelled the mystery of my birth.
JOCASTA: No! In God's name—if you want to live, this quest
> Must not go on. Have I not suffered enough?
OEDIPUS: There is nothing to fear, Though I be proved slave-born
> To the third generation, *your* honour is not impugned.[5]

These and numerous other examples of dramatic irony arise easily
from a basic situation which is itself ironic. The Oedipus story belongs to the category epitomised in the Arabian legend of the man
who fled from his home in Damascus to escape a meeting with Death
which has been prophesied to him. Arriving in Baghdad, he meets
Death, who says: 'I did not know you were here. I was just going to
Damascus to fetch you. You have saved me the journey.' So Oedipus,
in flight from the evil he supposed to be at Corinth, finds it irrevocably in Thebes. It is a classic instance of an irony which can properly
be called tragic because of its inherence in the destiny of the individual. But the incidental irony, which consists in the unrealised
ambiguity of the words of Oedipus and other characters, should be
called 'dramatic' rather than 'tragic'. If over-stressed it could become comic ('He is really *too* unperceptive'), which the basic irony
could never be.

Rich in both kinds of irony, the *Oedipus Tyrannus* entirely lacks

---

[4] *King Oedipus*, pp. 32–3. Trans. E. F. Watling in *The Theban Plays*
(Penguin, 1947).
[5] Watling, *op. cit.*, p. 58.

another element sometimes considered essential to tragedy. There is no conflict. Instead, there is a contrast—between the prosperity of the hero when the play opens and his misery at the close, between his imagined destiny and his real destiny, even, if one likes, between the world as he wishes and believes it to be and the world as it is. But the two opposites do not clash. There is no struggle in the hero's mind (or anywhere else) to preserve or attain the one and reject the other.[6] There cannot be, because he is not aware of the disparity until it is far too late to do anything but submit. We cannot even say that he beats against the walls of a trap, since he does not know that he is in one. We witness his suffering or anguish, but only at the end, in the prolonged recognition. It is not the anguish of a man torn between two alternatives, but the agonising contemplation of a disaster which has already occurred. Here we have a tragic hero in an indubitably tragic situation which does not entail conflict.

We must now look at another tragedy in which the elements are quite differently disposed.

5

Hamlet

One of the more curious features of this curious play is that the recognition occurs near the beginning. In Act I, Sc. 5, his father's ghost reveals to Hamlet that he was betrayed by his wife, Hamlet's mother, and murdered by his brother, who now reigns in his place. For Hamlet, this is the greatest horror that life can hold. It crowns his disgust and misgivings, already expressed in an earlier scene, at the sight of his mother 'incestuously' married to his despised uncle within a few weeks of his father's death. He now knows that this death was not an accident, that his mother may have consented to it, and that it occurred in such circumstances that his beloved father, having had no opportunity to confess his sins, is undergoing the torments of hell. Hamlet's immediate reaction is the same as that of other tragic heroes at the moment of recognition. He utters a speech of 'wild and whirling words', beginning:

> Oh, all you host of Heaven! Oh earth—what else?
> And shall I couple Hell? Oh fie, hold my heart,

[6] But surely he struggled initially when he tried to escape the oracle by leaving home? Apart from the fact that this is outside the play, it still does not qualify as tragic conflict. If a traveller lost in a wood believes he is going north when he is going south, there may be *hamartia* but not conflict.

And you, my sinews, grow not instant old,
But bear me stiffly up.

How far the hysteria which underlies this speech and recurs throughout the rest of the play in Hamlet's words and conduct involves true madness (however that may be defined) is a moot point which it is perhaps not necessary to argue all over again. It can, however, be said that Hamlet's 'madness' from then on does not appear to be always feigned—notably in his dealings with Ophelia— and that it is most satisfactorily explained as a disguise assumed through necessity rather than as an effect of pure calculation. The necessity springs from the shock induced by the realisation of the true facts, after which Hamlet can never again be confident of behaving rationally, since his rational world has collapsed. All this remains within the classic framework of the tragic recognition. The hero sees and understands the horror; it throws him off his balance, momentarily at least; he then usually commits suicide, having no further use for life.

If Hamlet does not commit suicide (though he contemplates it), a sufficient reason, in the context of the play, is that the recognition also contains a call to action. He must live on to avenge his father. It is worth noting, however, that even if he succeeds in this, revenge will not diminish the horror he has experienced. His mother's infidelity and the manner of his father's death are irrevocable.

It might be objected that Hamlet does not accept the disclosure as certain. He suspects that the Ghost may be an evil spirit sent to lead him astray by a false accusation of his mother and his uncle. The warrant for this is found in one or two passages *before* the Ghost has spoken,[7] and therefore quite inconclusive in themselves, and in one later passage at the end of Act II:

> The spirit that I have seen
> May be the Devil, and the Devil hath power
> To assume a pleasing shape, yea and perhaps
> Out of my weakness and my melancholy,
> As he is very potent with such spirits,
> Abuses me to damn me.

After saying this, Hamlet proceeds to test the Ghost's good faith

---

[7] Particularly Act I, Sc. 4:
  Be thou a spirit of health or goblin damn'd,
  Bring with thee airs from Heaven, or blasts from Hell, etc.

by means of the play-within-a-play of Act III, which traps his uncle into betraying his guilt.

None of this, however, really weakens the force of the original disclosure by the Ghost. It is impossible to conclude that Hamlet doubted it at the time, and improbable that he seriously doubts it later. Just before uttering the lines quoted above, he has been blaming himself bitterly for his inaction:

> ... for it cannot be,
> But I am pigeon-liver'd and lack gall
> To make oppression bitter, or ere this
> I should have fatted all the region kites
> With this slave's offal, bloody, bawdy villain,
> Remorseless, treacherous, lecherous, kindless villain!
> O Vengeance!

These are hardly the words of a man who still believes that his uncle may be innocent, and the stratagem of the Gonzago play seems devised less to clear up a genuine uncertainty than to lead the criminal to convict himself by his own reactions. (It may be seen as a phase in the duel between Claudius and Hamlet, which is one of the main dramatic motifs of the play.) Add that Hamlet is keenly aware of his own procrastination and is ready to clutch at any excuse which will justify it and at the same time set a term to it. When his uncle betrays himself, Hamlet's reaction is ironical and triumphant, not horror-stricken. There is certainly no recognition at this point, nor anywhere else but in the original encounter with the Ghost. The only plausible reading is to see *that* as the moment of truth and Hamlet's later actions as an obsessive circling around it.

One could therefore say that Shakespeare's play depends as much on a recognition as does the *Oedipus*, but after that there is a wide divergence. The two recognitions have this much in common: each shatters the hero's world. But whereas the whole tragedy of Oedipus is a leading-up to the recognition, which provides it with its force and its climax, the recognition in *Hamlet* is the point of departure from which the tragedy stems.[8] The recognition in the *Oedipus* establishes the hero's guilt—whatever its nature may be—but in

---

[8] A *climactic* recognition could only occur in *Hamlet* if the Ghost's word proved false; if, having destroyed Polonius, Ophelia, Rosencrantz, Guildenstern, Laertes, Gertrude, Claudius, and himself, Hamlet realised that he had been deluded. A powerful play, and conceivably a powerful tragedy, but still unwritten.

Hamlet it reveals a situation for which the hero can in no way be held responsible. The acts which led up to it were committed by others, not merely without his knowledge but with no reference whatever to him. They would have been the same if he had never existed. In this respect, Hamlet is in the position of a man who witnesses some fearful disaster and feels compelled to do something about it simply because he is there. Yet that would make him little more than a witness or a Chorus-character, whereas he is certainly something else. He—and not Claudius or Gertrude—is unquestionably the tragic hero. He is involved, one might then say, because the characters initially concerned in the disaster are his own people. He is tragically involved because he is the son of his parents. Ultimately, one might continue, he is tragic because he is the man he is—exactly like Oedipus. It is a neat analogy, but will it do?

We have just said that the events disclosed at the recognition would have been the same if Hamlet had never existed, and we have also called them a disaster. But they are not the final disaster which makes the tragedy and, although it is true that factually they would have been the same without Hamlet, it is only when they are realised by Hamlet and begin to work upon his mind as a stimulus to action that they assume a tragic potential. Hamlet has to know the truth before the tragic machinery can be set in motion, while with Oedipus it was the direct opposite. The machinery only functioned because he remained in ignorance. This, however, is a difference of situation and not necessarily of personality. It does not make of Oedipus and Hamlet two essentially different types of tragic hero.

Let us put forward another analogy, which may prove more rewarding. In both plays,

The final disaster is inherent in—alternately, is made inevitable by— the events preceding the play.

Such is the morally neutral definition. A parallel definition, this time morally loaded, is

An evil deed has been committed and it has to be expiated.

What are the respective positions of the heroes in the (identical) tragic situation just defined? Both are the instruments by which the final disaster/expiation is brought about. In the case of Oedipus this appears more fitting because he was the perpetrator of the evil deed, or, in other terms, is identified with the preceding events and so with the final disaster; but this need not differentiate him from Hamlet as a tragic character—it can still be attributed to the situation. He is the instrument which provokes the catastrophe (by his insistence on discovering the truth) and is all the more effective because he is an unconscious instrument. Hamlet is a conscious instrument in the progress towards disaster/expiation, and he is an imperfect one. He is too delicate, or too subtle, for the purpose.[9] It is somewhere here that the differentiating factor lies.

It is clear that a less self-questioning hero would have been a better instrument. This can be illustrated by a comparison with the Orestes of Greek tragedy, whose position is similar to Hamlet's. Orestes' father Agamemnon has been murdered by his mother Clytemnestra and her lover Aegisthus, who now rule the kingdom together. Orestes, who has been sent out of the country as a child, returns secretly as a grown man to avenge his father. Unlike Hamlet, he has never been ignorant of the true situation, but, like him, he is obeying a supernatural command, that of Apollo. His vengeance is to be more terrible than that of Hamlet, who was enjoined by the Ghost not to harm his mother, since he is to kill both his mother and her lover. Nevertheless, he does not hesitate,[10] but goes straight to work and succeeds.

All three of the great Greek tragic dramatists treated this legend. Aeschylus and Euripides show Orestes pursued by the Furies (which might, though questionably, be taken to symbolise the pangs of conscience) *after* the killing. Sophocles closes the account when blood has been paid for with blood. But none, with the exception mentioned in footnote 10 below, shows any slackening of Orestes' determination *before* the deed.[11] Whether this is regarded as a plain tragedy of re-

---

[9] It is worth recalling how nearly (following the plot literally) he fails. In Act IV his uncle, now fully on his guard, packs him off on the ship with Rosencrantz and Guildenstern, who bear a sealed request to the King of England to put him to death as soon as he lands there. That ought to be the end of Hamlet, but two lucky flukes—his discovery of the sealed despatch and the episode of the pirate ship—save him and enable him to return to Denmark. Shakespeare is even bolder than Sophocles in his rough handling of probability when the story requires it.

[10] Except momentarily in the version of Euripides, before killing Clytemnestra though after he has killed Aegisthus.

[11] The point, however, has been much debated in the case of the *Choephori*, Aeschylus' tragedy on the subject. A convincingly balanced discussion is found in H. D. F. Kitto's *Form and Meaning in Drama* (Methuen, 1956). Professor Kitto remarks: 'A development from hesitation through conflict to a decision is not in the picture at all. That is what I meant in calling this [first] part of the play "static" ; all its elements are there from the beginning: the decision, the prayers for help, the hatred of the murderers and usurpers, the indignation of the two children of Agamemnon

venge, of crime-and-punishment, or of evil springing from evil, Orestes is the ideal instrument to carry it out. He is of the type which drives straight on because he must and asks questions—perhaps very painful ones—afterwards.

That Shakespeare was aware of the type and ready to contrast it with Hamlet is shown by the use he makes of Laertes. This son of Polonius was abroad in France when his father was killed in what, to him, were mysterious circumstances. He does not at first know that Hamlet was the killer and suspects Claudius. At the head of a mob of supporters he breaks down the palace doors, overpowers the bodyguard and angrily demands an instant account of his father's death (Act IV, Sc. 5):

LAERTES: Where is my father?
KING: Dead.
QUEEN: But not by him.
KING: Let him demand his fill.
LAERTES: How came he dead? I'll not be juggled with.
         To hell allegiance: vows, to the blackest devil.
         Conscience and grace, to the profoundest pit.
         I dare damnation: to this point I stand,
         That both the worlds I give to negligence,
         Let come what comes:[12] only I'll be revenged
         Most thoroughly for my father.

If Hamlet had resembled Laertes in his unhesitating directness, the play would have been shorter. Or it would have been a different play. But it can hardly have been this familiar and simple point that Shakespeare intended to make when he indicated the contrast between the two types of avenger. His handling of the character of Laertes underlines Hamlet's hesitation and delay at a moment when, for all the audience knows, he is on his way to England, or already dead. That was surely Shakespeare's main purpose—to recall by implication his hero's tardiness even when he is not on the stage.

What reasons can be given for Hamlet's delay? It is possible to find three, not all of them necessarily exclusive of the others:

(*a*) It is a device to fill out the play, as just suggested, and give it a richer, more exciting plot.

---

[12] I.e., 'I don't give a damn for this world or the next, whatever happens.'

[Orestes and his sister Electra] that they have been excluded from their rights, the living wrath of the dead man, their hope that this wrath will come to their aid.' (*Op. cit.*, p. 45.)

(*b*) It increases the 'area of destruction'. If Hamlet had acted more expeditiously, the material disaster would have been limited to his uncle, possibly himself and—more dubiously—his mother. Polonius and his family would not have been involved, nor need Rosencrantz and Guildenstern—though this is a comparatively minor matter—have been sent to their deaths.

(*c*) Hamlet was that kind of man. The delay both typifies his character and gives fuller opportunities for it to be explored.

Reason (*a*) is too trivial to be worth discussion. Reasons (*b*) and (*c*) deserve to be taken with almost equal seriousness. The force of (*b*) is that it suggests that *Hamlet* is more than an ordinary tragedy of either retribution or revenge. The angry Ghost would have been satisfied with much less than it got—strictly, in fact, with one death, that of its murderer. Even if one supposes that Gertrude, Polonius and the two courtiers have been tainted by association with the murderer, though not directly involved in the crime, this does not extend to the entirely innocent Ophelia and her brother Laertes. What we seem to have is a wholesale contamination of the court of Denmark by the murder of the old King and the incestuous union of his brother with his widow. That little world is 'rotten' because of the evil which is abroad in it and which must run its course like a disease until every character of note has been destroyed. Even Hamlet's friend Horatio is about to commit suicide and so complete the shambles of the last scene; he is only dissuaded by Hamlet in order that one witness may survive to tell the tale. It is as though a force of nature has been released which dwarfs questions of personal innocence and guilt. It cannot abate until the old order has been extirpated and a new order, foreshadowed by the arrival of Fortinbras of Norway, is ready to take its place.

This reading greatly enlarges the theme of the tragedy. If accepted, it implies that *Hamlet* is concerned less with the destiny of particular characters or the consequences of one particular crime than with the problem and nature of evil in general. No doubt it can be accepted, but not to the extent of obscuring the interest of the hero as an individual. Its greatest value is that it provides a basis-in-nature for what would otherwise be a somewhat arbitrarily melodramatic juxtaposition of events, and also that it corrects the old theatrical tendency to subordinate everything in the play to the character of the hero. That, reinforced by the claims of star actors, has always been the temptation. It can be recognised as exaggerated without reducing Hamlet to a cipher or indeed removing him from the fore-ground position which he has always occupied and which is his rightful place.

But it must be conceded that reason (*b*) is hardly sufficient in itself. It happens that the delay serves the plot and gives an oppor-tunity for the disaster to become more complete. But if that were all, it would have only a mechanical relationship to the notion of the all-pervading effects of evil.[13] The latter is a moral factor, existing independently of whatever plot may embody it. We think that, in addition to the function which it fulfils in (*b*), the delay must be considered in relation to (*c*), that is, in relation to Hamlet's charac-ter. There is a natural link between the two if we conclude that the generalised concept of evil is focused on Hamlet, or, better perhaps, *through* Hamlet. The audience is aware of it almost entirely through his consciousness. The two chief culprits, Claudius and Gertrude, become aware of it only after he has shown them their guilt.[14] If Hamlet, as we have said, would be a poor instrument in a plain crime-and-retribution tragedy, he is a perfect instrument in this kind of tragedy which postulates a dissemination of evil through awareness of it to a point at which it cankers everything.

But one cannot stop there. If Hamlet were merely a catalyst, some passively clairvoyant character, some Teiresias, could perform his function. Hamlet is also the hero and one cannot contemplate the play without realising that the working of evil or guilt *through* him is not more important than its effects *upon* him. One must take notice of his reactions as they operate within himself. One must, to return to a familiar and inescapable position, recognise that the psychology of the hero—of this particular hero—is, of prime im-portance in the tragedy.

'Psychology' has become a suspect word in modern dramatic

[13] This becomes more evident if comparison is made with the 'delay'—of some fifteen years between the committing of the crime and its open consequences—in the *Oedipus*. (See above, p. 82.) The conclusion that this was a mechanical plot-device is somewhat attenuated by the fact that it came to Sophocles as part of the traditional story and so could be used by him with verisimilitude. But on analysis it fulfils no other function than to make the plotting of the story possible; and, just arguably though much more doubtfully, to give time and scope for the growth and spread of evil, as in the (*b*) of *Hamlet*. But it becomes quite unlike the 'delay' in Hamlet in that it has no integral relationship with the hero's character.

[14] See Act III, Sc. 3 (CLAUDIUS: Oh, my offence is rank, it smells to Heaven, . . . etc.) and Act III, Sc. 4 (GERTRUDE: O Hamlet, speak no more. Thou turn'st mine eyes into my very soul, . . . etc.).

analysis. But one can use it for want of a better without being led to the extreme and false conclusion that *Hamlet* is a psychological study of a particular kind of individual. While it is not a 'study' but a play, within the framework of this play Hamlet's acute self-awareness, with all the implications which stem from it, is an organic factor without which the rest would be unable to exist. If one were to isolate subject, plot, situations, theme, and moral assumptions, and try to put them together again without Hamlet as characterised by Shakespeare, the drama would be ineffective. One would have *Hamlet* without the Prince of Denmark, an old but not so foolish tag to which it is possible to give renewed significance. Shakespeare has introduced an element which was visibly not in Greek tragedy. Whereas Orestes and Oedipus can be satisfactorily described as 'instruments' because of the functions they are called upon to fulfil,[15] the personage of Hamlet cannot be defined so easily. Hamlet suffers, for example, before he has been given any function (Act I, Sc. 2). One can—though, in view of what has been said a few lines above, one probably should not—imagine him suffering in the same way in different circumstances.

A possible summary of the *Oedipus* tragedy would read: 'A man kills his father and marries his mother in ignorance. He becomes happy and prosperous. Then the truth is discovered.' If one supposes for a moment that the original was lost, this tragedy could be reconstructed around any reasonably noble hero. The hardest problem for the reconstructor would not be the characterisation of the protagonist, who could be a virtual stereotype, but the devising of a plausible plot. Once this had been convincingly done, the play would be effective and would answer Aristotle's requirement that 'the story ought to be so plotted that if one heard the bare facts, the chain of circumstances would make one shudder and pity. That would happen to anyone who heard the story of the *Oedipus*.'[16]

To an objection which may have occurred to the reader half a page previously, that the *Oedipus*, as much as *Hamlet*, only comes alive because the situation is viewed through the consciousness of the hero, the passage just quoted from Aristotle gives a reply. One can surely accept it, to the extent of agreeing that the events in themselves make the tragedy and that all that is needed for the personage

---

[15] The basic analysis is not affected by the fact that Oedipus is—ironically—led to take vengeance *on himself*.

[16] *Poetics*, Ch. 14. Potts, *op. cit.*, pp. 34–5.

of Oedipus is a respect-worthy man who can say, 'Horror, horror, horror' in a rising crescendo as the climax takes shape.[17]

On the other hand, one could summarise Hamlet thus: 'A king is murdered by his brother, who marries his widow and takes the throne. The murdered king's son feigns madness the more easily to obtain revenge. He finally succeeds after a series of vicissitudes and blunders in which half the court are killed, and dies himself at the moment of triumph.'

The events in themselves do not suggest a tragedy but a rich melo-drama, such as was adumbrated in the narrative 'source' of the play, and as was presumably realised in the earliest Elizabethan *Hamlet*, generally ascribed to Kyd, and is certainly found in the crude German version, *Fratricide Punished*, which may have been inspired by it. There, in essentials, is the story, but no amount of skilful plot-doctoring would turn it into a work of the same class as the *Oedipus*. The character of Hamlet had to be conceived and integrated into the whole structure before the play could get off the ground with any chance of rising to a tragic altitude.

It is really not enough to speak of Shakespeare's richer character-isation. It is not merely richer, but differently motivated, taking account of a new human dimension. For better or worse, the 'psy-chology' of the hero now matters. One can perhaps sum up the distinction by saying that in Greek tragedy the principal stress is on moral issues, as defined by the actions of the characters; in Shakes-pearean tragedy the characters do not so much define the issues as contribute to their creation. This they do by a combination of action with cogitation and argument. The two latter are Aristotle's 'thought',[18] but it is no longer realistic to separate 'thought' from

[17] In the same Chapter 14, Aristotle, with his preoccupation with 'action' and his plain conception of 'character', gives what might well be an antici-patory condemnation of *Hamlet*: 'These are the only possible alternatives. One must either act or not act and either know or not know. Of these alternatives, to know and to be about to act, and then not to act, is thoroughly bad—it is disgusting without being tragic, *for there is no emotional crisis* . . . [my italics],' Potts, *op. cit.*, p. 36.

As already pointed out, the main *emotional crisis*, identified with the recognition, occurs in *Hamlet* near the beginning, whereas Aristotle assumes that it will always occur at the end. *Hamlet* follows an entirely different pattern from any tragedy that Aristotle knew. To *open* with the main crisis and continue to the end without falling into a non-cathartic anticlimax, presents problems which he never needed to envisage. It would appear that a dramatist could only solve them by recourse to 'psychology'.

[18] See above, pp. 43–4.

either 'action' or 'character', even for the purpose of analysis. One can no longer speak of character-in-action but of character-with-action, and one must recognise that 'thought' is at once an internal action inseparable from the external action and a factor in the composition of 'character'. This latter, however it is made up, acquires a dynamic force which was dramatically impossible in a system based on character-as-type.

It must, however, be remarked that the 'psychological' element found in Shakespeare is an addition, or a potential addition, to the concept of the dramatic character in general, and need not be exclusive to tragedy. While therefore it increases the complexity tragedy, and so the difficulty of its analysis, it appears to bring no basic change to the theoretical tragic components. Hamlet is a different kind of hero from Oedipus. He might be described as 'more human', 'more credible', 'more interesting', 'more complex', and by various other comparatives. But rigorously he is not 'more tragic'.

6

Macbeth

In the shortest survey of tragic drama it would be unthinkable to omit *Hamlet*, whose influence on both the practice and theory of tragedy has been incalculable. It is, however, an unusual and refractory play, and hardly representative of the whole Shakespearean conception. It is worth considering briefly at least one other example, which at first sight conforms more nearly to the conventional principles of tragic drama. In *Macbeth* all the following features can be found:

(1) The rise and fall of an outstanding man (Macbeth).

(2) The murder of a King (Duncan) by a male-and-female couple who usurp his power—though, unlike the couple in *Hamlet*, the woman in *Macbeth* is actively guilty and does not stand in the same close relationship to the murdered King.

(3) Retribution. The play contains both the crime and its punishment.

As an incident in the general march of retribution, there is also a sub-motif of personal revenge: the eventual killer of Macbeth is Macduff, who is avenging the murder of his wife and children.

(4) The prevalence of evil. A climate of 'unnatural' wickedness is

96

established from the beginning of the play, which opens with the direction: *Thunder and lightning. Enter three witches.* It continues to be stressed throughout, by the reappearances of the witches, the portents on the night of Duncan's murder, the episode of Banquo's ghost. By such external means it is suggested that there is something very rotten in the state of Scotland, i.e., that Macbeth's crimes are related to forces larger and even more sinister than the actual deeds.

(5) Tragic recognition. The precise point at which Macbeth fully realises that he is doomed is when his adversary Macduff reveals that he was 'untimely ripped from his mother's womb'. Macbeth's reliance on the prophecy that 'none of woman *born*' should harm him thus fails and he abandons hope. There has been an earlier, partial, recognition of the same kind when Birnam Wood appeared to move towards Dunsinane, shaking Macbeth's faith in another misleading prophecy.

(6) Irony. The main irony is in the ambiguous nature of the prophecies just noted. Macbeth had gone to the witches for reassurance. What they in fact gave him was a literally exact forecast of the manner of his defeat and death.

All these features are in *Macbeth*, though very unequal in importance. To take them almost in the reverse order: The recognition is not essential to the tragedy. It finally extinguishes Macbeth's already waning faith in his star, but it cannot be said that the hero's whole position has been built up from the misleading oracles, as it was in the *Oedipus Tyrannus*. The witches, like Banquo's ghost, might almost be regarded as mechanical or scenic exteriorisations of Macbeth's unconscious fears and desires, but for the fact that Banquo also sees them on their first appearance. At the end, there is no sudden realisation of horror and the attendant disaster—mainly because Shakespeare's conception of Macbeth's unconfident character rules it out. The hero has always been apprehensive.

As the recognition lacks force in this tragedy, so does the irony which depends upon it. This is obvious if one recalls again the more basic irony which is bound up with the recognition in the *Oedipus*.[19]

Evil: the supernatural machinery of evil is much in evidence (more than in *Hamlet*) and the corollary that the country is 'diseased' is

---

[19] For a different example, one might postulate a tragedy on Joan of Arc in which the heroine was led to disaster by blind faith in her 'voices', which in the end she was obliged to recognise as deceptive. The predictions made to Macbeth never attain that authority. If, as is possible, the dramatist intended that they should, he was not entirely successful.

expressed notably by the Doctor attending Lady Macbeth ('Unnatural deeds do breed unnatural troubles,' Act V, Sc. 1) and in the dialogue between the Doctor and Macbeth (Act V, Sc. 3). The cause of the disease is Macbeth's crimes, as is plain at this point in the play. *Before* any of the crimes were committed, when the good King Duncan still reigned, there might perhaps be said to have been a disease-potential, of which Macbeth (though still innocent in deed) was the carrier. The play seems designed to stress all this. Nevertheless, the impression of a *general* climate of evil must strike one as more artificially contrived than in some tragedies. In spite of the witches and the ghosts, the whole evil can be related to the individual psychology of Macbeth and Lady Macbeth.

Retribution is a main theme, but it is not the whole point. The sympathy created for Macbeth, or at least the understanding of his position, attenuates the force of the plain moral lesson—if such a lesson were intended. The revenge motif, as has been said, is incidental. It is fitting that Macduff should be the agent of final retribution, but the tragedy would hardly suffer if Macbeth were killed by another hand.

The murder of a King (with the attempt to install a new order by usurpation) gives status to the crime and enlarges its consequences. It necessarily involves not merely two individuals, their victim, and the immediate connections of each, but the well-being of the whole realm. This theme is 'pure' in *Macbeth*, uncomplicated by questions of incest or family relationship.

In a sense *Macbeth* is also a rise-and-fall tragedy, in which the hero is shown reaching the heights of eminence, only to be cast down. This is a variety of the 'Fortune' tragedy. To use the common medieval symbol, still familiar to the sixteenth century, the Wheel of Fortune carries a man up to the top (greatness, happiness, or prosperity), then spins him down to misery and disaster. His fall can in itself be a sufficient theme for a tragedy, though clearly it is rather a thin one.[20] Unfortified, it resolves itself into contemplation

[20] This was the only meaning attached to 'tragedy' in the Middle Ages, when the word was not in common use and there was no tragic drama. See Chaucer's gloss on *Boethius* (Bk II, prose 2): 'Tragedye is to seyn a dité [tell a tale] of a prosperité for a tyme, that endeth in wrecchidnesse.' The Monk's Tale in the *Canterbury Tales* concludes with eleven short verse-stories on great men who ended in misfortune, including Nero, Holofernes, Julius Caesar, and Croesus. The Monk explains to his audience that these are 'tragedies' in that they show how Fortune has humbled

of the fickleness of Fortune and pity for the hapless and possibly guiltless hero-victim. Fortified by other elements, it may run through more substantial tragedies, such as the *Oedipus Tyrannus*. When, however, the hero rises through his own deliberate acts and falls through causes capable of some material or moral explanation, the concept of Fortune is weakened, perhaps to vanishing point. What remains is the image of the ascending and descending curve (which links naturally with the theme of crime and retribution). It is present in *Macbeth*, though made less conspicuous by the construction of the play and the character of the hero. Macbeth rises factually to supreme power, but hardly to the enjoyment of it. His frantic efforts to secure himself, stemming from his fears and misgivings, prevent him from ever seeming poised firmly enough on the height of prosperity for the effect of his fall to be shattering.

As in *Hamlet*, it is impossible to ignore in *Macbeth* the psychological interest of the chief character. This dominates and to a certain extent obscures the tragic themes and situations which form the ossature of the play. Any interpretation of the tragedy must take account of the fact that Macbeth is an unconfident villain, a man with too much imagination for the deeds which his ambition impels him to commit. Before killing Duncan, he sees the horror of the crime. He commits the murder as though in a nightmare, after experiencing the hallucination of the blood-stained dagger. When Duncan is dead and Macbeth king, he is still beset by fancies and delusions which involve him in further acts of savagery, so committing him to a hopeless policy of ruthlessness. But he is only externally ruthless: he is not tough at the core. What weakens him is not exactly a sensitive conscience, which would set up stronger feelings of guilt and remorse than he displays, but the fear of retaliation, the perception of hostile forces all around him carried to the point of superstition.

In contrast, Lady Macbeth seems to be hard all through. She reveals no imagination in the material pursuit of her ambition. If this were a pure tragedy of retribution, that would be sufficient. She would be the agent who incites Macbeth to crime, who supplies—to adopt Shakespeare's viewpoint—the male stiffening against his

---

the proud when they least expected it. The Knight and the Host, evidently lacking the tragic sense, like neither the name nor the thing and protest loudly against it. 'Hoo!' quoth the Knyght, 'good sire, namoore of this!' etc. (*Prologue of Nun's Priest's Tale*, line 1 *et seq*.)

unmanly weakness. For retribution a violent death for her at the end would be fitting, and if it were at the hands of Macduff, whose wife has been killed on Macbeth's order, it would be a nicely symmetrical piece of poetic justice. But Lady Macbeth is presented as more than an agent, a character necessary to the action. In her consciousness she is all steel, but she cannot command her unconscious and it is from this interior source, inaccessible to the will, that the breakdown comes. So she dies in her bed of a 'mind diseased' at a moment when no one has time to pay much attention to her.

As with Hamlet, one must beware of regarding the Macbeth pair either as portraits or as psychological studies transposable outside the context of the play. But the material is certainly in them, and here again it does more than enrich the tragedy. It transforms it into a different work than it would otherwise have been.

To illustrate this, one might consider the three possible interpretations, of which only one seems tenable:

(1) *Macbeth* is a drama of retribution with a particularly interesting hero.

(2) Macbeth is a particularly interesting case who becomes involved in a drama of crime and punishment.

(3) The tragedy of *Macbeth* results from the placing of a particular kind of man in a particular set of circumstances.

7

Phèdre

The story of Phaedra and Hippolytus has been treated by a number of dramatists, beginning with Euripides. Seneca wrote a by no means negligible version and several French dramatists, from the sixteenth century on, attempted the subject before Racine. Among these versions considerable differences of emphasis are to be found, some of them sufficient to alter the significance of the tragedy. One common factor, however, is inherent in the story and distinguishes it from the stories of the other tragedies considered in this chapter. This is the theme of passionate love, conceived as the basis of a tragic situation. No dramatist has brought this out more powerfully than Racine, whose play also demands consideration as an outstanding example, after the Greeks and the Elizabethans, of the tragic drama of the French.

In Racine's version Phèdre, the wife of Thésée, King of Athens, is tormented by a secret passion for her stepson Hippolyte, a chaste young athlete who so far has had no use for women. At the beginning of the play, however, he finds that he has fallen in love with Aricie, a young princess who is the last survivor of a rival royal family and who lives as a virtual captive at Thésée's court. Thésée is absent on a mysterious journey and has not been heard of for some time. A report of his death is brought, whereupon Phèdre, persuaded by her nurse, Oenone, seeks out Hippolyte ostensibly to beg him to protect her own young son, now fatherless and a potential successor to the throne. When Phèdre and Hippolyte meet, she is unable to conceal her passion for him and the truth, which she had been determined never to reveal, breaks out. Hippolyte's reaction is one of horror. Phèdre fully realises his disgust and is overwhelmed with shame at her own weakness. At this point it is learnt that the report of Thésée's death was false and that he has just returned home.

Phèdre believes that she is in mortal danger: she expects Hippolyte to denounce her to his father. To save herself, she allows him to be accused of having attempted to rape her. Again it is the Nurse who leads her on and who plans and makes the actual accusation. Hippolyte protests his innocence, but stops short of openly inculpating his father's wife. Phèdre begins to relent and is about to plead for him, but she is shocked into silence by learning for the first time that he is in love with Aricie. Until then she had thought that he was incapable of loving any woman; now she finds that he has preferred another woman to herself. She turns savagely upon the Nurse, whom she blames for having made things worse by her meddling. Oenone flings herself into the sea.

Meanwhile Thésée, acting in blind fury, has already called down the vengeance of the god Neptune upon his son. Setting out, as he believes, to banishment, Hippolyte is driving his chariot along the coast when a monster emerges from the sea and causes the horses to bolt. Entangled in the reins, Hippolyte is dragged over the rocky ground to suffer the particularly violent death which figures in all the versions of this tragedy. Phèdre confesses Hippolyte's innocence and her own guilt to Thésée, then dies, poisoned by her own hand. Thésée is left with the inconsolable Aricie, whom he promises to bring up as his own daughter.

The tragic hero of Racine's play is Phèdre. It is necessary to say this because in Euripides it is Hippolytus, who is punished for his disdain of Venus and his contempt for women in general, Phaedra being the instrument of his downfall. In the Greek play his destruction—it is at least arguable—is due to his defiance of a natural force, while his status of tragic hero is confirmed by the striking and agonising death which he suffers at the climax. The fact that this death is retained by Racine, following precedent, should not be allowed to confuse the issue. The Hippolyte of his play is not punished for having offended Venus. At the beginning he obeys her 'laws' by falling in love with Aricie.[21] The entire wrath of the goddess, if one conceives the tragedy in those terms, is concentrated upon Phèdre.

As it is, the tragedy is built upon the suffering, almost beyond the limits of endurance, of the central character. There is no rise-and-fall. Each turn of the plot serves simply to intensify her anguish. On her first appearance she is sick with the effects of a concealed and unsatisfiable passion and wishes only to die. The false report of her husband's death brings her no real hope, but merely the pretext of a meeting with Hippolyte which produces the added torment of seeing her love rejected with dismay. The final turn of the screw is the torment of jealousy, inflicted by the disclosure that Hippolyte is in love with Aricie. Phèdre, in this cruel tragedy, is thus a helpless and almost passive sufferer, who remains alive until the end only to suffer more and see her burden of guilt increased at each faltering step she takes. This guilt is not based on positive acts, of which she commits none. She merely has reactions, spontaneous and inevitable in view of her condition. In the presence of Hippolyte she is incapable of concealing her passion for him. At the shock of learning of his love for Aricie she is incapable[22] of proceeding with her intention of pleading his innocence to Thésée. If 'guilty' at all in any objective moral sense, she is simply so by her negative attitude at moments when she is weakened by extreme distress. The harshness of the situation is that she is condemned for effects which flow from her inability to react with sufficient force. The positive acts which

[21] This indeed (his involuntary capitulation to Venus, not his resistance to her) is singled out as Hippolyte's only 'weakness' in Racine's preface to his own play. Hippolyte is 'in some degree guilty' towards Thésée for having fallen in love with the daughter of his enemies. This attempt at a moral justification for Hippolyte's destruction, founded on a degree of 'guilt', need not be taken too seriously. In the play itself it is never in evidence.

[22] In both instances, psychologically incapable. But one might say with equal truth, physically incapable. This is one of those cases in which no clear distinction can be drawn.

produce an external 'crime' from her internal sickness are conceived and executed by the Nurse. The Nurse can, of course, be thought of as the other face of Phèdre—the incarnation of her baser nature—but much more plausibly as a separate character, sinning through blind faithfulness to her mistress. In terms of the various kinds of *hamartia*, the 'fault' which provoked the disaster was the treacherous denunciation of Hippolyte by Oenone; the 'error' which led to it was Phèdre's decision, after the report of her husband's death, to go on living and to see Hippolyte; the 'flaw' which bred the error was Phèdre's proclivity to violent physical desire, expressed in Racine's play as a curse laid upon her and other women of her family by Venus.

There is a disease or, if one likes, an evil element in Phèdre, which goes much deeper than her conscious intentions. This element brings disaster to the whole group in which she is placed: death to Hippolyte and Oenone, misery to Thésée, Aricie, and the dependent confidants. But it is not possible to say, as it was of *Hamlet* and more questionably of the *Oedipus*, that the whole group are 'contaminated'. Hippolyte and Aricie remain morally healthy and innocent until the end. Thésée, who might—if this were a different tragedy—be seen as the poisoned source who corrupts the whole of his kingdom,[23] remains curiously outside, despite his obvious emotional involvement. His chief importance is that of the agent whose decision sets the final catastrophe in motion. There is indeed no suggestion of a general atmosphere of evil. Though the acts which result from Phèdre's sickness are disastrous to the group, the sickness is confined to herself. This leaves her markedly isolated and increases still more the pathos of her situation.

8

What becomes of the various tragic elements in this play? With Phèdre as the tragic hero, there is no recognition within the frame-

---

[23] Thésée was a notorious seducer who had aroused the desires of numerous women and then abandoned them. He leaves his wife and her stepson together and disappears on a journey which Hippolyte's tutor Théramène suspects may be only a new woman-hunt. He returns to the situation already described. How fitting that this should be the effect and punishment of his Don Juanism and that he should be the hero of the play! The subject, so conceived, seems rich in dramatic and ironic possibilities. But it remains that, like the alternative *Hamlet*, it has failed to attract a single dramatist.

work of the play. At her first appearance, Phèdre already knows the worst—that she is incurably in love with a forbidden object. If there was any one particular moment when this truth dawned on her, it was anterior to the tragedy. The subsequent revelations of Hippolyte's aversion to her and of his preference for Aricie are hardly recognitions. They are, as has been suggested, turns of the screw which increase her suffering but do not alter her basic despair. She knows already that she is damned; these new shocks are bullets fired into a dying body. If the tragic hero were Thésée, following the implication of the last footnote, there would be a recognition for him when he learns that his son, whose death he has just caused, was guiltless. But Racine does not treat this as a recognition.[24] For him as for other dramatists, the error of Thésée is not at the heart of the tragedy: it is part of the machinery of the plot. It is thus necessary to describe *Phèdre* as a tragedy without a recognition.

It is also a tragedy without conflict. This is less immediately apparent. Phèdre, it might be objected, is being torn between physical desire and moral obligation, between 'must' and 'must not'. If this were so, it would be a clear-cut and poignant dilemma—'nature' pitted against 'virtue', passion against will. But in Racine's play there is no conflict of this kind. There has been one in the past,[25] as there may have been a recognition, but it does not belong to the actual tragedy. When this opens, the battle is already lost—or won, perhaps. Phèdre has realised that she cannot surmount her passion (which might be called a defeat), but is determined to conceal it and die (which might appear a victory). But defeat or victory, that issue is now irrelevant and is not reopened. Phèdre does not debate what she should do: there is no contention of great forces within her or round her. She is pulled momentarily out of her despair by the Nurse, as a drowning person might be, given a flicker of hope, and then pushed back. What goes on in her mind is, first, a reflex struggle for life, then a ferment, but hardly a conflict of opposites.

Next, irony. There are plenty of incidental opportunities for this, which a good playwright is unlikely to neglect. Thus, because Phèdre has made a show of persecuting Hippolyte to keep him away from her, his behaviour towards her is at first governed by the conviction

[24] In Euripides, Theseus does experience a recognition, though without becoming the hero.
[25] Phèdre recalls it in Act I, Sc. 3, lines 269–95: '*Mon mal vient de plus loin*, etc.'

that she dislikes him. 'I will spare her my odious presence,' he remarks in all sincerity. It is ironical too that the great scene between the two of them, in which Phèdre expresses her passion openly and uncontrollably (II, 5), should follow immediately after Hippolyte has made his declaration to Aricie, who now fills his mind. At no other moment could he be more indifferent to Phèdre. Later, the irony of her jealousy of Aricie strikes Phèdre herself as she rails against the young princess:

Aricie must be destroyed, My husband's anger must be aroused against that offspring of a hateful breed. And he must not be content with a light punishment. She is more wicked than her brothers were. I'll plead with him with the whole force of my jealous rage.

But what am I doing? Has my reason deserted me? I—jealous, and begging Theseus to avenge me? My husband alive, and I still hot with passion! For whom? Whose heart am I hoping to win?[26]

To these examples one might add the underlying irony of Thésée's anger against Hippolyte, who is innocent, and his championing of Phèdre, who is the culprit. This, like most of the rest, springs from ignorance, or a misunderstanding, of the true facts, and can be more or less underlined according to the dramatist's detailed handling of his plot. But in none of these instances is the irony essential to the tragic situation, which centres upon the martyrdom of Phèdre. There is essential irony, which may be called authentically tragic although it is not expressed in words, in the fate of a secondary character, the Nurse. She tries to serve her mistress faithfully, she means well. But the result of her good intentions is catastrophic and her reward is to be disowned by Phèdre and to commit suicide.[27]

[26] Il faut perdre Aricie. Il faut de mon époux
Contre un sang odieux réveiller le courroux.
Qu'il ne se borne pas à des peines légères.
Le crime de la soeur passe celui des frères.
Dans mes jaloux transports je le veux implorer.
    Que fais-je? Où ma raison se va-t-elle égarer?
Moi jalouse! Et Thésée est celui que j'implore!
Mon époux est vivant, et moi je brûle encore!
Pour qui? Quel est le coeur où prétendent mes voeux?
                  (Act IV, Sc. 6, ll. 1259–67.)
[27] If one follows the late nineteenth-century tendency always to identify the tragic with tragic irony, then Phèdre's whole position could be called ironical, as well as tragic. She would be exactly comparable to Hardy's Tess of the D'Urbervilles: ' "Justice" was done, and the President of the Immortals, in Aeschylean phrase, had ended his sport with Tess.' This

Finally, there is retribution. This again applies to the Nurse, who is certainly guilty (though, as she thinks, in a good cause) and is punished heavily. But it hardly applies to the protagonists. When the tragedy opens, no 'crime' has been committed, but Phèdre is already being 'punished'. (What she feels as her 'crime' at this stage is her lust for Hippolyte, so far not exteriorised. Perhaps it might be classed as a 'sin of intention'.) When the only specific 'crime' of the tragedy is committed—the denunciation of Hippolyte—it leads to the spectacular 'punishment' of its victim, Hippolyte . . . Obviously *Phèdre* contains no simple theme of crime-and-punishment such as might be embodied in a coherent moral code. With ingenuity various moral meanings can be extracted from it, as that the heroine is expiating a hereditary tendency to sexual aberration, which has been insufficiently punished in her ancestors. And over it all, as in the *Oedipus*, hangs a great irremovable question-mark on the nature of guilt. Euripides dealt with this summarily by implying that divine justice is not human justice, but Racine lets it stand.[28]

[28] One should not be over-impressed by Racine's Preface, written after the play most probably with a view to placating ecclesiastical critics of the theatre and asserting the moral respectability of his art. His remarks are either deliberately tendentious or they reflect a parochial view of morality and the drama whose interest is now mainly historical. He wrote:

> To conclude, I will not venture to claim yet that this play is definitely the best of my tragedies. I will leave it to my readers and to the passage of time to decide its true value. What I can claim is that none of my other tragedies lays more stress on virtue than this one. In *Phèdre*, the slightest faults are severely punished. The mere thought of crime is regarded with as much horror as the crime itself. The weaknesses of love are presented as real weaknesses. The passions are represented only to show the confusion and misery to which they lead; and vice is depicted throughout in colours which reveal it as repugnant and ugly. Such is surely the aim which every man who writes for the public should have before him. And [continues Racine, invoking Athenian tragedy in support of his contentions] such was the principal object which the earliest tragic poets had in view. Their drama was a school in which virtue was taught no less effectively than in the schools of the philosophers. That was why Aristotle was ready to lay down the rules of dramatic poetry, and why Socrates, the wisest of the philosophers, did not disdain to collaborate in the tragedies of Euripides.

reading depends on the meaning one attaches—or better, which Racine's contemporaries attached—to the concept of 'Venus'. The point is returned to below, p. 121.

6

Some Constants of
Dramatic Tragedy

1

The four tragedies examined in the previous chapter form a short cross-section of the world's tragic drama. Small though it is, the plays in question represent widely differing types of drama and they also have the advantage of being generally recognised as great tragedies. It is from some such place that a theoretical discussion should start, and not *vice versa*. It is comparatively easy to build up a theory of tragedy and then decide which plays fit it and which do not. It is more interesting, if perhaps more difficult, to accept certain major works as 'given' phenomena and to deduce principles from them.

The tragedies reviewed have at least this much in common: each has an individual hero who occupies the foreground. In some instances the hero might be said, with varying degrees of plausibility, to be compounded of two characters, as Phèdre-Oenone, Macbeth-Lady Macbeth, and some case could even be made out for an Oedipus-Jocasta combination. But, whether single or multiple, the hero possesses an independent *persona* and is not merely representative of a group. The destiny of the group is affected by his nature and his actions, as conversely his destiny is influenced by their nature and actions, but this means no more than that in drama, as in life, action and indeed existence are impossible to conceive in isolation; the hero cannot operate in a human vacuum. It is questionable whether any more organic connection can be established. Sophocles, as we have seen, begins by suggesting that Oedipus will 'take upon himself' the sins of Thebes, then drops the theme. It is equally doubtful whether Hamlet either takes upon himself the sins of Elsinore, or expiates them. Macbeth does not personify 'unhappy Scotland', he is the clearly objective cause of its unhappiness. As for Phèdre, the evil is in her,[1] not in her environment. In none of these plays can the hero be seen as the representative of a corrupt group, neither can he be consistently described as a good man placed in opposition to the group's corruption. In general, then, the hero's relationship to the group varies widely. He may be a scapegoat, or an avenger, or an outsider. There is no fixed pattern of interaction between him and the community, and this is a further reason for rejecting the Corn King theory of tragedy, which would require him to be always explicable as an expiatory victim.

One will, however, say this with rather less conviction if by 'community' is meant, not that of the characters of the play, but the 'community' of the audience and the society to which they belong. Cannot the tragic hero be a sacrificial victim for them? In order to be so, his suffering must surely be relevant to a type of transgression of which they are conscious. To be logical, we must then suppose a widespread addiction to incest in the Athenians, to fratricide—or better, to a reluctance to avenge fratricide—in the Elizabethans, to excessive physical passion in the contemporaries of Racine. The characters of Oedipus, Hamlet, and Phèdre must be taken to expiate these addictions vicariously. But even if they do so, which is far from certain, their sacrifices will no longer make sense in societies with different addictions. The punishment of a sheep-stealer can have little meaning in a community of market-gardeners. One must therefore conclude that these tragedies lose their main significance when removed from the social environment in which they were originally composed, or that their significance becomes symbolical, or that the sacrificial aspect is not the most important one. The last explanation is by far the most satisfactory, for while it is inevitable that a tragic drama, like any other work of art, should lose part of its original significance when it ceases to be contemporary, it is impossible to concede that that part was its *raison d'être*. If that were so, what empty entertainments we must be prepared to witness when we sit down to a performance of Sophocles, of Shakespeare, or even of

---

[1] Or in her family. But this family, labouring under the curse of Venus, does not constitute the 'group' of the play, which is composed of characters who are not her blood-relations.

Ibsen! That is, unless we are capable of employing a quite exceptional degree of historical imagination, or else a no less exceptional power of transposing the sins of the past into the different sins of the present.

The hero of dramatic tragedy is not, in any consistently definable sense, an emanation of either the fictitious group made up by the other characters or of the real community represented by the audience. The most one can say is that he is related to both, perhaps dependent on both, in senses which may well vary from play to play. He is, as has been deduced from Aristotle by different commentators, the most important component of tragedy, but he is a more complex phenomenon than Aristotle suggests. He cannot easily be conceived of in terms of 'neither wholly good nor wholly bad', unless the spread between those two absolutes is taken to be so wide that it can contain almost every human case. There are not, really, many redeeming features in Macbeth and none in his wife; Phèdre, according to the two possible points of view, is either totally innocent or incurably vicious, judged by any normal standard, Hamlet is quite innocent. But all these statements imply moral judgments such as Aristotle was careful not to make[2] and which suppose some fixed scheme of ethical values. Not only does dramatic tragedy not require this but, as will be seen later, it requires freedom from any such scheme.

The theme of *retribution* as a constant of tragedy is consequently weakened. It is fairly clear-cut in *Macbeth*, in which regicide and other murders are explicitly condemned and punished. It is found in *Hamlet*—though here its incidence is by no means as simple—but it is, as has been seen, a highly debatable concept in the *Oedipus* and *Phèdre*. And if it can be said that the two Shakespearean tragedies embody a moral position from which it is possible to establish a definite relationship between punishment and crime, neither these nor the other two plays can be reduced to the single theme of retribution. The most that can be said of all four tragedies is that certain things are done and certain people are brought together—in varying circumstances and with varying degrees of awareness on the part of the characters—and that certain consequences follow. If those consequences, which in each case are disastrous, were consistently interpreted as a punishment, then the 'moral utility' of tragedy would be established and its nature could at once be defined: a tragedy is a morality. But the limitations which such a definition

[2] See above, pp. 39–42 (*hamartia*).

sets up are plainly unacceptable. A reconsideration of the tragedies themselves would raise all over again the questions of what offences were being punished and why certain characters were included in the punishment. There seems to be no moral position from which the answers to all the questions can be given.

Before examining what the true position is, we must consider again the notion of a 'tragic conflict' in relation to the four plays. The simplest form of this conflict occurs, in theory, when the hero is torn between two courses of action, both equally painful. It is exemplified in the classic anecdote of the man travelling with his family in the troika who must throw out one of his children to the wolves to give the rest of them a chance of escape. The agonising choice with which the father is faced would constitute the tragic dilemma, while the tragic conflict would be identified with the attempt to resolve it. Essentially this same dilemma and conflict are found in such a play as Racine's *Andromaque*. The heroine, who is the widow of the Trojan prince Hector, must choose between marrying her Greek captor, Pyrrhus, or virtually condemning her young son Astyanax to death: for if she refuses Pyrrhus, he will hand over Astyanax to the other Greeks who intend to kill him. In that event, Hector's line will be wiped out for ever (together with all hope of a revival of Troy through its ruling family). But if Andromaque takes the other course and accepts Pyrrhus she will be betraying her dead husband in a different manner by unfaithfulness to his memory. Her natural feelings are also painfully balanced. Either she must give up her son to destruction or she must enter into a marriage which she finds repugnant.

It is difficult to apply another adjective than 'tragic' to such a dilemma. It entails the clash between right and right, or, if one likes, between wrong and wrong. It is insoluble[3] and takes place within Andromaque. If it is not tragic, what is it? One might sit up until dawn with a good dictionary without finding an acceptable alternative. Yet, as has been seen, no such conflict figures in the four tragedies we have considered.

In other terms, a tragic situation certainly need not rest on a problem of choice clearly envisaged by the characters, though one

[3] The fact that Andromaque does find a compromise solution (she will marry Pyrrhus, having secured his promise to protect Astyanax, and kill herself immediately afterwards) has been found *untragic* by various commentators. Those who approach tragedy through philosophy sometimes describe this type of conflict (when unresolved) as Hegelian.

cannot go so far as to exclude such problems from the domain of tragedy altogether.

There is, however, another kind of conflict, more fundamental because it is not fully exteriorised, which might appear to form the essence of the tragic. This conflict is between two opposing forces or conceptions of too profound or too general a nature to be expressed as a 'dilemma' and which happen to clash within the hero or the tragic group. This was the basis of Unamuno's conception of the tragic sense. There it was a conflict between the old order, regarded as predominantly spiritual, and the new order, seen as predominantly materialistic; between nostalgia-aspiration on the one hand and the possibilities of fulfilment on the other; between, in short, two worlds, the one 'ideal' (wherever situated), the other 'real'. What becomes of this is our four tragedies?

Of Oedipus it is possible to say that the state in which he is living when the play opens is good, but illusory; the state which is revealed to him in the course of the play is intolerable. But if there is a sharp contrast between the two states, there is, as has been already remarked,[4] no conflict between them. In addition, it would be somewhat far-fetched to look upon the two states of Oedipus as two 'worlds' between which he is divided, even if unconsciously. The 'ideal' world in that case would have to be a world of non-incest, in which a man can escape from his parents and form new relationships elsewhere. But this is represented in the tragedy as the 'real' world—as it undoubtedly is also for the majority of mankind outside drama—whose laws Oedipus is punished for infringing. It is, in fact, so difficult to apply the two-world theory to the *Oedipus* that the only reasonable conclusion to come to is that the tragedy does not contain that conception, even by implication. The present writer cannot think of any Greek tragedy which does contain it, and it may well be that it was not a conception which occupied the Athenian mind.[5]

It is rather easier to believe that it could have occurred to Shakespeare. There is some sort of conflict in *Hamlet*. First, that which is

[4] See above, p. 86.

[5] It is true that Greek tragedy may contain two conflicting 'laws', as that of Apollo and of the ban on matricide in the *Oresteia*, that of Aphrodite and of Artemis in the *Hippolytus*, but these laws are external to the protagonist. He is not divided between them in any intimate sense, as one might expect him to be from the standpoint of modern psychology. The absence of a struggle of conscience, and indeed of a faculty corresponding to 'conscience', strikes one forcibly when reading Greek drama.

See also below, p. 115, footnote 8.

exteriorised in the hero's hesitations, his doubts about whether to act, or how to act. But important though this may be in the story, it hardly attains the 'tragic' intensity of the conflict which divided Racine's Andromaque—unless, that is, one adopts the simple view of Hamlet as a chronic contemplative for whom *any* decision regarding action is a form of torture—a view which the events of the play hardly support. Secondly, there are hints of a disparity between two worlds in Unamuno's sense. The 'real' world is that of which Hamlet is made aware by the Ghost. It is 'out of joint' but uncomfortably present. 'O cursèd spite/That ever I was born to set it right!' (Act I, Sc. 5.) The contrasting 'ideal' world is a state of innocence: that, no doubt, in which Hamlet's father would be still alive and still king and no responsibility would be placed upon himself. It would depend upon his father's presence combined with his mother's innocence, and the conflict would take place between that reluctantly relinquished state of felicity and the reluctantly admitted nastiness of the actual situation. Some support can be found for this, particularly in the scene in Gertrude's room (Act III, Sc. 4), in which Hamlet fiercely blames his mother for having betrayed the ideal order:

> You are the Queen, your husband's brother's wife,
> *But would you were not so.* You are my mother, ... *etc.*

But although these two worlds can be discerned in the psychological background of the play, and more distinctly in certain passages of the text, it would be a strained and partial interpretation to base the tragedy upon the contrast—and much more, the conflict—between them. There are too many other elements of at least equal prominence. And after all, is Hamlet's ideal world, as we might ingeniously reconstruct it, a sufficiently compelling image to form the second half of a tragic dichotomy? Is it really much more than the general longing for security and freedom from guilt which can be read into so many human situations and which a dramatist may well imply without committing his hero to that self-destructive pursuit of it which the logic of tragedy seems to require?

Equally with Macbeth. His ideal world, no doubt, is one in which he would be securely established on the throne of Scotland as its loved and honoured king. The reality is certainly different, but it would be even less true of *Macbeth* than of *Hamlet* to say that the tragedy depends on a clash between the two states. The main 'conflict' in *Macbeth* is, obviously, an external one between the usurper and the supporters of the legitimate royal line. If there is another conflict in Macbeth's mind, it is between his chronic misgivings and his ambition—his desire for security and his desire for power. There is a potential dilemma here (as well as an opening for irony), for the more crimes Macbeth commits in his search for security, the more enemies he creates and the more precarious his power becomes. But this is the dilemma of any tyrant who attempts to rule by violence. If it is to attain a tragic pitch, it requires a specially sensitive hero who is conscious that every step he takes towards his goal is in fact setting him farther away from it. That is hardly Shakespeare's hero in this play.

As for Racine's Phèdre, it might be possible to construct a dream-world for her in which her passion for Hippolyte was not illicit and Hippolyte responded to it. But this plays no part whatever in the tragedy itself and, as has been seen, there is no conflict there of any other kind.

One could extend this examination to other recognised tragedies with equally negative results. Neither a conflict engaged on a conscious level nor an unformulated conflict between obscure forces would be found in them. One would be led to conclude that the tragic, on the evidence of dramatic tragedy at least, need not depend on an incompatibility between the ideal and the actual. In that case, Unamuno's conception of the 'tragic sense' (quite apart from its sociological application) seems to lack universal validity. It is note-worthy that he attributes it to a number of moralists, theologians and poets, but invokes no tragic dramatists at all.[6] The work which he chooses to symbolise the 'tragic conflict' in the Spanish soul is by Cervantes, an almost exact contemporary of Shakespeare—a writer with whom Unamuno was also familiar, but to whom he omits to attribute a 'tragic sense'. And when all allowance has been made for the fact that for a Spaniard meditating on the national temperament *Don Quixote* is an obvious choice, it is still a revealing one. The tradi-tional classification into which this work of Cervantes falls is romance and, even if it is burlesque romance or satirical romance, it remains in that category. This suggests that the ideological struggle which Unamuno read into the book should not properly be called tragic at all, but romantic. The word is not used, of course, in any pejorative sense, but in an attempt to use critical terminology as accurately as

[6] See above, pp. 58–9.

possible and so perhaps arrive at a valid distinction. We will define the romantic attitude as an attachment to an imagined order of things which is consciously preferred to the actual order.[7] The strength of the attachment is the important factor. If it becomes so great that to break it will constitute a 'final disaster'—in other words if the imagined order has been so thoroughly substituted for the actual order that the latter has lost all attraction in the subject's mind, the resulting situation may well be tragic. The collapse of the first is the collapse of the *only* order in which the subject can conceive

[7] Two of the main senses of *romantic* come together to justify this definition.

(A) As a category of literature, romance embraces fictitious stories about imaginary characters, as distinct from factual stories about historical or real characters. In earlier literature, the latter class included the chronicle and the epic, in both of which the events and characters were regarded as having had a real existence. The romancer, on the other hand, was free to invent both, together with the setting. His imagined world was, and is, usually an exciting and attractive place, governed by laws conducive to a happy ending. It is clear that the reality or historicity of non-romance is often a matter of faith, which is variable. The *Odyssey* can today be read as a romance. The Court of Charlemagne as it appears in the French epic *chansons de geste* is not now regarded as much more historical than the Court of King Arthur in the romances, but the principle remains. The epic tends to become romantic as it gets further away from its national origins, or from identification with a social ideology. It was of some importance to Frenchmen of the twelfth century to believe that Charlemagne and his Peers had existed, more or less in the form in which the *chansons de geste* represented them. It was of no importance to sixteenth-century Italians such as Ariosto. The same process is observable in the evolution of the 'historical romance', in which the reader accepts the invention of characters and episodes and is aware that he is not reading 'history'. While the relationships between history, epic, legend, and romance are of such complexity that it is doubtful whether any absolute distinctions can be established, it can at least be said that romance is set in the world furthest removed from the contemporary conception of 'reality' and usually conceived as a desirable place to escape to.

(B) In the Romantic Movement, the word acquires wider and less easily definable connotations. But the sense in which we are interested runs forcefully through all the works of Romanticism, however much the subsidiary characteristics may vary. The awareness of two worlds is here intensified until in many writers it becomes a repugnance for the actual world and an irresistible longing for the ideal world. To move into the second is no longer a pleasurable intermittent pastime but addiction. This addiction can be called spiritual, and particularly so when the actual world is regarded as essentially materialistic. It can be called religious and may be so when identified with the aspirations of an established religious faith. But the most striking feature of the European Romantic Movement as a whole was the proliferation of pseudo-religious 'ideal' worlds, due to reasons which are examined later in this book.

the possibility of living.[8] But this is a tragic development of a basically romantic situation. The concept of two incompatible orders is not of itself tragic. It becomes so because of a particular combination of character and circumstances within an ideology. A similar combination within a different ideology might well lead to a comic development, as indeed it appears to do in *Don Quixote*. It is impossible, without preconceptions, to read the last pages of that book (which describe, still with humorous touches, the Knight's sober renunciation of his 'madness' and his calm return to reality) as the culmination of a 'tragedy'.[9]

But it is important not to shut any doors. We will willingly concede the possibility of romantic tragedy, based on the realisation of a tragic potential in the romantic attitude to life. But we will not see that attitude itself as fundamentally tragic and will accept—as we must, on the evidence of some of the great dramatic tragedies—the presence of some other tragic potential in material which is *not* romantic in the sense defined above.

[8] But is not this, it may be asked, exactly what happens in the classic 'recognition' of Oedipus? In a sense it is, but with the difference (1) that there has been no preceding conflict of choice, and (2) that the imagined order has only to be seen for what it is to be at once detested, precisely because it was 'unreal'. There is no nostalgia.

This can be illustrated by re-shaping the *Oedipus* as a romantic tragedy, containing the duality conflict of nineteenth-century Romanticism and the psychological theories which derive from that. In that case, Oedipus has an obsessive longing, implanted in the pre-natal and early post-natal phases of life, for the intimate companionship of his mother. In his ideal world mother and son continue to live together in an exclusive and all-satisfying relationship. He is at once child and lover, protected and protector. Against this ideal world is set the real world in which incest is defined and condemned as a crime, in which his father stands in the way—and can only be removed by another crime—and in which the child is required to tear itself away from the maternal warmth and unite itself with an unfamiliar mate. These are the two worlds implied by such generalisations as 'the Oedipus complex' and incidentally exploited in Cocteau's play, *La Machine Infernale*. The disparity and conflict between them are evident and may well be tragic, but, as we have seen, they are not what constitutes the tragic in Sophocles' play. In that, both Oedipus and Jocasta have done everything possible in the past to avoid an incestuous relationship, which they saw when it was predicted to them as the ultimate horror. When, after all, that horror is realised, both find it intolerable. There is no question of either of them looking back for a single moment to their marriage as a felicitous, if forbidden, state.

[9] Unamuno's claim to interpret *Don Quixote* as he likes (see above, p. 60) implies that he is reading it with a nineteenth-century sensibility, which enables him to find it tragic. But we are more concerned here with what Cervantes 'actually did put into it' in the seventeenth century.

2

To sum up what has so far been put forward, we first have a number of negations. These bear on elements which may sometimes be present in tragedy but are not always present, and therefore cannot be reckoned among the essential conditions of the tragic. Tragedy *need not* contain:

(1) A conflict, whether conceived as a conscious dilemma or as a deeper struggle between two incompatible forces.

(2) The idea of retribution in the punishment of the hero for transgressions committed either knowingly or unknowingly.

(3) More broadly, the idea of expiation through the hero for the transgressions of the community as a whole.

(4) As a consequence of (2) and (3): judgments made from any fixed moral standpoint.

To these may be added the conclusions of the previous chapter, that a tragedy *need not* contain:

(5) Irony.

(6) A recognition.

Against all this we are so far able to place a single affirmation. All the tragedies we have examined contain a hero, placed in varying relationships to a group, who always suffers, though in various ways and degrees, and always come to final disaster as a result of something having gone wrong somewhere.

We can also go on to make a further affirmation, of a much more general nature. It is, that while dramatic tragedy is not a moral *demonstration*, based upon a pre-established set of values, it is very frequently, and perhaps always, a moral *exploration*. This is particularly noticeable in Greek tragedy, in which the hero is placed in certain positions or circumstances either to see what happens to him or, if it is known through familiarity with the story or from the mere fact that the play is a tragedy, that he must end in disaster, to see how the disaster comes about and/or how he reacts to it. In spite of such features as the moralisations of the Chorus,[10] the main design in the Greek tragedies is exploratory rather than exemplary.

[10] It might be truer to say that the comments of the Chorus underline the exploratory nature of the plays. The Chorus are generally in the dark and when they draw conclusions these often have to be revised as the action proceeds. They are nearer to observers attempting to interpret an unfinished experiment than to all-knowing spectators.

The characters in Greek tragedy move among unknown or half-known forces, represented by Fate, the gods, or other men. Among these, it is perhaps not so important as it once appeared to establish a hierarchy, or to attempt to define the particular fields in which each can operate. All are potentially dangerous—they have at least that common quality. To live in the same world as the dangers they embody dramatically is the inescapable human condition, and if tragedy 'demonstrates' anything at all, it is no more than this. The question asked is ultimately the question of *power*. In its simplest form: What will have power to harm, and how and in what circumstances will it take effect? (This alone is sufficient to account for the prevailing atmosphere of evil found in some tragedies. 'Evil' is synonymous with the harmful but not clearly identified forces which threaten the hero and sometimes the group. There is no difference between saying that danger may be anywhere and that evil appears to be everywhere, independently of any question whatsoever of a moral retributory principle. Cp. a ship sailing among uncharted rocks.) The answers which tragedy gives—all tragedy, not merely that of the Greeks—do not amount to a 'law' even within the limits of any one culture. That is the professional domain of the theologian on one hand and of the scientist on the other.[11] The impulse behind tragedy is best defined as curiosity, undogmatic and perhaps irrational but never frivolous, about the nature and sources of power as it affects the human subject. This power is of three main kinds, which also furnish the three broad classifications of the subject-matter of dramatic tragedy.

The first is the power attributed to natural and divine forces in their impact upon man. The dividing-line between these forces cannot be clearly drawn and the less scientific the culture the hazier it will be. The thunderbolt killed but it may have been Zeus who hurled it. That is the simplest case, but a similar ambiguity is necessarily present in any conception of a spiritual force working through physical agencies. For our immediate purposes the precise distinction between the divine and the natural is irrelevant, so long as the source of power remains in some way mysterious. The important feature of this kind of power is that it is envisaged as located in some extra-human part of the universe.

A second kind of power corresponds to forces within the in-

---

[11] Who both approach the tragic the further they move from their professional certitudes.

dividual. Love, jealousy, hatred, ambition are regarded as originating within man, but no more predictably than the extra-human forces of the first type. One can treat this either as a transference of attention from the 'universe' to the individual, or as a recognition that the individual is part of the substance of the 'universe' (i.e., that Nature includes human nature). On either hypothesis, human nature is seen as uncharted and as potentially dangerous to its possessors and to those with whom they are in contact as the external forces appear to more outward-looking minds. The 'psychological' interest thus created is evident in Shakespearean tragedy and seems to have made its first appearance in drama at about that date.

The third kind is political power. This is primarily power exercised over the community by human agents, who are, however, raised well above the common level by the community's institutions. It is the highest kind of power attainable by purely human means and can be instantly recognised as important because of its direct material bearing on the fortunes of the community. On those grounds alone its interest is obvious when it is dramatised as a story of kings, usurpations and conspiracies, or merely of the downfall of the ruler in whom power is vested. But since the 'supreme power' which the ruler exercises in the most material sense is also conceived as the collective power of the community, it can be notionally transformed in some degree at least into spiritual power, so shading into type (1). It lends itself equally well to a symbolic interpretation. The traditional tragedy organised round the figure of a 'king' is thus virtually the prototype.

All these three kinds of power may well enter into the same tragedy and they may not be clearly distinguished. But on analysis one or another will generally prove to be dominant and it is important for both a critic and a producer to decide which this is.

Oedipus might appear to be a borderline case. We concluded that, approaching this tragedy at the deepest level, the failure was found to lie *within* the hero and that his personality was identified with his calamitous destiny.[12] But if the failure was internal, the power which caused the destruction can only be called external. Even if we discard the plain theory of a malignant fate, we still have to account for the oracles and for the existence of a taboo upon parricide and incest which was not of Oedipus's making, however strongly he acquiesced in it. The failure of Oedipus was that he proved to be

[12] See above, pp. 78–80.

118

the man who had committed these universally condemned crimes. That is not the same as maintaining that he was destroyed through an addiction to parricide and incest, as one might be through addiction to a drug or through the presence of an acute psychiatric condition. Psychologically, Oedipus was a completely healthy man, at least according to modern standards. He was not suffering from a 'mind diseased' or from any inordinate passion. Therefore, although we concluded that his personality was inseparable from the acts which led to his destruction, we cannot say that his personality was conceived in such a light as to make it the cause of those acts.[13] Sophocles did not explore it from that angle and was not concerned with its composition, only with its identity.

One may go on to make the generalisation that in Greek tragedy the exploration of power bears primarily on existence, in which the extra-human plays an important part. It does not bear on the essence of human personality. Once this has been characterised (once its 'quality' has been indicated) by the dramatist, it is a postulated factor in the play, unmysterious and not in itself a source of power.

The same does not hold good of Shakespeare. Hamlet, as we have remarked, can neither be typed as *merely* irresolute nor defined as *merely* the agent of vengeance which the plot requires. What goes on inside him is of great importance, not so much to assist an actor in 'characterisation' as for its influence upon the course of events and the fate of the other characters. It was the dangerous forces within him which moved him, for example, to destroy Ophelia There was no necessary external cause. One might argue that this particular destructive impulse was set off by his mother's betrayal of his father, but there was no destiny, no family curse, no general rule to decree that her infidelity should have had that effect upon him rather than another.[14] Again, it seems necessary on the plane of 'action' that Hamlet should either kill his uncle or should not. A

[13] The conviction of nineteenth-century commentators that his personality *must* contain the cause explains their obsession with *hubris*, as the only discernible flaw in his composition. Hence their mistaken identification of a superficial characteristic with a self-destructive psychological component. See above, pp. 79–80.

[14] A different man in the same situation might well have broken away from his mother and the whole distasteful older-generation complex and opted instead for the young and pure Ophelia (Hippolyte in Racine's *Phèdre* does something like this). But he would have to be a 'different' man, which reinforces our argument.

'character' of the clear-cut Orestes-Laertes type will kill. A shambling, weak 'character' will fail to do so. Hamlet does kill in the end, but what a confused, half-bungled business it is. And the interest by that time is certainly not in the fate of Claudius, if it ever was so. It has long since established itself as lying in the reactions of Hamlet. Are there any new discoveries to be made of *him*? The question of his madness and the difficulty of deciding how far it is simulated reinforces the same atmosphere of doubt about the human psyche and the hidden forces which may lie within it.

So with Macbeth, though his case is less complicated; so with Lear—who, as a type-character would be only the foolish father of the fairy tales,[15] but who is developed into something much greater and more dangerous. So, to a lesser degree, with Othello (the Jealous Moor *plus*) and certainly with Iago (the Envious Man *plus*), with Brutus (the Conspirator *plus*) and so on. To speak of the psychological interest, or complexity, of these characters is one way of putting the point. Another is to say that Shakespeare was ready to site power within the individual to an extent which no Greek tragedy appears to recognise.

3

Racine's *Phèdre* poses a more difficult question. Was the force which produced the disaster here internal or external? Adopting one modern point of view, it is easy to describe it as the first. Psychologically and physiologically, Phèdre is a woman suffering from an erotic obsession for a particular male and it is unnecessary to look beyond this self-sufficient explanation. Racine himself and his contemporaries, it might be argued, did not seriously look beyond it. But the dramatist preserved part of the divine apparatus of his Greek original, with its implication of an external influence (Venus). He did this, it might be said, in obedience to dramatic tradition, following a line of plays on the same subject. If he gave it deeper thought than that, his motive was to attenuate conventionally for contemporary taste the direct physical implications of the story and to allow his characters a wider imaginative margin in which to evolve, fear, and suffer.

[15] The tales of the *Cap O' Rushes* family, in which a father mistakenly rejects a loving daughter in favour of her two evil sisters. Through this theme Cordelia can be related not only to the heroine of *Cap O' Rushes*, but to the Cinderella of Grimm's version.

The objection to an unqualified acceptance of this is that we cannot know precisely in what light Racine and his generation regarded the case of Phèdre and the text of the play gives no clear answer. While it is unlikely that the seventeenth century would have conceived it exclusively as an essay in natural psychology, what meaning was attached to *the wrath of Venus* is hard, and perhaps impossible, to determine. The phrase itself, if transposed from its poetic context to the Christian-conditioned world of reality in which the audience normally lived, would of course become symbolic. But again, symbolic of what? In his Preface, which has some evidential value although, like any other preface, it may not accurately represent the true implications of the play, Racine observed that Phèdre 'is involved *by her destiny and by the wrath of the gods* in an illegitimate passion by which she is the first to be horrified . . . her crime [i.e., her passion for Hippolyte] is *a punishment inflicted by the gods* rather than an effect of her own will.'[16] For the (Greek) 'gods' read 'God' in his Christian puritanical aspect, possibly. The disputed problem of Racine's Jansenism hinges on questions such as this, which can be answered either way. The play itself allows of both a theological and a natural interpretation. The 'destiny' which, according to the passage just quoted, also involves Phèdre in her guilty passion, is equally open to different attributions. Indeed, the lasting interest of this play rests largely on the fact that it remains as moving and as 'true' whether one holds that destiny is shaped in heaven or in the viscera of the individual. But there is one element which, even on a modern non-religious view, transcends the limits of the individual heroine. Phèdre's proneness to illegitimate passion is inherited. She had, on any view whatsoever, no control over heredity. The destructive power within her had been placed there by other hands, whether these should be called human or not.

If we refuse to be bogged down in the question of moral responsibility (which we have seen to be not immediately relevant to tragedy) and concentrate instead on the question of power, we find that Phèdre is comparable to the bearer of a charge of explosive which goes up, killing her and some of those around her. How she came to have the explosive and why it blew up at that particular point are by

[16] Incidentally and, I think, quite unconsciously, Racine drives yet another coach-and-four through the simple retribution theory in this sentence. If Phèdre's 'crime' *is* her punishment, the moral question of what she is being punished for still remains totally unanswered.

no means otiose questions, but they are secondary to the interest of watching her frantic and vain attempts to avert the catastrophe which she carries with her or within her. If Racine is to be acquitted of having perpetrated, intentionally or not, a work of highly sophisticated sadism, it must be on this that the main exploration bears— on this and on the effects on her entourage. It does not bear, as we think it might in Shakespeare, upon the nature of the destructive force. For Racine's contemporaries the devastating power of an unbridled passion is taken for granted and is not subjected to analysis any more than dynamite need be in the parallel suggested. There is therefore no place for the kind of psychological exploration that occurs in Hamlet, and in this respect Phèdre is nearer to the characters of Greek tragedy—which is not unexpected, given her dramatic ancestry. Yet she differs very perceptibly from such a character as Oedipus, whom we have been able to describe as a completely healthy man, not suffering from any particular addiction. She differs also from Phaedra, her original in Euripides, chiefly by being more fully and sympathetically drawn, with a consequent magnification. She is promoted from being the instrument of destruction into being its source, or at least the centre from which it proceeds. Of Racine's story, one could plausibly say: 'But for Phèdre, there would have been no disaster.' One could not say this with any confidence of Euripides' story. There would still be Hippolytus's slighting of Aphrodite, Aphrodite's resentment and her rivalry with Artemis to threaten danger.

One can perhaps sum this up by saying that the power is in Phèdre, though it is much more calculable and less personal than the power in Hamlet. How it got there is left indeterminate, though one need not affirm that it was deliberately planted in her by a supernatural force.

In all the four tragedies under review there is some question of political power. In each of them a throne is at stake. Macbeth is an open usurper, whose criminal seizure of the royal authority is the mainspring of the plot. Hamlet's uncle also has committed murder to obtain the throne, with the additional factor that he has taken the queen, his victim's wife. Oedipus, though he has acted in ignorance, has done exactly the same thing; and there is the further theme of political rivalry between him and Jocasta's brother, Creon. In *Phèdre* there is an extensive sub-plot concerning the succession to the throne. When the old king, Thésée, is reported dead, his second wife Phèdre, his son Hippolyte, and the princess Aricie all have rival claims to it. Hippolyte quickly renounces his in support of Aricie, while Phèdre is too overwhelmed by her personal suffering to undertake any effective action. A potential struggle for the throne is in any case cut short by Thésée's return, but the basis of it is clearly laid down. In some versions of the story it is fully developed.[17]

But it is obvious that the 'political' theme in these plays, similar though it is in all of them when it is abstracted and defined, does not occupy the same place in any two of them. Only in *Macbeth* can it be said to be dominant. In the others it is of varying importance, until in *Phèdre* it is so faintly marked that one tends to overlook it altogether. Yet the fact that it is always present, even when hardly utilised, points to the existence of some basic requirement which the great tragic dramatists usually tend to fulfil.

This is partly due to the persistence of the traditional tragic theme of the fall from high prosperity to abjection. Kingship represents the highest temporal office and it is from this eminence that the fall is steepest and most impressive. A second function of the King in drama is that of the judge. He is the authority who metes out rewards and punishments, thereby both representing and enforcing the standards of conduct of a social order. In this rôle he stands apart from the other characters. But when he is involved in the action, either through his personal acts or through usurpation of his office, then there is a challenge to the authority of the judge-and-ruler which throws open the whole question of material power: either in relation to other forms of intra-human power or, on a hierarchical view (the King is next to the gods), to extra-human power. Thus not only an individual, not only an office, but the validity of a social law which shades imperceptibly into a moral law may be brought under scrutiny in the 'political' theme of a tragedy.

4

We can now reaffirm that dramatic tragedy is based on a preoccupation with the various kinds of power which influence human existence. When power is dangerous it is synonymous with evil. Tragedy

---

[17] For example, in Pradon's *Phèdre et Hippolyte* Phèdre deliberately plots to exclude Thésée from the throne and to have Hippolyte crowned as her consort.

assumes that all power is potentially dangerous, but makes no assumptions on the manner or the circumstances in which it will prove so. *Certainty* about the results of a course of action will not yield a tragic situation.[18] Equally, neither will acquiescence in the impossibility of attaining at least some degree of certainty. Tragedy will not flourish in areas either of strong faith or of strong scepticism. In the first, the sort of power with which it is concerned operates according to absolute principles, knowledge of which is conceptualised as Truth. In the second there are no absolute principles and a search for them would appear futile or absurd. The field of tragedy lies between these two. The tragic sense is alive wherever there is unsatisfied curiosity about the nature of power allied to the belief that *some* valid discoveries about it are possible.

The *method* by which the tragic investigation is conducted in drama and other literary forms is to put forward the tragic hero as an exploratory agent. He is, in this sense, an unconscious agent—the conscious exploration is undertaken by the spectators. He must engage the sympathy of these by some personal quality, for otherwise they would be watching an irrelevant experiment on an alien subject. He must not be a passive victim, for that would rob the experiment of its interest in another way. He must be unable to foresee the final outcome, since if he did so it would no longer be a genuine experiment. It is here that the mistake, defect, or failure enters in. Not being a passive victim, the hero will make an attempt to avoid the dangers which surround him. Owing to some uncalculated factor the attempt fails and he comes to disaster, which may or may not be the disaster he feared initially.[19]

But why, envisaging tragedy as an exploration, must there necessarily be disaster? Why, after the dangers have been encountered and, as it were, reconnoitred, should there not be a happy ending if the catastrophe is not to be conceived as a 'punishment'? The most convincing answer rests on the principle that the 'perils' of tragedy are of the highest stature. The characters of tragedy are not trivial either, but when it comes to an encounter between them, it is the characters who must go under. The character who comes through triumphant is a 'hero' in the heroic sense and is out of the

[18] See above, p. 9 *et seq.*

[19] *Phèdre*, as has been seen, is almost a passive victim. She would be one if the disaster consisted in her suicide and nothing more; the story, though lamentable, would not then be tragic. The real tragic disaster consists in the consequences for the other characters.

domain of tragedy.[20] The character who merely eludes the dangers by a combination, perhaps, of luck and cunning, not only falls short of tragic stature himself but, more important, brings some contempt upon the perils themselves. The latter represent the gravest threats conceivable to human well-being and it would diminish them to find that a man could be exposed to them and escape without mortal damage. The exploration is sufficiently serious to exhaust all that is in him. It is not fitting that he should survive to be utilised a second time, as though he were the hero of an adventure story.[21]

We thus have the tragic hero, surrounded by the tragic group, committed to a course of exploration in which he will ultimately be destroyed. His experiences will illuminate certain danger-areas for us, but only momentarily, only partially. They will not confirm a preconceived judgment any more than they will establish a new rule. They have no didactic value, in spite of anything that has been said by the moral apologists of tragedy. The disasters which tragedy contains are not exemplary. The fact that they occurred in certain circumstances gives no guarantee that they will occur in the same way in other circumstances. *Qu'est-ce que cela prouve?* Such was the misconceived question asked of *Phèdre*, and derided often enough, if sometimes for the wrong reasons. What does *Hamlet* prove, or the *Oedipus*? In the sphere of practical behaviour, absolutely nothing. The conviction that they should prove something underlies every debate on guilt-and-punishment in tragedy. The debate is irrelevant. Tragedy does not deny the possibility of a transcendent principle of justice—it denies nothing—but it does not affirm it either. Its nature is to remain constantly empirical. It is only on that condition that

[20] This disposes in part of the vexed problem of the dramatic 'tragedy' with a 'happy' ending. Another road to a happy ending is opened when a metaphysical power (necessarily personified) relents and allows the hero to survive. Both types of development occur in plays classed as tragedies, but one would say that, though the explorations they embody may attain tragic height and seriousness, they fail as wholes to be completely tragic.

[21] Oedipus does reappear in another play, *Oedipus at Colonus*, probably written some twenty years after the *Oedipus Tyrannus*. The two plays have no organic connection and, though it is possible to read the second as a tardy epilogue to the first, it really deals with a different subject and its existence hardly diminishes the 'final' impact of the *Oedipus Tyrannus*. In Aeschylus' Oresteian Trilogy, as quite possibly in other trilogies, now lost, some of the same characters appear in more than one play. It then becomes a matter of finding the 'tragic hero' and of deciding whether, or in what sense, he/she has survived.

it can persist as a concept in different cultures, each with their different ethical and philosophical orders.

Around the exploratory tragic hero so conceived the various para-tragic elements fall into place. They can be seen as the *means* by which the tragic theme is developed as a 'story'. The 'tragic' riddle, problem, or conflict (according to context) is an exteriorisation of a basic uncertainty; it is one way of rendering the hero's hesitation as he gropes his way among unknown dangers. The fact that he eventually takes what proves to be the wrong road for him opens the door to irony. There is potential irony in any situation based upon a mistake. The degree to which it is emphasised depends on the nature and prominence of the mistake, as well, to a large extent, as on the dramatist's handling of the story and his metaphysical assumptions. In the *Oedipus* the mistake is evident and all-important and the irony is correspondingly pervasive. In *Hamlet*, where the mistake is much harder to define, the ironical element hardly exists. As for the recognition, this may also be a matter of emphasis and handling. If one requires the tragic hero to arrive, at the end, at a full knowledge of his failure (here again, the *Oedipus* is the outstanding example) the recognition will be stressed. But not every tragedy requires this.

Taken separately, neither conflict, irony, recognition, nor the concept of retribution are essential to tragedy. But without any of them it would seem impossible to construct a story bearing on the serious exploration of power. It is therefore virtually certain that one or more of them will be present in any embodiment of tragedy in a verbal art-form.

An Anti-Tragedy: 'Candide'

1

The inadequacy of generalisations about particular periods and societies has already been noticed, but they can hardly be avoided altogether. They can perform the function of yielding comparisons which are broadly true and usefully light up changing concepts of the gods, of the psychology of the individual, the composition of the fictional character, and so on. The traditional image of the eighteenth century as the Age of Reason has done good service and need not be rejected today, provided that it is hedged with certain qualifications. These will include the abandonment of crude antitheses between emotion and intellect, after which it is perfectly possible to introduce into a pantheon of higher powers no longer exclusively engaged in battle, vengeance and whoring, the goddess Reason alongside other relatively gentle and enlightened deities. She is fully entitled to an equal place with Justice, Mercy, and Chastity, since as an ideal she is as 'spiritual' as they and does not necessarily bring Materialism in her train.

The Age of Reason only becomes a serious misnomer when it is taken to exclude metaphysical anguish and when this is identified with the 'tragic sense'. The eighteenth century was patently no more free of apprehension or less conscious of the horrors and brutalities inherent in human existence than most other ages. The madness of some of its poets, the nausea of some of its intellectuals when confronted with the social scene is at least partial proof of this. One might not look in such an ostensibly academic poem as Gray's *Ode on a Distant Prospect of Eton College* (1747) for evidence of the tragic sense—awareness of the uncertainty of the human lot and of the perils which attend it—but it would be a mistake not to:

> Alas, regardless of their doom
>> The little victims play!
> No sense have they of ills to come,
>> Nor care beyond today.
> Yet see how all around 'em wait
> The Ministers of human fate
>> And black Misfortune's baleful train!
> Ah, show them where in ambush stand
> To seize their prey the murth'rous band!
>> Ah, tell them, they are men!

Gray and his contemporaries certainly possessed a tragic sense of this kind, though it is equally true that they possessed no authentic tragic drama. The net result of the eighteenth-century productions of Shakespeare was to take the sting out of him. Voltaire, whose 'tragedies' dominated the French stage of his time and were the models of the genre in Western Europe, never produced a play comparable to those of the great earlier periods. His plays, at least in intention, were exemplary, and the fact that they assumed certain fixed moral standards is enough in itself to disqualify them as tragedies according to the evidence we have so far assembled. Voltaire, however, was much more than a dramatist and if any one figure can be taken as representative of the rationalism of the century his claim is hardly disputable. If he were found to be totally devoid of the preoccupations associated with a perception of the tragic, the case would be strong for an incapacitatingly blind spot in the rationalistic outlook. But these preoccupations are visible in his nondramatic work. In this he is again typical of an age which was liable to express its tragic awareness anywhere but in the theatre.

As is well known, Voltaire was profoundly affected by the great earthquake of 1755 which destroyed Lisbon in a few minutes and caused the death of some 30,000 people. His reactions were expressed in the long *Poème sur le désastre de Lisbonne* which he wrote very soon after the event and from which it is necessary to quote:

> Philosophes trompés qui criez: 'Tout est bien',
> Accourez, contemplez ces ruines affreuses,
> Ces débris, ces lambeaux, ces cendres malheureuses,
> Ces femmes, ces enfants l'un sur l'autre entassés,
> Sous ces marbres rompus ces membres dispersés;

Cent mille infortunés que la terre dévore,
Qui, sanglants, déchirés, et palpitants encore,
Enterrés sous leurs toits, terminent sans secours
Dans l'horreur des tourments leurs lamentables jours!
 Aux cris demi-formés de leurs voix expirantes,
Au spectacle effrayant de leurs cendres fumantes,
Direz-vous: 'C'est l'effet des éternelles lois
Qui d'un Dieu libre et bon nécessitent le choix'?
Direz-vous, en voyant cet amas de victimes:
'Dieu s'est vengé; leur mort est le prix de leurs crimes'?
Quel crime, quelle faute ont commis ces enfants
Sur le sein maternel écrasés et sanglants?
Lisbonne, qui n'est plus, eut-elle plus de vices
Que Londres, que Paris, plongés dans les délices?[1]

Here, a savagely impressive disaster is contemplated with pity and with a horror which is hardly excessive in the circumstances, though fear is absent and there is no obvious place for it. Having experienced these at least partly tragic reactions, the poet goes on, however, to ask just those questions which, if answered, will lead away from the tragic. By what 'law' was the disaster caused? Can this be an example of retribution? But the questions immediately prove to be rhetorical. Voltaire does not really expect an answer in terms of 'God' and 'laws' and uses his irony to deride those who claim to give one:

 ... Ainsi du monde entier tous les membres gémissent.
 Nés tous pour les tourments, l'un par l'autre ils périssent.
 Et vous composerez, dans ce chaos fatal,
 Des malheurs de chaque être un bonheur général!
 Quel bonheur! O mortel et faible et misérable,
 Vous criez: 'Tout est bien!' d'une voix lamentable.

[1] Deluded philosophers who cry: 'All is well', gather round and gaze at these dreadful ruins, this rubble, this torn flesh, these miserable remains, these women and children heaped on top of each other, these severed limbs under these broken blocks of marble; a hundred thousand victims swallowed up by the earth, who, torn and bleeding and still breathing, end their lamentable lives in horrible agonies buried under their houses with no one to help them.
 At the sound of their dying, half-articulate cries, at the dreadful sight of their charred remains, will you say: 'This is the effect of the eternal laws which dictate the choice of a God who is both free and good'? Will you say, on seeing this pile of victims: 'God has taken vengeance; their deaths are the penalty of their crimes'? What crimes, what faults have been committed by these children lying crushed and bleeding on their mothers' breasts? Did Lisbon, now destroyed, have more vices than London or Paris, wallowing in pleasure?

L'univers vous dément, et votre propre coeur
Cent fois de votre esprit a réfuté l'erreur.
Eléments, animaux, humains, tout est en guerre.
Il le faut avouer, *le mal* est sur la terre.
Son principe secret ne nous est point connu.
De l'auteur de tout bien le mal est-il venu?[2]

Under the civilised prosody is a kind of scream. Voltaire's keenly felt awareness of a tragic situation—that of humanity and indeed of all creation beset by appalling and inexplicable dangers which he conflates with *evil*—leads him to reject the comfortable reassurances of Optimistic philosophy. So far, he is still in the domain of tragedy and the way might still be open for an exploratory attitude towards the forces which influence the human condition. But Voltaire's satirical bent causes him to react against the Comforters with excessive sarcasm, which will lead him away from tragedy towards complete negation. By concentrating his indignation on the fools who refuse to see that existence is too bloody to be explained so simply, he becomes cornered in the position of maintaining that it is too bloody to be explained at all. There is thus no point or interest in investigating it further. Had he instead conceded the possibility, as we have in a previous chapter, of regarding such things as earthquakes as the effect of pure chance, and had refused to generalise from these to other types of disaster, he might well have remained in the tragic field.

Voltaire's outlook ultimately becomes untragic not through lack of sensibility, not because of his rationalism, but because an obsessional impatience with the advocates of the providential solution drives him into a nihilistic agnosticism. When, a few years later, he writes his best-known story, *Candide*, his nihilism is dominant and his treatment of the tragic elements is systematically destructive—though whether or not by conscious design it is difficult to say.

2

From the point of view of this study, *Candide* can well be considered as an anti-tragedy written—as it only could be—by a man with an almost complete tragic endowment,

[2] So all the creatures of the whole world groan. All born for torment, they perish by one another. And in this murderous chaos you would concoct a general good from the misfortunes of each individual! What a good! O weak and miserable mortal, you cry: 'All is well!' in lamentable tones. The universe gives you the lie and time and again your own heart

130

It is the story of the fantastic misadventures of a small group of characters in a contemporary eighteenth-century setting. The hero, Candide, is an innocent but clear-minded young man who has been brought up in the household of a rustic German baron. From the family tutor, Pangloss, he learns a simplified perversion of the doctrine of Optimism:

'It is proved,' Pangloss used to say, 'that things cannot be other than they are, for since everything was made for a purpose, it follows that everything was made for the best purpose. Observe: our noses were made to carry spectacles, so we have spectacles. Legs were clearly intended for breeches, and we wear them. Stones were meant for carving and for building houses, and that is why my lord the baron has a most beautiful house ... And since pigs were made to be eaten, we eat pork all the year round. It follows that those who maintain that all is well talk nonsense. They ought to say that all is for the best.'[3]

The truth of these optimistic assertions is soon put to the test. Thrown out of the house for making love to the baron's young daughter, Cunégonde, Candide is forcibly enlisted in the army, undergoes a collective flogging by his regiment for attempted desertion, escapes after the carnage of a murderous battle and embarks on a series of adventures which take him over half Europe, across to South America, and back again to the Old World. He is shipwrecked, involved in the Lisbon earthquake, imprisoned and flogged by the Inquisition, becomes fabulously rich after visiting Eldorado, and is swindled out of most of his wealth before finally settling on a little farm near the Bosphorus with a selection of other characters. Between them these have survived practically every brutality which it is possible for humanity to inflict, from rape to hanging. They include the philosopher Pangloss, who has endured worse physical hardships than Candide, but argues almost to the last that good is the ruling principle of the universe. Another philosophical character, Martin, quietly maintains that the ruling principle is evil. An old woman, born a Pope's daughter and once a ravishingly beautiful

---

[3] *Candide or Optimism*, translated by John Butt (Penguin, 1947). Most of the other extracts from *Candide* quoted in this chapter are from the same translation.

---

has refuted the error of your mind. Elements, animals, men, all are at war. There is no concealing it, *evil* is upon the earth. Its hidden principle is unknown to us. Did evil come from the author of all good?

princess, does the washing for them. She lacks one buttock, cut off during a siege to make a meal for the famished soldiery. But the steepest fall, in the context of the story, is that of Candide's youthful sweetheart, Cunégonde. The quest for her has been the guiding light of all his travels, but now that they can be united she is no longer desirable. Privation and suffering have aged her prematurely and turned her into an ugly, acid-tongued woman. However, they marry and settle down with the others to a dim but tolerable existence. To the battered little community Candide imparts the philosophy which experience has taught him. The only way to make life bearable is to work at the practical task which lies immediately before one. It is useless to argue about transcendental and insoluble problems. Their best hope of at least a limited happiness is to cultivate their farm.

Before this conclusion is definitively reached, Candide and his companions consult a dervish, famous for his philosophical wisdom:

'Master, we have come to ask a favour. Will you kindly tell us why such a strange animal as man was ever made?'

'What has that to do with you?' said the dervish. 'Is it your business?'

'But surely, reverend father,' said Candide, 'there is a great deal of evil in the world.'

'And what if there is?' said the dervish. 'When His Highness sends a ship to Egypt, do you suppose he worries whether the ship's mice are comfortable or not?'

'What ought to be done then?' said Pangloss.

'Keep your mouth shut!' said the dervish.

The pervading lightness of style and tone and the refusal to entertain answers to such momentous questions as the meaning of human destiny provide the two general features of an anti-tragedy. Another anti-tragic feature of a general kind is that *Candide* reaches a moral conclusion—'the thing to do is to work humbly in our garden'—and is indeed an exemplary tale. The fact that its moral is not uplifting does not change its category. In more particular respects also *Candide* is the obverse of the tragic coin. Several of the characters are left for dead after undergoing the most soul-destroying experiences, yet in some later chapter they reappear, practically unaltered in the psychological sense. This faculty of bobbing up again like so many puppets ought to dehumanise them to the level of comic automata and so destroy the reaction of sympathy in the reader. Curiously enough, it does not do this. One still hopes, temperately, that Candide will succeed in his aims. One can still experience disappointment in his disappointments—though again temperately. But if the characters possess a limited human quality and can conceivably command pity, they certainly have no tragic stature. They are in no way above the norm of the spectators. Failing to fulfil this condition, they ruin another condition which we concluded was essential to tragedy. They reduce the stature of the perils they encounter. For if such characters —who could certainly never be regarded as heroic—can emerge undestroyed and, to a considerable extent, undefeated, from the worst calamities, it becomes impossible to take the calamities themselves very seriously. As the old woman with the crippled posterior remarks, after recalling her tribulations at the hands of pirates when she was still young and beautiful: 'But let's not dwell on that. Such things are so common that they're really not worth mentioning.'

This casual attitude towards the most terrible experiences runs through the whole story. It appears very plainly in the episode recounted in Chapter 26, in which six dethroned kings sit down at table together at an inn in Venice, to eat a supper for which some of them can hardly pay. The old theme of the fall of the mighty is sufficiently evident, but Candide's companion makes light of this classic reverse of fortune.

'It is no more unusual,' said Martin, 'than most of the things which have come our way. It is very common for kings to be dethroned. And as for the honour of having supper with them, it is a trifle which does not deserve our attention.'

3

Almost systematically *Candide* negates all the main characteristics of tragedy. The tale has been described as anti-metaphysical, anti-religious, and immoral, but though it may be all these things incidentally in certain senses of the words, its most consistently evident quality is the anti-tragic. Its attitude towards the dangers which threaten humanity is an advance on the *Poème sur le désastre de Lisbonne*, for in that work Voltaire was still prepared to join, even if sceptically, in an argument on the transcendental causes of misfortune. In *Candide* the characters who do this are derided. Either by words or events they are shown to be indulging in a useless occupation, in speculations *which do not concern humanity*. If one develops the dervish's parallel of the mice on board the ship, one will conclude that the universe is indeed a planned machine working under the remote control of some omnipotent Sultan, but that it works without reference to mankind and its purpose is for ever beyond their comprehension.

But if the mice cannot comprehend, they can dream. They can construct a fantasy-world in which they will come into their own, a place where mice are happy, good, and on top of their destiny. *Candide* contains examples of two such worlds.

The first is material. In their wanderings in America, Candide and his companion Cacambo reach Eldorado, a country isolated by impassable mountains to which they are carried by the current of an underground river. On leaving Europe, they had already hoped to find their better world in the New Continent, for 'when you don't have satisfaction in one world, you find it in another.' Eldorado seems to fulfil this promise. 'This probably is the country in which all goes well,' remarks Candide, 'for there must necessarily be some such place.' It proves to be a Utopian region in which gold and precious stones are as common as dirt, and prized no higher, in which exquisite food, music, architecture, and manners are universal, and whose inhabitants are naturally cultured, law-abiding, equalitarian, humane, and contented.

But for Candide this earthly paradise is not enough. After a few weeks of tranquil happiness he feels the urge to move on. Ambition and love supply his motivations:

'It is perfectly true,' he says to Cacambo, 'that the castle in which I was born couldn't compare with this country. But there is no Cunégonde here and I expect that you have some mistress in Europe as well. If we stay here, we shall be no different from the others. But if we go back to our own world, with only twelve sheep loaded with the stones of Eldorado, we shall be richer than all the kings put together and it will be quite easy to recover Cunégonde.'

So they leave Eldorado for a still more alluring prospect, the imagined country of power and perfect love. Their eventual disillusionment has already been described. Their money melts away, and with it the dream of material dominion. The quest for beauty in the person of Cunégonde is frustrated by the reality of human physical decline. Neither this nor the tameness of Eldorado would, in Voltaire's time, suggest consciously anti-tragic features, in view of the concept of tragedy up to that date. What they do suggest is a prefiguration of the Romantic concept of two worlds, to be incorporated into a new image of tragedy and evidently germinating already in the Age of Reason.

4

The immediate reaction to situations of extreme horror is not a tragic one. If expressed, it is more likely to be Rabelaisian than Aeschylean, as with troops living under the strain of the worst battle conditions. In such circumstances and others of perhaps acuter but more short-lived horror, the apprehension, the questioning, the 'recognition' associated with tragedy would be entirely out of place. In order to cope with the situation, or even to exist through it, the anticipatory and reflective faculties must remain numb, the alternatives being hysteria or madness. The tragic qualities simply are not survival-qualities. If there is a reaction, it can only take the form of crude mockery, expressed at its crudest by some physical manifestation of disassociation. Some protective psychological mechanism at first disconnects the process of verbal articulation, with the result that the situation is not allowed to emerge into conceptual existence at all. If it did, it would be overpowering. The protective mechanism then appears to re-route the dangerously constructive processes of thought. It initiates, with apparent infallibility, a mental transposition of the most pressing perils from the level of the sublime and the terrible to that of the familiar and the ridiculous.[4] When reality is too massively horrible to be surmounted, the human mind instinctively attempts to burrow beneath it. This is surely the explanation of the notion (which should never become a definite concept) of the absurd, current in generations who suspect the futility of either a heroic or a tragic response.

In *Candide* the absurd is conspicuous enough. To be raped several times a day, be knocked on the head, contract plague, and eventually be sold as a slave, is represented as commonplace and laughable. So with the other hugely disastrous events of the story. But on the other hand both the author and his characters are highly articulate. They try to make rational sense of the disasters which occur, though without measuring them in either material or psychological terms. It can be argued that this rationalisation, which is shown to be ineffectual,

[4] These considerations would lend support to our hypothesis that the tragic exploration (as in the great periods of tragic drama) is most likely to be undertaken from a position of strength. See above, pp. 73–4.

is itself part of an all-embracing notion of absurdity. Not only is the human situation ridiculous, but so is the human reaction to it. That, in *Candide*, would be a fair statement of Voltaire's position. (And he thus rejoins earlier, Christian-orientated, writers in demonstrating the inadequacy of Reason; unlike them, however, he concludes for reasonableness, on purely practical grounds of existence.) But the effect of a plain reading of the work is to separate him somewhat from other practitioners of the absurd—particularly more modern ones—without altogether denying his kinship with them. The style and the organisation of the story betray an intellectual coherence which is not that of a man writing under the immediate impression of horror. This apparent detachment can be ascribed partly to literary technique—there have been few periods in which perception and the means of expression have been less well-matched than in the eighteenth century—but one must take the work as one finds it. Very possibly there was a Kafka struggling inside Voltaire. But, as he never got out, that, for the literary critic, is the end of the matter.

We are therefore left with a work in which the absurd, as later understood, is foreshadowed conceptually but not exploited emotionally or aesthetically. Negation of an earlier attitude, which coincides very closely with the tragic attitude, is the dominant characteristic. It is not necessary to speculate on the author's conscious intentions to recognise *Candide* as an anti-tragedy and to value it as a contribution to an understanding of its opposite.

III

The Duality Conflict

8

Two Worlds or One? Neoplatonism, Pascal

1

We can now return specifically to the question which has haunted so many of the pages of this book. It is that of the Two Worlds between which the tragic protagonist is assumed to be divided, with a resultant irresolvable conflict, the perception of which has been held to constitute the tragic vision.

We were unable to find a conflict of this kind in the Greek, Shakespearean, and Racinian[1] tragedies we examined. We may as well add that it figures nowhere in Aristotle's analysis. Oh the other hand, the nineteenth-century commentators and those who inherited their outlook, beginning with Unamuno, have seen it as the essential of the tragic human condition. The point is put with great clarity in an essay by Matthew Arnold on the French prose-poet, Maurice de Guérin, who was a disciple of the Christian socialist Lamennais:

> The intuition of Guérin, more discerning than the logic of his master, instinctively felt what there was commanding *and tragic* [my italics] in Lamennais's character, different as this was from his own; and some of his notes are among the most interesting records of Lamennais which remain:
>
> 'Do you know what it is,' M. Féli [Lamennais] said to us on the

[1] Except, perhaps, incidentally, in *Andromaque* (see above, p. 110). Andromaque's Other World can be connected with the cult of the dead and the power of its attraction must depend, in general terms, on how dead the dead are considered to be (cp. Ibsen below). For Racine's tragedy it is at least dubious that this particular conflict is the central theme of the play and, even if it is, whether it should be treated as a struggle between two worlds.

evening of the day before yesterday, 'which makes man the most suffering of all creatures? It is that he has one foot in the finite and the other in the infinite, and that he is torn asunder, not by four horses, as in the horrible old times, but between two worlds.'[2]

This particular essay of Arnold's was written in 1861. The passage he quotes from Guérin's diary belongs to 1833. It is true that the word *tragic* is Arnold's and is not used here by Guérin or by Lamennais, who merely calls man 'the *most suffering* of all creatures'. But it seems legitimate to conclude that they would have allowed this suffering to be called tragic suffering, as has been done so often since. Man, by his nature, is 'torn asunder' between two worlds, which Lamennais characterised as 'finite' and 'infinite'.

If, as appears to be the case, this view of the human condition only became important in the nineteenth century, and particularly in that part of it when Romanticism was dominant, what was there before? Rational empiricism is only a very small part of the answer. It hardly accounts even for the whole of Voltaire. And before Voltaire stretch endlessly precedent generations immemorially aware of the dichotomy of body and soul, earth and heaven, the contingent and the absolute, the cabbage and the king.

Two main influences canalised and nourished this duality concept in the European mind: Platonism and Christianity. The fact, which is indeed obvious, has often been pointed out,[3] but is worth looking at again.

Plato's own theory of Ideas or Forms seems to have originated in purely, or predominantly, intellectual speculation on the possibility of abstracting qualities from particular instances; or, to put it the other way, of establishing categories of things or acts according to the quality which they have in common. To begin with, it was hardly more than the process of generalisation which is necessary in all co-ordinated thinking about 'real' phenomena:

> It seems probable that the *Euthyphro* is the first dialogue in which either of the words *idea* and *eidos* appears, in its special Platonic sense; and both appear there. The passages are as follows: 5 d, 1–5, 'Is not piety in every action the same? and

[2] Matthew Arnold, *Essays in Criticism* (Macmillan, 1937; first published 1865).

[3] Recently by Morse Peckham in *Beyond the Tragic Vision: the Quest for Identity in the Nineteenth Century* (Braziller, New York, 1962). Certain sections of this book are highly relevant to the subject of this chapter and the next.

impiety, again, is it not the opposite of all piety? Is not everything that is to be impious the same as itself, having, as impiety, a single Form (*idea*)?' And 6 d, 9–e 6, 'Do you remember that I did not ask you to give me one or two examples of piety, but to explain that very Form (*eidos*) which makes all pious things to be pious? Do you not remember that you once said there was one Form (*idea*) which makes impious acts impious, and pious acts pious?... Tell me then, what is the nature of this Form (*idea*), so that by looking to it and using it as a pattern I may say that any act done by you or another that has such a character is pious, and any act that has it not is impious?'[4]

Although *piety* is a moral quality, and its use as an example in the above passage might seem to tilt the emergent theory in an ethical direction, the mention of other generalisable qualities in other Dialogues show that there is no such necessary bias. Thus, quickness, courage, health, numerical evenness, bed, and beauty, are all considered in various passages as having or being *ideas*.

As this curiosity about general qualities was developed and elaborated through Plato's subsequent writings, the notion of a quality as a 'universal', distinct from each particular instance, developed also almost inevitably. The seeds of this growth were already contained in the words translated above as Form and 'pattern'. *Outside* the particular phenomenon, and with an independent 'real' existence, was the Form, pattern, or model enshrining its quality in perfect form (the last word is inescapable). The Form or Idea was of necessity pure (unmixed), it was 'higher' than the phenomenon, it was outside space because not sensible, outside time because unchanging. The logical compulsion of his premiss caused Plato to postulate, if not gods (though the Idea of 'good' very nearly becomes God[5]), at least a number of intellectual idols or transcendent values which easily lend themselves to deification. He himself seems to have moved a considerable way along this path. The earliest Neoplatonists (the Alexandrian philosophers of the third century A.D.) went much further in the mystical significance which they attached to the Ideas. The revival, or rather re-working, of Neoplatonism by Italian scholars of the fifteenth century completed a doctrine of transcendences in which attention was now concentrated

[4] Sir David Ross, *Plato's Theory of Ideas* (Oxford, 1951), pp. 12–13.
[5] See Ross, *op. cit.*, pp. 39–44. Ross denies that Plato himself identified God with the Idea of good, while recognising that this interpretation has been widely held and is a 'very natural' misunderstanding.

upon the 'highest' ideas such as Love and Beauty, to the exclusion of the numerous 'lower' Ideas which could not become objects of exaltation. This doctrine, or the main conceptions which it embodied, permeated the literature of Western Europe during the Renaissance. It is typically expressed in a sonnet of Du Bellay's, published in 1550:

> Si notre vie est moins qu'une journée
> En l'éternel, si l'an qui fait le tour
> Chasse nos jours sans espoir de retour,
> Si périssable est toute chose née,
>   Que songes-tu, mon âme emprisonnée?
> Pourquoi te plaît l'obscur de notre jour,
> Si pour voler en un plus clair séjour
> Tu as au dos l'aile bien empennée?
>   Là est le bien que tout esprit désire,
> Là, le repos où tout le monde aspire,
> Là est l'amour, là le plaisir encore.
>   Là, ô mon âme, au plus haut ciel guidée,
> Tu y pourras reconnaître l'Idée
> De la beauté qu'en ce monde j'adore.[6]

In such a poem the abstract Universals which Plato originally postulated have become charged with force as objects of desire. The poet, conscious of the transitory nature of his physical life, 'imprisoned' and 'in darkness', longs emotionally to satisfy his desires, spiritualised, in some free, bright, heavenly, eternal day.[7] This paradise, while containing nothing which might not have been developed from Plato, has much in common with a Christian heaven. The sixteenth century was, indeed, the age when Platonism and Christianity became most closely intertwined, and nowhere does this appear more markedly than in some of the works of Spanish mysticism. The fusion is very evident in the poems of Luis de León, whose *Noche*

---

[6] If our life is less than a day in eternity, if the recurring seasons disperse our days without hope of return, if all things born are perishable, why do you delay, my imprisoned soul? Why does the darkness of our (mortal) day give you pleasure, if, to fly up to a brighter abode, you have a well-fledged wing on your back? There is the Good which all minds desire, there the repose to which all men aspire, there is love and pleasure also. There, O my soul, guided to the highest heaven, you will be able to recognise the Idea of the beauty which I worship in this world.

[7] This sonnet is a free imitation of the sonnet by Bernardino Daniello beginning: *Se'l viver vostro è breve oscuro giorno / Presso a l'eterno . . .* The French version develops the Neoplatonic theme considerably beyond the Italian.

Serena ('Clear, Calm Night') considerably expands the theme briefly
sketched in Du Bellay's sonnet:

> Cuando contemplo el cielo
> de innumerables luces adornado,
> 1   y miro hacia el suelo
> de noche rodeado,
> en sueño y en olvido sepultado,
>
> El amor y la pena
> despiertan en mi pecho una ansia ardiente;
> 2   despiden larga vena
> los ojos hechos fuente;
> la lengua al fin dice con voz doliente:
>
> Morada de grandeza,
> templo de claridad y hermosura,
> 3   mi alma que a tu alteza
> nació, qué desventura
> la tiene en esta cárcel baja, oscura?
>
> Qué mortal desatino
> de la verdad aleja así el sentido,
> 4   que de tu bien divino
> olvidado, perdido,
> sigue la vana sombra, el bien fingido?
>
> El hombre está entregado
> al sueño, de su suerte no cuidando,
> 5   y con paso callado
> el cielo vueltas dando
> las horas del vivir le va hurtando.[8]

[8] (1) When I gaze at the sky, adorned with innumerable lights, and look
down at the earth covered in darkness, buried in sleep and oblivion,
(2) love and anguish awaken an ardent longing in my breast. My eyes
become a spring and let fall great floods (of tears). At length my tongue
speaks in sorrowful tones: (3) Abode of greatness, temple of brightness
and beauty—my soul which was born at thy high level, what misfortune
keeps it in this deep, dark dungeon? (4) What mortal error so separates
(human) understanding from truth that, forgetful of thy divine good, lost,
it follows a vain shadow, an imaginary good? (5) Man is sunk in sleep,
heedless of his fate, and the revolving heavens with silent step are stealing
away the hours of his life from him.

Ay! despertad, mortales.
Mirad con atención en vuestro daño.
6   Las almas immortales
hechas a bien tamaño,
podrán vivir de sombra y de engaño?

Ay! levantad los ojos
a aquesta celestial eterna esfera;
7   burlaréis los antojos
de aquesa lisonjera
vida, con cuanto teme y cuanto espera.

Es más que un breve punto
el bajo y torpe suelo, comparado
8   a aqueste gran trasunto
do vive mejorado
lo que es, lo que será, lo que ha pasado?

Quien mira el gran concierto
de aquestos resplandores eternales,
9   su movimiento cierto,
sus pasos desiguales,
y en proporción concorde tan iguales . . .

. . . Quién es el que esto mira
y precia la bajeza de a tierra,
10   y no gime y suspira
por romper lo que encierra
el alma, y de estos bienes la destierra?[9]

Aquí vive el contento,
aquí reina la paz; aquí, asentado
11   en rico y alto asiento

[9] (6) Mortals, awake! Be watchful against the dangers which threaten you. Can immortal souls, created for such great good, live on shadows and illusion? (7) Ah, raise your eyes to that eternal heavenly sphere; you will laugh at the fleeting whims of this false-flattering life, with all its fears and hopes. (8) Is the low and heavy earth more than a tiny point compared to that great copy in which lives perfected what is, what will be, and what has been? (9) Whoever looks on the great ordering of those eternal lights, on their sure movements, on their different orbits so well concerted in their harmonious relationship . . . (10) What man can look on that and prize the lowness of the earth, or not groan and sigh to break out from what confines the soul and exiles it from these good things?

está el amor sagrado,
de honra y deleites rodeado.

    Inmensa hermosura
aquí se muestra toda, y resplandece
12   clarísima luz pura
que jamás anochece;
eterna primavera aquí florece.

    O campos verdaderos!
O prados con verdad frescos y amenos!
13   riquísimos mineros!
O deleitosos senos!
repuestos valles de mil bienes llenos![10]

This poem, which I have quoted almost in full, contains as comprehensive a picture as can be found in general literature of the Platonised heaven of a sixteenth-century Catholic. It is compounded of the physical sky—space with its stars and planets—and of a metaphysical empyrean in which Happiness, Peace, Love and Beauty exist in their supreme form (stanzas 11 and 12). The physical aspect which was not—or only faintly—indicated in Du Bellay's sonnet is strongly evident. The significance of this should perhaps not be over-stressed. Sixteenth-century general science did not always draw a clear distinction between the heaven of the astronomer and of the mystic, both of which were equally inaccessible by material means to man. It can also be argued that the 'sky with its innumerable stars' was a good imaged starting-point for a meditation on the common enough theme of 'Cast your eyes upwards', and that one would be absurdly literal-minded to fail to recognise its symbolism. Nevertheless, it is difficult to ignore the stronger sensory impulse which runs through this poem, when compared with Du Bellay's. The ecstatic contemplation of the clear, glittering sky begins as a sensation and culminates in the closing stanzas in imagery which easily yields an erotic interpretation, particularly when it is remembered that the same writer made a translation, with a commentary, of the *Song of Songs*.

[10] (11) Here contentment dwells, here peace reigns; here, seated on a rich, high throne, is holy love, surrounded by honour and delights. (12) Boundless beauty shows herself here complete; and pure and brightest light which is never dimmed shines forth; eternal spring blossoms here. (13) O real fields! O truly cool and pleasant meadows! Richest mines! O delightful hollows! Secluded valleys filled with a thousand joys!

Another development beyond Du Bellay is the use of the words *verdad*, *verdadero* (stanzas 4, 13) to qualify the things of heaven. These alone are 'true' or 'real', in contrast to the things of earth which are 'vain shadows', 'imaginary', 'illusions' (stanzas 4 and 6). Reality thus belongs to the ideal and the immaterial and not to the earthly and the material. The former is by its nature eternal, immortal, or unchanging (all words containing the same concept), while the latter is short-lived and variable. This familiar philosophic conception is also thoroughly Christian, so far as it goes. Christian also, up to a point, is the warning (stanzas 4–7) that men are in danger of losing the divine good if they remain sunk in the 'sleep' and illusions of daily life. The call to them is: 'Awake. Realise your danger and raise your eyes to the heavenly, eternal values.'

All this is compatible with Lamennais's view of man as having 'one foot in the finite and the other in the infinite', but the parallel extends no further. For Lamennais, the two worlds so qualified are mutually opposed—so sharply that man is 'torn asunder' between them, with consequent suffering. But the Neoplatonist's True or Ideal World is not opposed in this way to the material and finite. At most, it is contrasted with it, as the greater is to the less. Conceived as a pattern, it is composed of elements which are all present in a less pure state in the material world, of which, to change the metaphor, it is a distillation. The ascent to it is begun, in Luis de León, by an exaltation of the senses—the physical eyes looking up at the night sky—and it is by the natural and exhilarating process of the senses transcending themselves that the distance between earth and heaven is bridged.[11]

To accomplish this, it is true, 'body' must give way to 'soul'. But, first, there is no question that the soul can achieve the ascent. It is 'immortal' and was 'created for such great good' (stanza 6), just as in Du Bellay's sonnet it had the 'wings' or the power to rise to heaven, which is its true element. On earth, it is 'in exile' (stanza 10). Secondly, there is little question that the soul is regarded as the essential part of the human entity. Although it may be temporarily weighed down by the body, its liberation will not bring a loss of any 'real' factor in

[11] This is a slight, but scarcely misleading, simplification of the fully developed theory of Neoplatonism. According to this there are several superimposed 'spheres of being' which would each have to be traversed in the process of return to the great Source of All. The ascent is thus more gradual than Du Bellay or Luis de León suggest, but no less sure. The multiplicity and gradation of the spheres of being attenuate further the notion of a painful duality.

the personality. On the contrary, its ascent will satisfy not only the spiritual (transcendental) longings of man, but also—in an intenser and more durable way than is possible on earth—his physical longings also, and so the whole of him. There is no trace of a fundamental duality, no irresolvable conflict of the kind so agonisingly experienced by the nineteenth-century sensibility.

Yet, it might be objected, Luis de León does experience anguish. It is, in fact, 'love and anguish' which lead to an 'ardent longing' or a burning desire (stanza 2). He 'groans and sighs' to break the mortal envelope which restrains his soul (stanza 10). If one takes up the commonest terms used by the mystic and metaphysical writers: 'prison', 'dark', 'low', 'heavy', and their opposites: 'freedom', 'light', 'high', 'winged', etc., one sees at once that the physical phenomena to which they correspond are those either of sexual tension, of the child in the uterus, or of the plant germinating beneath the soil. 'Winter' does not figure explicitly in this particular poem, but 'eternal spring' does. Its image supplies the joyful climax.

2

A hopelessly fundamental incompatibility can only occur when certain Christian or quasi-Christian factors are introduced. One thinks of these as typically Calvinist and it is clear that Luis de León, who was certainly a Christian of some kind, could hold his faith whole-heartedly without them, as many others have done. He touches upon them in stanzas 4–7, but hardly in a tone which would make them the crux of human suffering. In those verses it seems relatively easy for man to shake off his sleep or sloth by an effort of will, after which he will surely recognise the superiority of true values over false and will as surely follow them.

But the grimmer view assumes that the aspirational struggle can be frustrated, either by external forces (the World, the Devil) or, more intimately, by an element in human nature itself. It is here that the concept of original sin takes on its full horror, if it is interpreted as meaning that the upward urge in man is no more integral to his psyche than the downward urge, and no stronger. Then indeed he is agonisingly torn between the two, in a conflict which can be represented in several ways: the true life of the plant is as much in its roots as in its stem; the evolved bird is still attached by its skeletal structure to its reptilian origins; the sexual urge is blocked by impotence; the death-wish exactly counterbalances the life-wish; the desire to remain in the uterus exerts as powerful a pull as the desire to break free of it (e.g., the Freudian Oepidus). Though they lie deep below the level of consciousness, the two opposing forces are generally expressed in religious terms, as in the well-known entry in Baudelaire's journal:

> There are in every man at every moment two simultaneous aspirations, one towards God, the other towards Satan. The urge towards God, or *spirituality*, is a desire to rise; the urge towards Satan, or *animality*, is a joy in descent.

But that again is a voice from the nineteenth century, and the question of immediate interest is whether such a conflict was intimately felt and consciously recognised in any terms at an earlier period.

An excellent test-case is that of Pascal, both because of the frequency with which the 'tragic vision' is attributed to him by modern commentators, and because historically and biographically he seems to be situated at a crucial stress-point. Born in 1623, he grew up in a France where the Counter-Reformation had triumphed after bitter internal strife, but where deep marks of spiritual dissension still remained. To the consequent *malaise* in theology and religion was added a new source of scission in the growing claims of the lay intellect. Mathematics and science were preparing to offer a new interpretation of the universe, presented with a rigour and confidence unknown to the previous century. French society, in its more sensitive members, stood as plainly at a spiritual crossroads as the Spaniards of Unamuno's generation two and a half centuries later. Pascal, by constitution and circumstance, was as precisely placed at the nerve-centre as Unamuno in his day. A brilliant mathematician, particularly gifted in geometry, he combined with an abstract habit of thinking a practical talent for experimental physics and mechanics. Concurrently, he and his family were preoccupied with religious questions. Their sympathies had been won by the Jansenist sect of Catholic reformers—the nearest approximation within the Roman Church to the Calvinists, both in doctrine and in austerity of life. Pascal's elder sister, Gilberte, married a Jansenist supporter. The younger, Jacqueline, determined to make religion the whole of her life and entered Port-Royal as a nun. Pascal's own approach to religion was at first predominantly intellectual. He revelled in theological controversy, in which he later engaged with biting brilliance in defence of his Jansenist friends. But, though deeply committed to their movement, he did not join them irrevocably. He remained in the secular world, keenly enjoying its intellectual opportunities and, for a time, the social life of a group of cultured aristocrats. Was he torn between this and a spiritual world? Was he agonisingly aware of some impediment in his own nature which prevented him from either clearly opting for one or the other or achieving a reconciliation of the two?

In his early thirties there were signs of a psychological crisis, probably precipitated by his growing ill-health. Through his sister Jacqueline he sought the advice of the ecclesiastics of Port-Royal and was prepared to submit to their spiritual direction. To this point in his life belongs the so-called *Mémorial*, which records a night of ecstatic revelation and is the most immediately personal document which he has left. It has to be quoted in full.

THE YEAR OF GRACE 1654

Monday 23rd *November*, feast of St Clement, Pope and Martyr, and others in the Martyrology.
Eve of St Crysogonus, martyr, and others.
From about half past ten at night until about half past twelve.   5
Fire.

'God of Abraham, God of Isaac, God of Jacob.'
Not of the philosophers and the learned.
Certainty. Certainty. Feeling. Joy. Peace.
God of Jesus Christ.   10
Deum meum et deum vestrum.
'Thy God shall be my God.'
Forgetfulness of the world and everything except God.
He is only to be found by the ways taught in the Gospel.
Greatness of the human soul.   15
'Righteous Father, the world has not known thee, but I have known thee.'
Joy, joy, joy, tears of joy.
I separated myself from him.
Dereliquerunt me fontem aquae vivae.   20
['They have forsaken me, the spring of living water.']
My God, wilt thou forsake me?
Let me not be separated from him eternally.
'This is eternal life, to know thee as the only true God, and him whom thou hast sent, Jesus Christ.'
Jesus Christ.   25
Jesus Christ.
I separated myself from him, I fled him, denied him, crucified him.

149

May I never be separated from him.
He is only to be kept hold of by the ways taught in the Gospel.
Total and sweet renunciation, etc.　　　　30

Total submission to Jesus Christ and to my director.
Eternally in bliss for one day of travail on earth.
Non obliviscar sermones tuos. Amen.
['I shall not forget thy words. Amen.']

After Pascal's death nearly eight years later, the *Mémorial* was found on a much creased piece of paper sewn in the lining of his coat, together with a fair copy on parchment which added the three final lines after the word 'etc'. Considered first as a psycho-physiological document, it transcribes with considerable faithfulness a reduction of hypertension more nearly cerebral than sexual. Pascal's death at the age of thirty-nine, which was followed by a crudely conducted autopsy, has been ascribed most plausibly to intestinal tuberculosis combined with a haemorrhage of the brain. It is at least certain that since his early twenties he had suffered from painful headaches of the kind also associated with the less serious ailment of migraine.[12] A frequent symptom of these is the appearance of flashes of light before the eyes, which might explain the word 'fire' (line 6) which heads the account of the ecstasy proper. There is a striking if loose relationship with Luis de León's heavenly 'lights', the stars of the probably objective sky which set off his meditation. The mention of 'fire' or 'light' is so common in accounts of the mystic experience that one is tempted to interpret it symbolically as the light of truth dispersing the darkness of ignorance. But this interpretation need not rule out in every case the possibility of a physical 'illumination'. Presumably it was not a mere figure of speech which knocked St Paul off his feet.[13]

One can conclude that Pascal saw, or thought he saw, fire vividly enough to record it prominently near the beginning of the *Mémorial*. The second physical reference is to 'tears': 'Joy, joy, joy, tears of joy' (l. 18). This is reinforced by the biblical quotation (*Jeremiah*, ii, 13) in line 20. It seems significant that, among the many possible ways of qualifying God, it was as 'the spring of living water' that Pascal thought of Him at that moment.

Here again, there is a parallel with the 'floods of tears' of Luis de León's second stanza. Tears, in moral terms, express contrition, an opening of the heart, a softening-up of the hard shell of sinful

---

[12] Simone Weil suffered from a similar affliction.
[13] *Acts*, ix. 3–4.

resistance. Their flow, seen as streams of water, signals the break-down of some restricting substance (ice, rock) and the end of aridity, the parched and sterile state. There is almost no limit to their symbolical connotations, all possessing some basis in nature. Pathologically also they are a discharge from the painfully swollen lachrymal ducts in the migrainous type of tension, and it is surely unnecessary at this date to attempt to draw a distinction between the physical relief which Pascal probably felt and the mental release which follows the solution of a tormenting problem.

Having experienced something similar to the Aristotelian medico-emotional catharsis, and rejected the intricately criss-crossed intellectualism of the 'philosophers and the learned' (l. 8), Pascal notes his mental state as, 'Certainty, certainty, feeling [the original French is *sentiment*], joy, peace'. 'Contentment' and 'peace' also reigned in Luis de León's heavenly world (stanza 11). 'Certainty', 'joy', and 'feeling' were all no doubt too obvious to be named explicitly, but they underlay the climax of the poem. 'Love', even qualified as 'holy' (L. de León, stanza 11) is not named by Pascal, though the reiterated 'Jesus Christ' of lines 24–6 almost certainly transcribes the same basic concept; in Pascal's later writings it figures prominently as 'charity'. Only 'beauty', stressed by the Spanish mystic in stanzas 3 and 12, is totally absent from the *Mémorial*. It is of course a neoplatonic ideal which Christian doctrine has consistently refused to sanctify and certainly Pascal, on the evidence of his writings as a whole, felt no particular need of it.[14]

In this document he has 'found God' through a direct revelation, prepared, evidently, by a study of the Bible, from which he quotes several times. The 'world' is to be forgotten (l. 13). Separation from

[14] Much the fullest and almost the only discussion of beauty is in the essay entitled *Discours sur les passions de l'amour*, whose attribution to Pascal is doubtful. If it is his, it would stamp him as an anti-Platonist, for the argument is that each individual has his own particular conception of beauty ('the original') which he projects on to humanity in general in his search for a woman to love ('the copy'). (Cp. Stendhal's theory of 'crystallisation'.) Beauty in women—the only kind considered in the *Discours*—is therefore a relative and subjective quality, the opposite of the Neoplatonic Idea: '. . . That is why there is an age for blondes and another for dark women . . . Even fashion and the particular country often decide what is called beauty. It is strange that custom should have so strong an influence over our passions, but the fact remains that each man has his own idea of beauty by which he judges others and through which he establishes comparisons . . .' (*Discours sur les passions de l'amour*, in L. Brunschvicg, *Pascal: Pensées et Opuscules* (Hachette), p. 127.)

God is the greatest evil or the greatest fear and is the *motif* of about a third of the *Mémorial* (ll. 19–29). By line 28 it seems to have been definitely overcome. Pascal would hardly write: 'May I never be separated from him', if he did not feel he had already crossed the barrier between 'the world' and 'God'. His preoccupation now is to remain on the Godward side, which he believes he can do by holding firm to the truths taught in the Gospel (l. 31), by 'total *and sweet* renunciation', 'total submission'.

3

The relevance of this to the tragic conflict is that it does not contain one. One may imagine that a conflict preceded the night of the *Mémorial*, but on the occasion itself there is an unreserved adherence to the world of spiritual values and an unreserved rejection of what alone Pascal calls 'the world', i.e., that of the intellect and the senses. To the possible objection that 'the world' refused to lie down, so that the same conflict continued to recur during the remaining years of Pascal's life (in which case he might have kept the *Mémorial* about him to fortify himself in renewed struggles, and not as a record of a permanently acquired conviction), one can only reply that there is no support whatever for this view in Pascal's subsequent writings. And it is on these, which include all his important reflections on religion and human nature, that the case for his 'tragic vision' is necessarily based.

Some fourteen months after his Night of Illumination Pascal began publishing the *Lettres Provinciales*, a series of brilliant tracts attacking Jesuit casuistry in support of the Jansenist position. Probably at about the same time he conceived the idea of a much greater work, a defence and vindication of Christianity as the only truly satisfying way of life. Death prevented him from finishing it, but the voluminous notes and jottings which he left, published as *Les Pensées*, seem to contain the whole substance of his mature thought. They yield statements on the corruptness of (human) nature, on the insignificance of man in regard to the universe, on his helplessness and his 'nothingness', which have been taken to imply a tragic despair. In fact, they do nothing of the sort.

Pascal's guiding intention was to convince the agnostic and the apathetic Christian of the vital necessity of a positive faith. His book was planned to persuade these by the kind of arguments which he supposed that even the non-religious would be brought to accept, and in its grander and profounder way it would have been as much a work of polemics as the *Lettres Provinciales*. Its arguments, though never dishonest, are sometimes loaded in favour of a case which he passionately believed to be true.[15] He intended to develop this case along two main lines, which he summarised thus:

First part: Misery of man without God.
Second part: Happiness of man with God.
  Otherwise:
First part: That nature is corrupt. By [i.e. proved by] nature itself.
Second part: That there is a Redeemer. By [proved by] the Scriptures.[16]

In pursuance of this design, his analysis of 'man without God', or human nature in its 'natural' state, is concerned almost exclusively with human weakness, instability, vanity, and self-deception, the whole building up to an overpowering impression of man's inadequacy in his material and conceptual environment. But there is no suggestion that the gulf between this state and the state of 'happiness with God' is unbridgeable. The bridge is indeed shown in Pascal's alternate formulation above: 'There is a Redeemer.' Thanks to the Redeemer, man is capable of crossing the gulf. This must also be the significance of that oddly placed and otherwise inconsequential sentence in line 15 of the *Mémorial*: 'Greatness of the human soul'. It is identical with the affirmations made by Luis de León (stanza 3: 'My soul which was born at thy high level') and Du Bellay (the 'imprisoned soul' with the 'well-fledged wing'). It can only imply that, for Pascal as much as for the Neoplatonists, the human soul belongs to the divine world, in which it finds its fulfilment, comprehensively described in the *Mémorial* as, 'Certainty, feeling, joy/bliss, peace'. And the 'soul' again, for Pascal, signifies the true essence of the personality. Nothing that matters is lost by renouncing the 'world'

---

[15] One can say this of Pascal, as of other great advocates, without going so far as to maintain that they considered that the end justified the means.
[16] *Pensées*, La. 29; Br. 60.
Because of the nature of the unfinished manuscript, the order in which the *Pensées* should be read cannot be determined with certainty. Of the several editorial arrangements, that by Louis Lafuma is at present considered the most authoritative. But the earlier arrangement of Léon Brunschvicg is still current in several editions. There is another current arrangement, with parallel English text, by H. F. Stewart (Routledge & Kegan Paul, 1950), to which reference will be made on occasion.
Abbreviations: La.: Lafuma; Br.: Brunschvicg; St.: Stewart.
The translations given here are our own, with some debt owing to Stewart.

and discarding that corrupt 'nature' which is the element of the *moi* or self, The *moi*, is this sense, is 'hateful' because of its inevitable self-centredness, the quality which prevents the soul from looking beyond its prison and aspiring to find 'God' or absolute fulfilment. The *moi* is not, in human nature so conceived, an essential part of the personality whose disappearance would impair its wholeness. It can be removed like an appendix.[17]

The modern difficulty of accepting such a view of the human personality has given rise to the theory of Pascal's tragic conflict. But there is little doubt that Pascal held that view and that it is incompatible with a 'tragic vision'. One cannot attempt to interpret him accurately without allowing for his religious beliefs, to which the concepts of God and of grace are integral. Very naturally he cannot and does not affirm that grace—the supernatural aid which enables the human soul to rise to its proper sphere—is universally available, but his attitude towards it is one of hopeful expectancy rather than one of pessimism. His darkest descriptions of human nature, influenced at least partly by his polemical intentions, can hardly be expected to contain a saving clause in every instance; but one can fairly be said to run through the *Pensées* as a whole.

It does so even in the following passage, which represents as close an approach as Pascal makes anywhere to the anguished awareness of an irreconcilable duality. It figured among his papers under the heading: 'Second Part [the significance of this is uncertain]. That, *without faith*, man cannot know true good, or justice.' It continues:

> All men seek to be happy, there are no exceptions to that· However different the means they employ, they all work to that end . . . The will never makes the slightest move except towards that objective. It is the motive of all the actions of all humanity, including those who are going to hang themselves.
>
> And yet, in all the years of history, not a single man, *lacking faith*, has reached that state which is the continual aim of all. And all complain—rulers, subjects, nobles, commoners, the old, the young, the strong, the weak, the learned, the ignorant, the healthy, the sick, in all ages, in every country and class.

[17] The surgical metaphor is not too strong. It is a removal and not a reduction. E.g., *Pensées*, La. 141; Br. 455: 'The *moi* is hateful. You, Miton, conceal it, but you do not thereby *remove* it. So you are always hateful . . .' *Pensées*, La. 689; Br. 476 begins: 'One must love God only and hate only oneself,' and develops the familiar analogy of the body and its members. The foot (here, the *moi*) should gladly 'submit to the will which controls the whole body, to the point of consenting *to be cut off* if necessary'.

A test of such length, so continuous and unvarying, should indeed convince us of our powerlessness to attain the good *by our own efforts*, but we learn little from experience. It is never so completely uniform as not to admit some subtle difference, and this leads us to expect that our hopes will not be disappointed this time as they were last. And so, never finding satisfaction in the present, we are duped by experience and led on by it from one misfortune to another, until we reach their eternal culmination in death.

What is it that this eagerness and this impotence cry aloud to us, if not that there was once true happiness in man, of which nothing now remains but a hollow outline which he tries vainly to fill with everything he sees around him, seeking in absent things the comfort which he does not find in things present, but which all of them are incapable of giving, because this infinite void can only be filled by an infinite and changeless object, that is, *by God himself*.

He alone is man's true good, and since He left him the strange thing is that nothing existing in nature has proved incapable of taking His place: stars, sky, earth, elements, plants, cabbages, leeks, animals, insects, calves, serpents, fever, pestilence, war, famine, vices, adultery, incest. Since he lost the true good, anything can come to resemble it in his eyes, down to his own destruction, though this is contrary to God, reason, and nature alike . . .[18]

The saving clauses in the above passage are those I have italicised. The 'loss of Eden', which is the basis of the penultimate paragraph, contains a potential two-way anguish as long as it is accompanied by a persistent nostalgia for Adam's lost happiness. But since human nature was 'corrupted', i.e., altered, by the Fall, that happiness has become permanently irrecoverable in a 'natural' form. An anguish dependent upon it is a pseudo-anguish. For Pascal it is unchristian— and on the evidence of the *Pensées* as a whole, one might fairly add irrational and unrealistic—to harbour nostalgia for a state which does not belong to post-Adamic man. A correct appreciation of the human situation shows that man's new nature can never be assimilated to the old by reason of its composition. For the same reason it is incapable of providing any lasting satisfaction from within itself, for its corruption or its newness consisted in the withdrawal of God from man. This is not used by Pascal as a mere phrase. He equates God with true happiness and holds that this was the element in human nature which was lost at the Fall. To regain it, recourse must

[18] *Pensées*, La. 300; Br. 425; St. 250.

be had to a force outside nature, of whose existence Pascal felt that he had acquired a 'certainty' (*Mémorial*).[19]

The general motive of the *Pensées* is to lead others towards the same certainty. Luis de León reached it in a moment of emotional exaltation. So ultimately, it seems, did Pascal, but only after a period of strenuous intellectual preparation which he was unlikely to forget. He was therefore ready to use an intellectual system which can be deduced consistently from his notes—in spite of the fragmentary nature of some of them and their still disputed sequence—in order to demonstrate, not the truth of divine being, but the only way in which man can hope to be united to it.

His theory supposes three Orders, to one or other of which everything belongs. They correspond nearly enough to the traditional classification of body, mind, and soul, though Pascal names them variously in different contexts. The bodily or carnal order comprises not only all physical phenomena, from the firmament downwards, but the values which attach to them: material power, the prestige of kings, captains, and rich men, the pleasures and miseries derived from the senses operating through the 'passions'. The order of the mind (*esprit*) is immaterial and non-sensory; it comprises intellectual curiosity, reason, learning, knowledge, 'genius', and its values have no bearing on material power.[20] (Characteristically, Pascal does not trouble to define them further, considering their status to be self-evident.) The third order is that of Charity or Holiness. Charity is to be taken in its theological sense of divine or divinely-inspired love, as distinct from love of the physical order, which is *concupiscence*. ('Concupiscence' is not confined by Pascal to the directly sensual or sexual. He extends it in its fullest theological sense to 'desire' over a wide field, ambition, covetousness, even aspiration, but always with

[19] The gist of the above is contained concisely in *Pensées*, La. 14; Br. 560:

We cannot understand either the blissful state of Adam, or the nature of his sin, or its transmission down to us. These are things which occurred in the state of a nature quite different from ours and which are beyond the scope of our present capacity to understand.

It would be useless for us to know all this in order to win through. All we need to know is that we are wretched, corrupt, separated from God, but redeemed by Jesus Christ; and of that we have excellent proofs on earth.

[20] The distinction still persists, at least as an image with a certain foundation of truth. Vulgarised, it yields the figure of the 'disinterested' intellectual. It underlies the perennial conviction that no true scholar or scientist will engage in a rat-race.

an ultimately material object.) Into the Order of Charity fall God, the angels, the saints, and such qualities and faculties (some of them surprising) as justice, wisdom, faith, the heart, feeling, inspiration, intuition, and instinct.[21]

The Three Orders constitute a kind of hierarchy, but one in which there are no gradations. Pascal insists on this, because it is the basis of his position. They are 'different in kind'. There is 'no relationship' between the different types of 'greatness' to which they lead. They are all, in fact, 'infinitely distant' from each other, though while the distance between 'bodies' and Minds is unqualifiedly 'infinite', that between Minds and Charity is 'infinitely more infinite'. Out of context, this seems a nonsensical concept, but Pascal's meaning is clear enough. While the physical and the intellectual orders are absolutely separate ('From all bodies put together, one could not produce one tiny thought; that is impossible, and of a different order'), the Order of Charity is still more separate, for it alone is 'supernatural'.

The first two Orders are in human nature, or in man, within whom they wage a ceaseless battle:

> Internal strife in man between reasons and the passions.
> If only he had reason without passions ...
> If only he had the passions without reason ...
> But having both, man cannot be free of strife, since he cannot make peace with the one without having war with the other. So he is always divided and opposed to himself.[22]

At first sight this might seem to destroy the whole case against a duality concept. But it belongs, in the first place, to Pascal's constant denigration of reason. The reason of 'the philosophers and the learned' (*Mémorial*, 1. 9) is so easily thrown off its balance by the senses that it can never be a reliable guide to truth, in spite of the fact that it is the noblest faculty possessed by natural man. The senses, for

[21] The most explicit single passage bearing on the Three Orders is *Pensées*, La. 585; Br. 793. Most of what is said above derives from it. There are variations, of a relatively minor character, in other passages. Thus, *Pensée*, La. 721; Br. 460, begins: 'There are three orders of things: the flesh, the mind, *the will*.' The best interpretation of this interesting *Pensée* as a whole is to read it as a deflation of false *gloire* or worldly self-aggrandisement. Meanwhile, the general sense of our own analysis of the Three Orders is not affected.

[22] *Pensées'* La. 253; Br. 412. The same theme is developed in *Pensée*, La. 249; Br. 413, which adds: 'Some have tried to renounce the passions and to become gods; others to renounce reason and to become brute beasts. But neither group of them has been able to ...'

their part, are disturbed by reason (cp. La Rochefoucauld: 'We never taste anything pure'). To show that there is an inevitable conflict between the intellect and the passions, which incapacitates both of them, is thus part of Pascal's larger argument concerning 'the misery of man witl_out God', from whom neither of them come. Secondly— and this is crucial—the only serious aim of man being to rejoin God and so find true happiness, the conflict which goes on in human nature without Him is of very secondary importance. Compared to the vital issue of the destiny of the soul, it is a mere dogfight in a back-yard. Its occurrence emphasises the sordidness of the backyard, but it is well below a level which could be qualified as tragic.[23] Not only is it a conflict which ought not to matter to man, but it is one which demonstrably does *not* matter, except perhaps insofar as it distracts attention from a search for reality along the true direction. Whatever may be the part of human nature which it 'divides', that is not the part which is capable of experiencing God/happiness. We are brought back to the conclusion already reached on other grounds: that anguish arising from this particular conflict would be a pseudo-anguish.

4

After this, it is possible to illustrate Pascal's conceptions diagram-matically, in the hope that some inevitable simplification will be outweighed by the advantages of clarity in the essentials.

In the diagram opposite, the square A represents man's original nature, or the felicity of Eden in which there was no differentiation between, the natural and the divine. The square X represents man's new or present nature.

AB is the line of true happiness/God/Charity, along which human nature was originally orientated. At the point A^1 it deviated along A^1C and A^1D, the intellectual and physical orders respectively. Both of these run through man's new nature, though they tend in divergent directions, with the inevitable but subsidiary conflict discussed above.

All the three lines diverge from each other and, if prolonged to infinity, they would, in Pascal's words, be 'infinitely distant'. At the

[23] Note the scoffing tone of: 'Man is thus so wonderfully constituted (*si heureusement fabriqué*) that he possesses no exact source of truth and several excellent ones of falsehood. Now let's see how many . . . But the most comical (*plaisante*) cause of his errors is the war between the senses and reason.' (*Pensées*, La. 81; Br. 82, last paragraph.)

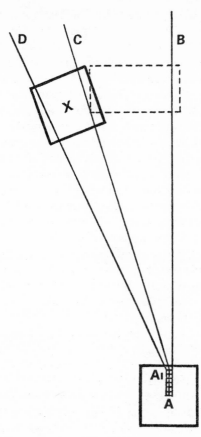

same time, if one admits of degrees of infinity, *AB* would become infinitely more distant from A^1C and A^1D than these two from each other. This seems to be the best interpretation of his reasoning.

The new and wrong orientation of human nature which occurred at A^1, with the consequent separation from *AB*, is theologically the Fall or Original Sin. Its existence as a fact is vital to Pascal's conception. He takes it as part of his data while accepting it as inexplicable (see above, p. 156 footnote 19) and insists elsewhere on its necessity in his scheme:

> Original sin is a folly according to man, but it is given as a fact. So you ought not to criticise me for the want of reason in this doctrine, since I postulate it as being unreasonable. But this folly

is wiser than all the wisdom of men. For without it, what shall we say that man is? His whole condition hinges on that imperceptible point ...[24]

Given the deviation at A^1 and the three fixed divergent lines or Orders, it is mathematically impossible to swing the square X back on to its true axis AB, as it would also be physically impossible if the same thing were conceived three-dimensionally. Yet it must be swung back if man is not to remain eternally miserable. That is the function of the dotted rectangle which overlaps both AB and X. This is the supernatural area in which the 'mysteries' of redemption and grace can operate to perform a miracle of conversion or reorientation in defiance of the laws of nature and geometry. This area is the ancient battle-ground of theology and of much besides. Its shape on the diagram has no significance; it is shown as a small rectangle merely for convenience. By definition it is not representable in geometrical or physical terms. Any other shape would serve as well or as badly, and it is arguable that it should occupy the whole picture and be infinitely extensible in all directions (immanence). The only point which is essential to Pascal's scheme is that the dotted area should impinge somewhere on the square X.

If it remained outside or tangential, it could be conceived as radiating a kind of magnetic field which would indeed set up an agonising and permanently indecisive conflict within square X. Square X has not the means within itself to abandon its axes A^1C and A^1D and to respond to the pull of AB. Some force from AB must enter X to enable it to behave in a way external to its nature.

This, Pascal maintains over and over again, is what does or can happen. Even the most pessimistic Christian apologist, so long as he was a Christian and sane, could never exclude that possibility. To do so would entail disregarding the doctrine of redemption and 'abandoning man to his own nature', i.e., consigning him irrevocably along the lines A^1C and A^1D. In that case, the line AB would become irrelevant to the human situation.

5

In spite of the evidence which Pascal furnishes and which may reasonably be taken as representative of the Christian outlook of his time, one would still be reluctant to deny the existence of a form of

[24] *Pensées*, La. 323; Br. 445; St. 384.

anguish which centres historically on the Counter-Reformation. As the 'Baroque anguish' it is unmistakably present in West European literature, extending from the late sixteenth century to about the middle of the seventeenth. It covers Shakespeare's period and can just be stretched forward to the time of Racine.

So far as it arises from the conflict between Reason and the Passions, which Pascal notes and concedes, it is mainly a secular anguish connected with the Renaissance conception of Stoicism. If severed entirely from the Christian tradition and yet endowed with sufficient spiritual force to be the centre of a whole human life, it could be the psychological effect of a tragic duality. But, though such a duality must have been experienced, it must also have been exceedingly rare and have seldom attained the concentrated intensity of the Romantic conflict. One looks in vain for its exteriorisation in dramatic literature. It is not in Shakespearean tragedy. If, making a loose generalisation which has numerous exceptions, one regarded Corneille's tragedies as illustrating the triumph of Reason, working through the will, over Passion, we should still not have a tragic duality. When Reason can be said to triumph in Corneille, the result is less tragedy than heroic drama (with a perceptible loss of psychological credibility). In Racine, as represented by *Phèdre*, Reason is really a non-starter as a contestant. It makes little appearance in his other plays, except possibly in *Bérénice*, considerably disguised as *raison d'état*, or political necessity. A variant conflict might perhaps be read into Marlowe's *Dr Faustus*, if this were interpreted as a struggle between Pascal's Divine Order and, principally, his Intellectual Order—strongly reinforced, however, by the Material Order. *Faustus* would then demonstrate the impossibility of attaining the true supernatural from a position on the two natural orders—particularly with the deceptive support of Satan.[25] However, Marlowe's tragedy does not easily fit this scheme. It is more satisfactory to regard it as an exploration of power as discussed in the previous chapter.

At this point the reader may perhaps recall the four lines of verse quoted above on p. 53. In themselves they would be perfectly appropriate to the nineteenth-century conflict, but they are, of course, by Fulke Greville, a contemporary of Shakespeare's. Before drawing the obvious conclusion, one must consider them in their full context. They are the opening lines of the *Chorus Sacerdotum*—the Chorus of

[25] Goethe's nineteenth-century Faust does succeed in attaining it. That is the vast difference.

(Mahometan) Priests—in Greville's tragedy *Mustapha*. The italics
are ours:

> Oh wearisome condition of humanity!
> Born under one law, to another bound,
> Vainly begot and yet forbidden vanity.
> Created sick, commanded to be sound.
> What meaneth *Nature* by these diverse laws?
> *Passion and Reason* self-division cause.
> Is it the mark or majesty of Power
> To make offences that it may forgive?
> *Nature herself* doth her own self deflower
> To hate these errors she herself doth give.
> For how should man think that he may not do,
> If *Nature* did not fail, and punish too?
> Tyrant to others, to herself unjust,
> Only commands things difficult and hard,
> Forbids us all things which it knows we lust,
> Makes easy pains, impossible reward.
> If Nature did not take delight in blood,
> She would have made more easy ways to good.
> We that are bound by vows and by Promotion,
> With pomp of holy sacrifice and rites,
> To teach belief in good and still devotion,
> To preach of Heaven's wonders and delights:
> Yet when each of us in his own heart looks,
> He finds *the God* there, far unlike his books.

Beginning with lines 5 and 6, the Priests are saying precisely what
Pascal said some fifty years later about the inconclusive war between
Reason and Passion. If we accept the Priests at their face value as
Mohammedans, there is no difficulty. As non-Christians they may
know good moral principles but they do not know the true God and
are therefore hopelessly confined within nature. The (natural) conflict which they experience would not be experienced by the Christian,
who has his way out through grace. That would be Pascal's position,
but is it Greville's?

It seems inevitable that the author, in order to write such a passage,
must have identified himself at least momentarily with his nominally
infidel speakers and that he himself could not have been unaffected by
the kind of conflict described. In that case, Nature would be something more for him than the corrupt element which the orthodox
Christian was ready to discard. Though harsh and apparently self-

contradictory in its laws, it would acquire transcendent standing as the only God conceivable, and the 'self-division' stemming from its indecisive tyranny would be tragic because inherent in the total condition of man. What, however, is 'the God' of the last line, which each priest finds 'in his own heart'? Is it Nature again, under her transcendent name, or is it Passion, 'far unlike' the teaching of the sacred books? Or is it self-will, the 'detestable' element in the Pascalian psychology?[26] Greville's modern editor, Geoffrey Bullough, in an introduction stressing the fundamental duality of his author's mind,[27] interpreted it as the voice of the true divine, *which is present in man*: 'Man's only stay, Greville hints, is the knowledge of God within the heart, that is to say, a *personal* religion.' We think this interpretation questionable, but it can hardly be ruled out. If accepted, it is basically Protestant, as was Greville in his outward religious allegiance.

Can anything conclusive be said about this without floundering ever deeper into the morass of Renaissance and post-Renaissance theology? It is at least clear that Greville, like many of his contemporaries, was attempting a largely personal reinterpretation of the Christian religion as it had emerged in Elizabethan and Jacobean England after the Reformation. His main basis was no doubt Calvinism,[28] but as a man of the world—he was a successful courtier-politician—he was also influenced by humanist Stoicism and even by Neoplatonism. These different influences co-existed in his mind; it is unlikely that he was consciously aware of them as distinct philosophies. (Atheism and various kinds of sorcery were also present in the contemporary ideology, not always plainly identified for what they were.) As a further complication, the moral ideas in his two plays, *Mustapha* and *Alaham*, are voiced entirely by Mohammedan characters, but one cannot really determine how far he intended to present them as the obverse of true religion and how far he was prudently giving them a trial run under the colours of a different stable. Most probably, there was something of both.

[26] Cp. BEGARBI: Who will, to hurt his foes, himself destroy?
      ROSSA: *Myself?* What is it else but my desire?
                                     (*Mustapha*, III, 2, ll. 23–4.)
[27] See Fulke Greville, Baron Brooke: *Poems and Dramas*, ed. G. Bullough, 2 vols. (Edinburgh and London, 1939.)
[28] But with a 'hopeful' attitude towards grace. See *Caelica*, Sonnets 98 and 99. E.g.: 'Down in the depth of mine iniquity / . . . Deprived of human graces, not divine, / Even there appears this *saving God* of mine.'

The resulting picture is one of rich confusion, not exclusive of anguish but fraught with a multiplicity of stresses rather than with anything that could be called a straight duality. In this respect, this interesting if secondary author typifies the mentality now usually described as Baroque. It is characterised, not by a plain two-way urge, but by turmoil. Man is conceived as

> A crazed soul, unfixed:
> Made good, yet fall'n, not to extremes, but to a mean betwixt:
> Where (like a cloud) with winds he toss'd is here and there,
> We kindling good hope in his flesh, they quenching it with fear.
> (Greville: *Alaham.*)

The *we* and *they* in the last line are the Good and Evil Spirits contending for the mastery of the universe, above and outside man, rather as in the medieval Moralities. As a result of their contention man 'toss'd is here and there'—a revealing metaphor when it is contrasted with the 'tearing-apart' metaphor of Lamenanis, the nineteenth-century Christian Socialist. The Baroque analogies are always with the storm or the whirlpool rather than with he tug-of-war. The personality is swirled about among competing forces or, if the disturbance is conceived as internal, is an area of perpetual confusion characterised by its mobility and instability and also by its moments of exaltation and exuberance. The psychological consequence of this state is anxiety (which, strictly speaking, ought to be distinguished from tension) founded on the all-pervading uncertainty. The opposite, so ardently desired, is 'certainty'—the first positive quality named by Pascal in his *Mémorial*—then peace or rest (the cessation of violent movement) and the assurance of permanent stability.

According to the Catholic Pascal, writing half a century after Greville in a country where the Counter-Reformation had triumphed and when the issues had had time to become clear to his exceptionally logical mind, the Baroque turmoil would be a wholly 'natural' phenomenon. Adopting his rigorous distinctions, the internecine war between Reason and the Passions, each of which 'misleads' the other[29] would not include the religious factor at all. If it seemed to do so, that would be a delusion produced by the action of the Passions and which might be entertained by the confused Protestant—in short, heretical—mentality, but not by the enlightened Christian. The latter

---

[29] See *Pensées*, La. 82; Br. 83.

remained convinced of the essential separateness of the divine line. Nevertheless, it is obvious that many minds on both sides of the Reformation were unable to draw or to accept this distinction in the post-Renaissance Age of Anxiety.

6

Small wonder, since, to conserve Pascal's terminology, God is 'hidden'. Much has been read into this word and M. Lucien Goldmann constructed an elaborate theory of the tragic vision upon it.[30] In a less debatable sense, the concept enters naturally into Pascal's scheme of things and indeed is a necessary part of it. As a Christian apologist he has to face the large question of why God's existence is not plain for all men to see. Why, for example, was Christ not recognised by the Jews, when their own prophets had foretold his coming? Why do other religions recognise godliness but not the true God? ('They have seen the effect but not the cause.'[31]) Obviously his existence is not plain to the unbeliever, but equally obviously He has always had the power to make it so. From this apparent discrepancy Pascal draws a proof of the uniqueness of his religion. Only it allows for the mystery of the true supernatural. If God were evident in 'nature', which includes 'the world' and natural man since the Fall, or if his existence could be demonstrated by pointing to the wonders of the physical universe (a method which Pascal has the scientific insight to condemn) then the fundamental distinction between God and 'nature' would be lost and, as far as humanity is concerned, the effects of the Fall would have to be disregarded. Yet, conceived as the Creator, God cannot be thought of as totally absent from nature, his creature. In another guise He enters, or re-enters it: as the Redeemer, through the Area of Grace. The paradox appears in *Pensées*, La. 699 (Br. 485; St. 578), which intellectually hardly makes sense and seems after all to come very near the Protestant notion of 'God in the heart':

> The true and only virtue is therefore to hate oneself—for one is hateful for one's materialism (*concupiscence*)—and to seek a truly lovable being to love. But as we cannot love what is outside us, we must love some being who is in us and is not us, and that is true of each individual man. Now only the Universal Being is of such a

[30] See above, p. 66 *et seq.*
[31] *Rem viderunt, causam non viderunt* (St Augustine). *Pensées*, La. 400; Br. 235.

kind. The Kingdom of God is within us; universal good is within us, is ourself, and is not us.

These are mysteries peculiar to Christianity. They are, as Pascal eagerly concedes, not amenable to rational explanation or proof. But that merely shows the limitations of the Intellectual Order. The Christian truths are 'foolishness', 'follies', *stultitia*, 'stupidity', from a rational point of view, but They Are. It is this burning, irrational conviction which allows Pascal to speak of the Hidden God with no sense of frustration or incompleteness—which might indeed be a form of the 'tragic sense'—but in the spirit of: 'Seek and ye shall find.' And if God seems to be either absent or silent in 'the world', in the precise and restricted sense in which Pascal uses that term, it is because we are using the wrong organs of perception to detect his presence.

He is not 'silent' or 'absent' for the believer, such as Pascal himself.[32] Neither is 'the world' or 'the body' regarded as anything but expendable once God has been 'found'. It was on the opposite assumptions that M. Goldmann based his case for Pascal's tragic vision (*Le Dieu Caché*, *passim*). It seems impossible to justify either of them.

A different assumption, contained in a recent and valuable book, George Steiner's *The Death of Tragedy* (Faber, 1961), must also go by the board if our analysis, or anything resembling it, is valid. Mr Steiner writes: '. . . at the heart of the Jansenist position is the effort to reconcile the life of reason to the mysteries of grace. This effort, *sustained at fearful psychological cost* [my italics] produced two tragic images of man, that of Racine and that of Pascal. In Pascal, an austere, violent compulsion towards reason plays against a constant apprehension of the mystery of God . . .'[33]

Here again is the persistent idea that the tragic must consist in a conflict, leading to a psychological tearing-apart; and the further assumption that Reason was a sufficiently powerful concept in the minds of seventeenth-century theologians to constitute an opposite pole of attraction to Faith. As far as we know, this never occurred. The theologians always regarded Reason as an instrument, hardly realising its dangerous potentialities, and continued to do so right into the eighteenth century. As we have already suggested, a conflict

[32] See in particular *Pensées*, La. 310; Br. 288.
[33] *Op. cit.*, p. 81.

resembling the one described could only occur, if it did, in the Stoic mentality—in which, however, the counter-pole to Reason would not be Faith. It would be either Passion or else Nature, amputated of the intellect.

The historical fact that Pascal and Racine were both associated with Port-Royal has probably given rise to more misunderstandings than true judgments. Our own view in a nutshell is that Pascal's vision was not 'tragic'. Racine's must be allowed to be, since he wrote good tragedies—and also one excellent comedy. But in what it consisted seems less a matter of Jansenist theology than of a detailed analysis of each play, for which there is no space in the present book.

7

Each of Pascal's three Orders includes the means of perceiving the things which belong to it: in the Physical Order, the eyes (and no doubt the other sense-organs); in the Intellectual Order, the mind; in the Supernatural Order, the heart.

Even at this date it is unnecessary to examine at length what Pascal understood by 'the heart'. The concept has not changed radically since his day. For him it is the faculty always associated with non-physical 'feeling' (*sentiment*) and with 'love', natural and divine, both of which it is capable of experiencing. Distinct from and superior to reason, it is the element in the human personality through which alone 'faith' can enter. Faith is the conviction of the existence of God, i.e., of a principle of total and permanent happiness/fulfilment which, moreover, is accessible.

'It is the heart which feels God, and not Reason. This is what faith is: God perceptible to the heart, not to reason.'[34] And: 'Faith is a gift from God . . .'[35]

The process by which faith is communicated to the heart is called by Pascal '*inspiration*', sometimes translated as 'revelation', but perfectly comprehensible in its literal sense of a 'breathing-in' of the divine influence.

All this is still familiar ground, both as regards religion and the natural emotions, and needs no further gloss on that score. Beyond it,

[34] *Pensées*, La. 225; Br. 278. Presumably one should distinguish between Greville's 'God *in* the heart' and Pascal's 'God *perceptible to* the heart', in spite of what appears to be the sense of *Pensées*, La. 699, quoted on pp. 165–6 above.

[35] *Pensées*, La. 376; Br. 279.

however, Pascal extends the term 'heart' to cover the intuitive understanding of things which one would now tend to associate with the
intellect, and at times he also equates it with 'instinct':

We know truth not only through reason, but also through the
heart. It is in this way that we have knowledge of first principles,
and it is in vain that reason, which has no part in them, attempts
to dispute them ... We know that we do not dream; however
powerless we are to prove it by reason, this impotence merely
demonstrates the weakness of our reason, not the uncertainty of
all our knowledge ... For knowledge of first principles, such as the
existence of space, time, motion, numbers, is as sure as any knowledge which reasoning gives us. And it is on this knowledge
supplied by the heart and instinct that reason must rely, founding
all its arguments (*discours*) upon it ... Principles are felt, propositions are deduced, and the whole with certainty, though by different
ways ...

Would to God that we never had need of reason and that we
could know everything by instinct and feeling. But nature has
refused us this boon. It has given us very little knowledge of this
kind; all the rest can only be acquired by reasoning ...[36]

For Pascal the 'heart' is a faculty which is within natural man, but
which is nevertheless capable of 'feeling' divine truth, as well as truths
of the other two Orders. It is the only human faculty which can do
this. As a guide to truth of any kind, the 'heart'—or its synonyms
'feeling' and 'instinct'—is infallible. Since it is the organ of love as
well as of knowledge, it may love the wrong objects—the world or the
moi. But it does this deliberately, knowing that it has gone astray.[37]
So it is still possible to say that as a means of perceiving truth the
'heart' cannot be misled.

But besides this infallible guide man possesses another faculty
which is very easily confused with it and which is a prime source of
error, 'all the more misleading because it is not always so, for it would
be an infallible measure of truth [by contraries] if it was an infallible
measure of falsehood'. Pascal's name for this faculty is Imagination.

[36] *Pensées*, La. 214; Br. 282; St. 630.
[37] The choices of the 'heart' can be exercised consciously:
The heart has its reasons which Reason does not know: there are
countless examples of this. I say that the heart loves the Universal
Being naturally, and the self (*soi-même*) naturally, according to the way
it turns; and it hardens itself against the one or the other as it chooses.
You [the unbeliever] have rejected the one and retained the other; is it
through reason that you love yourself?
Pensées, La. 224; Br. 277; St. 626.

One of the more fully-developed passages of the *Pensées* is devoted to it, as befits the chief of the 'misleading powers' in man, the formidable Queen of Error, whom even Pascal seems unable to regard without a certain grudging admiration:

> ... This haughty power, hostile to reason, which it loves to curb and dominate, to show how far its influence extends, has established a second nature in man. It has its own happiness and misery, its healthy and its sick, its rich and its poor. It suspends the senses or makes them feel. It causes reason to believe, to doubt, or to deny. It has its fools and its wise men, and nothing is more galling than to see how it fills its possessors with a satisfaction far greater and more complete than reason provides. Imagination's adepts find far more pleasure in themselves than thoughtful people can reasonably do. They look down commandingly on others; they argue boldly and confidently, while the others are timid and diffident, and their self-assured appearance often gives them an advantage in the minds of their hearers, since the imaginary pundit will always find favour with judges of the same kind, Imagination cannot turn fools into wise men, but it makes them happy—unlike reason, which only makes its partisans miserable. One covers them with glory, the other with shame.[38]

Imagination for Pascal was the faculty of make-believe, founded ultimately on self-interest (*amour-propre*), which could distort physical and mental realities for the immediate benefit of its possessor, but, in the long run, to his ruin or damnation. Under that or other names it was the bogey of sixteenth and seventeenth-century thought. It was inseparably linked to 'imaginary' (fears, pleasures, treasures, illness) and to the word 'image' in all the modern senses of that word, from the graven image of the idolator to the public image of the advertising-man, and not excluding the image and imagery of poetry, which came to be suspect because of the possibilities of exaggeration and misrepresentation which it opened up. The same with the other arts: the 'image' of the portrait-painter, even when not intentionally 'flattering', inevitably contained some distortion of the original. Such distortions were all the more insidious in that, as Pascal had observed, they were not without elements of truth.

As 'fancy' and 'fantasy' (whence 'fantastic') Imagination takes on relatively playful and harmless forms, but through 'phantom' and 'phantasm' it is again dangerous—whence the potential distrust of

[38] *Pensées*, La. 81; Br. 82; St. 75.

the Ghost in *Hamlet*.[39] It operates when the restraint of reason is removed, through sleep, illness, or any other cause. The dream, always mistrusted as a probable (but not certain) perversion of reality, is one of its principal fields of operation:

> Thus have I had thee as a dream doth flatter,
> In sleep a king, but waking no such matter.[40]

Much more explicitly, and about a century after Shakespeare:

> Dreams are but interludes which Fancy makes.
> When Monarch Reason sleeps, this mimic wakes,
> Compounds a medley of disjointed things,
> A mob of cobblers and a court of kings.
> Light fumes are merry, grosser fumes are sad,
> Both are the reasonable soul run mad.
> And many monstrous Forms in sleep we see,
> That neither were, nor are, nor e'er can be.
> Sometimes forgotten things long cast behind
> Rush forward in the brain and come to mind.
> The nurse's legends are for truth received,
> And the man dreams but what the boy believed.
> Sometimes we but rehearse a former play
> And night restores our actions done by day,
> As hounds in sleep will open for their prey.
> In short, the farce of dreams is of a piece,
> Chimeras all, and more absurd, or less.[41]

It is not difficult to assimilate the faculty which Pascal named Imagination to the Freudian unconscious. Or perhaps, so far as the parallel holds, it should be thought of as the emanation of the unconscious. To bring the latter into the daylight as the only guide we

[39] See above, p. 87.
[40] Shakespeare, Sonnet 87.
[41] Dryden, 'The Cock and the Fox', ll. 325–41, from *Fables Ancient and Modern* (1700). This fable is an adaptation of Chaucer's *Nun's Priest's Tale* and, like the original, contains a long debate on the reliability of dreams as a means of predicting the future. The conclusion is that dreams contain true omens and the debate is heavily weighted in this sense. But it is more significant that Dryden saw fit to insert the passage quoted above, which is almost entirely his own invention. It is an expansion of four lines of Chaucer's:

> For swevenes [dreams] been but vanytees and japes [tricks].
> Men dreme alday [always] of owles or of apes,
> And of many a maze [illusion] therwithal.
> Men dreme of thyng that nevere was, ne shal.

have, fallible or not, to the deepest levels of personality, and hence to the reality of the human condition, is a relatively modern preoccupation. To the seventeenth-century mind it was abhorrent, since it meant risking a release of all the uncontrollable forces in the depths of corrupt human nature; and they had seen the effect of this happening, when reason, it seemed, abdicated and men went mad.

However, between Pascal and Freud there occurred a revolution in the human conception of the human condition at least as great as the scientific and technological revolutions which changed the material circumstances of life. It did not lead in a single phase to Freudian psychology, but in the long run it made its development possible and perhaps inevitable. It was, of course, the work of the early nineteenth century.

9

Imagination Enthroned: Blake and Romanticism

1

To investigate the nineteenth-century ideological revolution in detail is not the business of this book and it would lead us far beyond our subject. All that seems necessary is to take a sampling which is decently representative of the changes which occurred. In the light of what we have already written about Pascal, Blake provides a fair and striking illustration of the new view of man. A 'visionary' of a novel kind, nourished on the eighteenth-century depolarised mysticism of such writers as Swedenborg,[1] contemporary with the American and French Revolutions and with the beginnings of the Industrial Revolution, he has one foot in each of the eighteenth and nineteenth centuries and belongs historically to the germination period of the Romantic Movement, many of whose features he incorporates or foreshadows.

For Blake, as for most of his successors, Imagination was a very different thing from Pascal's conception of it. He accepted its association with Art, not in order to denigrate either, but to glory in it. He looked upon the artist, not as a creator of distorting images,

---

[1] Swedenborg's intellectual (but not physical) composition recalls Pascal's. With a religious (Protestant) family background, he was at first a technological scientist and mathematician. A psychological crisis turned him towards mysticism. His later writings were inspired by the conviction that he had received a direct divine command to interpret the true meaning of the Bible. His temporal environment, however, was about a century later than Pascal's.

but as the highest type of man—in fact the only type capable of receiving a true vision of the divine:

> A Poet, a Painter, a Musician, an Architect; the man or woman who is not one of these is not a Christian.
> You must leave fathers and mothers and houses and lands if they stand in the way of Art.
> Prayer is the study of Art.
> Praise is the practice of Art.
> Fasting, etc. all relate to Art.
> Art is the Tree of Life.
> Science is the Tree of Death.
> For every pleasure Money is useless.
> Christianity is Art and not Money, Money is its curse.[2]

These sentences, taken from the many with which Blake surrounded his engraving of the Laocoon Group (their intended order is impossible to decide with certainty) might seem to be overinfluenced by the obsessions of a man who was himself a dedicated artist continually battling against commercialism and other forms of materialism, and who said 'art' where others say 'religion'. But in a wider sense his view of the Artist, and especially the Poet, as the inspired interpreter of God to man was to become the view of the whole Romantic era. In a wider sense still he was profound and consistent in linking Art to Imagination, Imagination to Vision, and Vision to God. This is expressed in words which would have been totally unacceptable to the generation of Pascal:

> The Eternal Body of Man is the Imagination; that is God Himself, the Divine Body, Jesus; we are His Members.
> It manifests itself in His Works of Art: In Eternity all is Vision![3]

To this must be added:

> All that we see is Vision; from Generated Organs [physical organisms], gone as soon as come; permanent in the Imagination; consider'd as nothing by the Natural Man.

and:

> Adam is only the Natural Man, and not the Soul or Imagination.[4]

[2] See *Poetry and Prose of William Blake*, ed. Geoffrey Keynes (Nonesuch Press, 1927), p. 764. All page references in this chapter are to this, the 'Centenary', edition.
[3] *Laocoon*, Nonesuch edn, p. 765.
[4] *Laocoon*, Nonesuch edn, p. 765.

'Nature' and 'natural man' receive a severe handling in Blake's poetic works, but the second is not the basically corrupted creature of the old theology. It would be difficult and possibly misleading to deduce a coherent system from the totality of Blake's works, but at least one consistent line can be traced: Nature, understood purely as the physical order and including 'natural man' with his sense-perceptions, is undeniably finite and impermanent, besides being raw material which lacks form. But through the human imagination, and pre-eminently that of the artist, the things which are physical and transitory in 'nature' take on a permanent form, which could be called God. This is the significance of: 'The eternal body of man is the Imagination, that is, God himself . . .'

One other quotation will reinforce this interpretation:

To Lord Byron in the Wilderness:
    What doest thou here, Elijah?
Can a poet doubt the Visions of Jehovah? Nature has no Outline, but Imagination has. Nature has no Tune, but Imagination has. Nature has no Supernatural, and dissolves: Imagination is Eternity.[5]

It is clear that Blake's Imagination is not opposed to the Heart, as in Pascal, but includes it, as both a receiving and a generating agent. It is at once a faculty, possessed by the human personality, of perceiving truth unerringly and of shaping it into an 'eternal body', which becomes tantamount to creating it (order out of chaos). A weak point in the Pascalian conception, as in most Christian thinking at his date, was to assume the existence of two intangible detector-faculties in man, the one fallible and the other infallible, but distinguishable only by the application of a supernatural test, which necessarily lay outside man. Blake's conception eliminates this weakness, though at a cost which will be apparent later.

Meanwhile, to return to the rôle of 'nature'—the physical order—Blake is at one with Pascal in recognising its limitations, as he also recognises the limitations of Reason and the dependence of the second on the first:

The Argument: Man has no notion of moral fitness but from Education. Naturally, he is only a Natural Organ, subject to sense.

[5] *The Ghost of Abel: a Revelation in the Visions of Jehovah seen by William Blake*, Nonesuch edn, p. 769.

1. Man cannot naturally perceive but through his Natural or Bodily Organs.
2. Man by his reasoning power can only compare and judge of what he has already perceived.
3. From a perception of only three senses or three elements none could deduce a fourth or fifth.
4. None could have other than Natural or Organic Thoughts if he had none but Organic Perceptions.
5. Man's Desires are limited by his Perceptions; none can desire what he has not perceived.
6. The Desires and Perceptions of Man, untaught by anything but Organs of Sense, must be limited to Objects of Sense.

Conclusion: if it were not for the Poetic or Prophetic Character, the Philosophical and Experimental would soon be at the Ratio of all things; and stand still, unable to do other than repeat the same dull round over and over again.[6]

The 'Poetic or Prophetic Character', elsewhere called the 'Poetic Genius', is synonymous with Imagination. It alone enables man to break out of the 'dull round' instituted by the Philosophic (the rational or intellectual) and the Experimental (the sensory) interminably reacting upon each other to project what Blake calls the Ratio. This is in effect a boundary—though not conceived here in terms of a boundary *line*—set up by the interrelation of two limited faculties.

However, the capital distinction between Blake and Pascal, which cannot be reconciled, lies in Pascal's insistence on the absolute separateness of the Three Orders. However far it is prolonged, the physical can never meet either the intellectual or the divine.[7] In the quest for true fulfilment the 'body' can and must be discarded. For Blake the 'body', regarded as the seat of the senses, is not discarded but at most outgrown in the upward flight of the Poetic Genius to complete fulfilment. The sensual nature of man contains within itself the force, which Blake names 'energy', to generate Imagination, which is of course inseparable from Desire[8] (the Love-*Caritas* of earlier generations) and in this aspect unites with the supernatural:

Man has no Body distinct from his Soul; for that called Body is

---

[6] *There is no Natural Religion* [First Series], Nonesuch edn, p. 147.
[7] See above, pp. 157 and 159.
[8] This is universally accepted. But for the seventeenth century 'imagination' was desire for unattainable or inexistent objects. For the Romantics,

a portion of Soul discerned by the five senses, the chief inlets of Soul in this age.

Energy is the only life, and is from the Body; and Reason is the bound or circumference of Energy.

Energy is eternal delight.[9]

A few pages later in the same work, the argument is developed in semi-mythological terms and is led to its inevitable and 'blasphemous' conclusion:

The Giants who formed this world into its sensual existence, and now seem to live in it in chains, are in truth the causes of its life and the sources of all activity; but the chains are the cunning of weak and tame minds which have power to resist energy . . .

This one portion of being is the Prolific [i.e., creative], the other the Devouring [i.e., destructive]. To the Devourer it seems as if the producer was in his chains; but it is not so, he only takes portions of existence and fancies *that* the whole.

But the Prolific would cease to be the Prolific unless the Devourer, as a sea, received the excess of his delights.

Some will say: 'Is not God alone the Prolific [i.e., the creative principle]'? I answer: 'God only Acts and Is in existing beings or Men.'[10]

2

The theory outlined in the last few pages bears certain apparent resemblances to Neoplatonism. Was it not perhaps simply a nineteenth-century revision, with a different jargon and an attempted new

---

[9] *The Marriage of Heaven and Hell*, Nonesuch edn, p. 191. These sayings are ascribed to 'The Voice of the Devil', but Blake agrees with the Devil. His theme is the reconciliation of apparent contraries: Good and evil, body and soul, Heaven and Hell.

[10] *Marriage of Heaven and Hell*, Nonesuch edn, p. 198.

Desire is linked to perception. Hence, in Blake's view, its object must exist. Further, and again for Blake, it must be attainable. See particularly: *There is no Natural Religion* [Second Series], Nonesuch edn, p. 148:

1. Man's perceptions are not bounded by organs of perception; he perceives more than sense (though ever so acute) can discover . . . 5. More! More! is the cry of a mistaken soul; less than All cannot satisfy Man. 6. If any could desire what he is incapable of possessing, despair must be his eternal lot. 7. The desire of Man being infinite, the possession is infinite and himself infinite. *Application:* He who sees the infinite in all things, sees God. He who sees the Ratio only, sees himself only. Therefore God becomes as we are, that we may be as he is.

mythology, of the sixteenth-century theory of he senses transcending themselves, in which the divine Form is once again projected out of the 'natural' impurity, and in which the aspirational drive of human desire is now happily identified with Imagination and 'energy'? A first, quite empirical, hint that this is not so is furnished by the observation that Neoplatonism, by and large, made its adherents happy, whereas Blakism, by and large, was to make them miserable. A stronger hint is in Blake's own remark that: 'The Gods of Greece and Egypt were Mathematical diagrams (see Plato's Works).'[11]

There are plenty of other indications that Blake did not consider himself a Platonist. The root distinction is that even a Neoplatonist must consider the Idea or Form as an abstraction, although it is an abstraction which somehow conserves the desirable qualities of the 'natural' phenomenon. Blake's Poetic Genius does not *abstract* (which for him was a 'mathematical' and passionless process), but *forms* the 'natural' into its true shape, using the elements which are always in it. The 'body', according to this conception, is not refined so much as improved. It remains as the source of 'energy', which is the same force whether it is considered physical or divine. There is no generic distinction between body and soul, and none either between God and man. If God exists only 'in existing beings or Men', He is dependent on the human personality in order to be at all, and the enlargement of this personality through Imagination will be an enlargement of God as well as of man. The Platonic theory required at least two spheres, the phenomenal and the ideal, while conceding that the transition from one to the other is humanly possible, and indeed normal. Blake's assumption is not of two spheres. His emphasis is on wholeness, in which the 'natural', though transcended, still plays a part. What he calls 'universal Man' contains everything within him: 'All deities reside in the human breast.'[12]

For the Romantics in general, 'nature' means the whole cosmos rather than man alone. But the two are not separated. Their essence is the same, their association is fundamental. In this all-embracing association, the divine is also included, or it is immanent—hence the Pantheistic tendencies of some Romantic writers. The divine element, like everything else, can be apprehended and known by the

---

[11] Engraving of the Laocoon, Nonesuch edn, p. 765.
[12] *Marriage of Heaven and Hell*, Nonesuch edn, p. 195. Blake's term, 'universal Man' should be compared with Pascal's term, 'the Universal Being' (God). See above, p. 165. (*Pensées*, La. 699.)

Poetic Genius or Imagination. For that matter—though not many seem to have drawn this extreme but necessary deduction—it can even be shaped by it. Blake himself was forthright about this, and in a passage which directly contradicts Pascal's strictures on Imagination, he sets it up as the supreme creative faculty. It includes Pascal's 'heart' and 'faith', has the dynamic of 'energy', and is not dissociated from the senses:

> The Prophets Isaiah and Ezekiel dined with me, and I asked them how they dared so roundly to assert that God spoke to them . . .
> Isaiah answered: 'I saw no God, nor heard any, in a finite organical perception; but my senses discovered the infinite in everything, and as I was then persuaded, and remain confirmed, that the voice of honest indignation is the voice of God, I cared not for consequences, but wrote.'
> Then I asked: 'Does a firm persuasion that a thing is so, make it so?'
> He replied: 'All Poets believe that it does, and in ages of imagination this firm persuasion removed mountains; but many are not capable of a firm persuasion of anything.[13]

3

God, in the Pascalian sense, is obviously out. There is no place now for an unknowable principle, belonging to a different order, and contacting man through the mysterious agency of grace. What is left of the concept of grace has become the Poetic or Prophetic Character, which originates within man. The concept of the Hidden God, so necessary to Pascal, is and must be discarded. Discarded also is the 'mystery' of Original Sin, for there is no place in this philosophy for some unimaginable fault which distorted human nature before it became aware of itself.

Several of Blake's prints and engravings show an ancient bearded figure which, under various aliases, is broadly identifiable with the Jehovah of *Genesis*. Wearing a look of concentrated power from which only intelligence is lacking, he creates an agonised Adam out of chaos. In a print inspired by *Paradise Lost* he hangs stiffly over a ghastly group of human beings stricken by plague, whose sufferings he will neither end nor alleviate. His beard has grown to conceal the

[13] *Marriage of Heaven and Hell*, Nonesuch edn, pp. 195–6.

whole body except the head and the hieratically outstretched arms, while a whitish cloud cloaks him in further pointless mystery. His eyes are now closed in somnolence or blindness. Elsewhere, the same figure with the same concealing beard broods with imbecile ferocity among slabs of rock shaped like tomb-stones. Once the Creator, he has been overtaken by his own creation. He crouches uncomprehendingly in it, reduced to beard, shadow, a vacant glare and one large motionless foot.

Such deities can still be dangerous, even when they have lost ninety per cent of their power, but they can also be approached mockingly. This is the ultimate fate of the Hidden God in a squib written by Blake in about 1790. It is entitled: *To Nobodaddy*:

> Why art thou silent and invisible,
> Father of Jealousy?
> Why dost thou hide thyself in clouds
> From every searching eye?
>
> Why darkness and obscurity
> In all thy words and laws,
> That none dare eat the fruit but from
> The wily Serpent's jaws?
> Or is it because secrecy gains females' loud applause?

The last line is perhaps a little cheap, but the sending-up of Jehovah the Mysterious and of the inexplicable fault in Eden are definitive enough to be taken with complete seriousness.

Concurrently with a revision of religious values went a revolt against the paternalistic principle which is being repeated in as extreme a form today and on similar grounds. At certain points in history, for reasons which are ultimately sociological and technological, it becomes blatantly apparent that the Wisdom of the Elders bears too little relevance to actual conditions. Experience, particularly that kind which has become sanctified or ossified in traditional dogma, grows meaningless in the face of new circumstances and new problems. It is rejected, more or less roughly and uncritically according to the tenacity of its claims, but in any case rejected. It is obvious from this distance of time that the European nineteenth century could never have followed out its development in a framework of moral assumptions inherited at latest from the seventeenth century. The general movement of thought known as Romanticism gropingly translated a half-conscious realisation of Nobodaddy's shortcomings into a new idiom, a new cosmology, and a new conception of man.

4

In taking over the Jehovah-Daddy's inheritance, nineteenth-century man was obliged to assume responsibility for it. The exhilaration was at first great but the strain, in process of time, proved intolerable. Everything, it will be recalled, was now within man. The sensual, the intellectual, and the divine were all present within each human individual. Theoretically they could be shaped by a faculty called Imagination into one harmonious, and indeed glorious, whole. That was the hope or the vision of some of our great-great-grandparents. But when Imagination proved inadequate, the feeling of guilt was as painful as in the past and there was now no metaphysical alibi. Looking back, it is easy to see that it would have been better for the health of Western society if the whole Christian tradition could have been jettisoned towards 1820 and if something like the Russian atheistic but progressive Revolution of 1917 had been ante-dated by a hundred years and extended on a European scale. The lunatic impracticability of such a hypothesis is enough in itself to indicate the complexities and contradictions which lay within a growingly industrialised and acquisitive civilisation. Meanwhile, the psychological consequences of rejecting the pattern of the past with no fundamental modification of the elements which composed it can be illustrated by another diagram which should be compared with that on p. 159 above.

As in the Pascalian scheme, the figure opposite still postulates an original innocence of the whole human race at point A, assumed by such writers as Rousseau (this is not the doctrine of Progress). But now there is no original deviation. The Natural and the Divine continue undifferentiated as far as square X, which represents human nature as it is; more exactly, in view of the Romantic insistence on the individualised ego, it represents each separate human personality in a sense which the more generalised Pascalian conception of man hardly possessed.

Within X, and no longer in some remote past, the Fall occurs. The dividing-point at A^1 gives an apparent choice of two orientations, either along A^1B (the line of God-Felicity-Imaginative Fulfilment) or along A^1CD, which represents the sensory and the intellectual orders, no longer at this date sharply distinguished. (Mind, con-

180

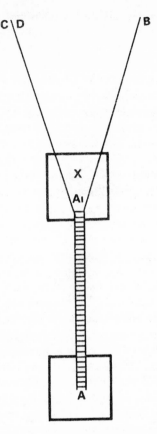

ceived as the reasoning faculty, is now compatible with Body. But Mind-Imagination follows the divine line.)

The choice of orientation, however, is illusory. The lines A^1B and A^1CD having both originated within X, neither can be abandoned for the other without a violent distortion, and consequent rupture, of the personality. Yet as long as the two trends are present within the same individual, there will be the unceasing two-way strain which Lamennais compared to quartering, Baudelaire to the struggle between God and Satan, and so on.

In short, man's physical nature is part of him, his divine nature is part of him. There is no external grace to swing him supernaturally from one to the other. He must try to do it himself, through Imagination, and he cannot.

The literature and thought of the nineteenth century are cluttered with the divided personalities and the unresolved conflicts which this conception of the human condition necessarily produced. The cost of denying a flaw in Man as a species was to transfer it to each new individual, implanting in his existence a potential personal failure, since it was apparent, in the plainest terms, that at point A^1 things generally still went wrong.

A subsidiary consequence, but of vast emotional importance throughout most of the century, was the growth of nostalgia as the prevalent malady.[14]

This can be ascribed to the feeling that Eden, the blissful state, really existed in the infancy, or immediate pre-natal existence, of

[14] Nostalgia has of course always existed. One can hardly ignore the theme of lost youth, of fading beauty, of the passing years, so frequently expressed by the poets of several languages that in the end it becomes conventional. But one may legitimately draw a distinction between this desire to immobilise the present and the desire to return to the past which is the true form of nostalgia. Nostalgia proper appears, e.g., in Dante: '. . . *nessun maggior dolore* / *Che ricordarsi del tempo felice* / *Nella miseria*', lines singled out by Byron as an epigraph to *The Corsair*; or in Villon's regrets for his care-free if misspent youth. But these and other examples are usually longings connected with some quite concrete memory, such as a prisoner's memory of freedom, or lovers' of their happiness before separation. The religious poets' complaints of 'exile' from heaven are often conventional, and bear on a state to which they confidently hope to return. A rare, possibly unique, case is Henry Vaughan (1622–95), who translates this traditional theme of banishment from heaven into a strongly personal experience and even includes the 'original' fault in his own life. See, e.g., *The Retreat*:

> Happy those early days, when I
> Shined in my angel-infancy,
> Before I understood this place
> Appointed for my second race,
> Or taught my soul to fancy aught
> But a white, celestial thought.
> . . . Before I taught my tongue to wound
> My conscience with a sinful sound,
> Or had the black art to dispense
> A several sin to every sense,
> But felt through all this fleshly dress
> Bright shoots of everlastingness.
>   Oh, how I long to travel back,
> And tread again that ancient track! . . .

Such instances are quite infrequent. Childhood innocence, in particular, is rarely sentimentalised before the late eighteenth century. Nowhere in previous European literature is there anything comparable to the great wave of looking-back, or looking elsewhere, which sweeps through Romantic lyric poetry.

each man, and had therefore been experienced by the same personality which later became conscious of its terrible duality. Thus it was sharper, because more conscious and intimate, than the diffused restlessness of the 'Baroque' mentality, explained by Pascal as a longing ignorant of its object.[15]

If this analysis is conceded, the view of human nature-in-existence as an area of continual conflict between two irreconcilable urges is more than understandable. That it should be called 'tragic' was a natural development, since this conflict was the intimate cause of an enormous volume of patently hopeless suffering.

The odd thing is that it produced so little tragic drama, and that most of what there was was of such indifferent quality that it has failed to last.

5

Romantic drama, whose historical field it is as well to define in broad terms, belongs to the first half of the nineteenth century and can be extended backwards in time to the last two or three decades of the eighteenth century in order to include the seminal contribution of German writers. It covers the *Sturm und Drang* movement, the work of Goethe, Schiller and others, English poetic drama and near-drama, the Romantic drama of France (Hugo, Vigny, Musset) and of Spain (Zorilla, Rivas). But, as has just been said, the tragic content, in terms of an intimate conflict, of all these varied productions is disappointingly small.

The Romantic hero—for now there can be less hesitation than ever in regarding the hero as the focal point of the work—is engaged in an effort of self-assertion which must be sustained at whatever cost. His position is usually pre-Blakian, ideologically if not in time. Although he questions or challenges the Jehovah-God, he has not reached the point of discarding him in Blake's confident manner. Defiance is his key-note. He is so single-heartedly intent on affirming the human ego against external powers that the internal conflict which theoretically should be splitting him apart remains smothered or subsidiary. For there still are external spiritual powers, either Christian, para-Christian, or recreated from some pagan mythology to give reality to the one completely authentic and irresistible impulse—that of revolt. These powers are not Nobodaddy, a concept

[15] *Pensées*, La. 300, quoted above, pp. 154–5.

which only comes into existence after the revolt has succeeded. They are still capable of destroying man, but no longer the whole of him. Some part of his essence is invulnerable to them. Even when the idea of damnation is retained, the hero wills it and welcomes it as a deliberately incurred consequence of taking command of his own destiny. In such cases, typical of the Byronic hero, revolt is a declaration of independence as a necessary prelude to the raising of man to an equal plane with the spiritual forces which surround him. After that, why not to a superior plane? The idea of such a progression would be the spiritual counterpart of the theory of physical evolution to be elaborated by Darwin soon after the mid-century.

If Byron and some of his contemporaries had not reached this point, at which Blake arrived intuitively thanks to his 'Poetic Genius', at least they seem to have had the impression of going somewhere very riskily but not hopelessly. This must reduce the tragic potential of Byron's poetic dramas and of any other works based on similar postulates. For, to return to our definition of tragedy,[16] the hero does not go down in 'final' disaster in the sense, for example, that Marlowe's Dr Faustus does. Neither is the partial disaster in which he is involved 'unforeseen' or 'unrealised', but deliberately courted and savoured. In fact he has not 'failed' but has succeeded in his basic intention, his will or his soul remaining unconquered. The result is therefore less tragedy than heroic drama, with the same kind of victory at the end. If it is straining words to call the ending of such a work as Byron's *Manfred* a happy one, it does contain an element of fulfilment and exaltation which is different from the final impression left by the *Oedipus*, *Hamlet*, *Othello*, or *Phèdre*.

In one department of Romantic ideology, therefore, the outstanding human individual is conceived as competing with supernatural powers on something approaching equality. His conflict is an external one, with a chance of success. If in his own past and personality is embedded some usually mysterious fault, it is regarded in a different way from the traditional fault which caused the Fall, so severing man from felicity/fulfilment. But it is not seen either as an organic part of the self, as it would be in the fully developed Romantic ideology expounded a few pages previously. Certain writers seem to represent a transitional stage in which the fault or weakness is neither wholly generic nor wholly personal and easily lends itself to an ambivalent exploitation. It is adopted into the ego as a soldier

[16] See above, p. 20.

might adopt his war-wounds, not self-inflicted but self-incorporated. It can thus become a source of pride, a pretext for defiance, a reason for rejecting the injustice of the supernatural.[17]

Other Romantics go less far. They are unable to reject the idea of an ultimate divine sanction, conceived more or less in traditional Christian terms, but they temper it to human requirements. In Goethe's *Faust*, Part II, the hero is saved, and indeed glorified, against the whole run of orthodox Christian theology. The earliest of the Don Juans, Tirso de Molina's, had gone down unequivocally to eternal torment after vainly calling for confession and absolution. Another seventeenth-century Don Juan, Molière's, went similarly to damnation, though unrepentantly. The nineteenth-century Don Juans fare, in general, much better. Sometimes they repent and work their passage to heaven in an aura of willed saintliness. Sometimes they are saved at the last moment by the power of the Love to which they have devoted their lives, incarnated in the person of the one woman out of many who has proved to be their true soul-mate. (This entails an un-Pascalian merging of carnal love with divine love.)

In both these broad categories of works, the supernatural still had a part to play. In the first it provided the opposition against which the increasingly audacious spirit of man measured itself. In the second, it permitted or tolerated the human revolt, which it could only be said to condone by its refusal to exact the ultimate punishment. Conceived as the paternal principle, the supernatural-divine was either not omnipotent (it was beginning its slide towards Nobodaddy) or it was benign; in the latter case it operated in a sense favourable and comprehensible to humanity obeying its natural impulses, which again was not Pascal's sense. Conceived as an external force, it did not

---

[17] This again was particularly Byronic, and perhaps inevitable at that date. It is disconcerting to find it recurring in 1942 in Sartre's first play, *The Flies*. The existentialist hero of this, Orestes, defies the declining god Jupiter, creator of a Nature no longer inevitably inclusive of Man, and also opts out of Society (in the form of the population of Argos) while taking its guilt upon his shoulders in a gesture which can only be described as self-glorifying. This he does in the name of *liberty*, conceived as that intimate and irreducible element in the self which the Romantics usually called *the will*, reserving the term 'liberty' for the object of the will. By having, as he says, 'the courage of his acts' and the determination to go it alone without remorse or repentence, Orestes bears a strong resemblance to Manfred and seems to be renewing a protest made a long time previously in more difficult circumstances. It is only by a trick of dubious psychology that the protest is made to appear novel.

warrant much attention for its own sake, as it seems to have done in Greek tragedy, because it could be overcome or manipulated. There was therefore no tragic exploration to be undertaken in its field. But at the same time its continued existence served to obscure or delay the anguished exploration of power regarded as internal to man—in other words, the psychology of the individual—by providing humanity with a certain alibi. The writers of the first part of the nineteenth century, particularly the dramatic writers, had not accepted the full implications of Blake's: 'All deities reside in the human breast,' which was equivalent to saying: 'All good and evil are within man.' Although the alibi of the superhuman was sometimes realised to be rather thin—hence the misgivings which lay at the root of the Romantic 'sickness'—nevertheless it veiled the true situation for long enough to inhibit the growth of a fundamentally serious Romantic drama at a period when Romantic ideology was at its prime in other domains, notably in lyric poetry.

6

Another aspect of the paternal principle which the Romantic temperament was bound to challenge was represented by Society. It was not a totally different aspect but a complementary one, since the incidence of an established social order and an established system of religious beliefs set up identical reactions as authoritarian pressures upon the individual. However, the open identification of God with Society, familiar though it may be to post-Marxists, was hardly yet a consciously held concept.

The chief exception to this, paradoxical though it may seem, is found in the doctrine of ultra-Catholic royalists such as Joseph de Maistre, who argued divine justification for the traditional social order. These writers, generally regarded as the lunatic fringe of reaction, harking back to a much earlier mystique, offered political authority in a transcendent envelope, whereas Marxist theory offers transcendent authority in a political envelope: the difference is purely one of presentation. Neither of these approaches was of much consequence in the first half of the century.

Revolt against Society, the man-made prison, at most ran parallel with revolt against an orthodox God, and often occurred independently. With it almost alone the positive and general cult of *liberty* was associated—political liberty no doubt whenever its connotations could be made precise, but shading out beyond this to a simple love of break-out for its own sake. This was one of the few occasions in history when a state of isolation, friendlessness, and exclusion could be idealised as a state of personal fulfilment. As foreshadowed in Voltaire's *Candide*, in which all the horrors except the Lisbon earthquake stem from humanity, the herd stank so abominably that it was necessary to get away from it in order to breathe. This impulse found a characteristic expression in historical and pseudo-historical drama, whose heroes defied contemporary society projected into the past and usually personified in a tyrant. Here again, the ardour of the external revolt and the assumption of its 'heroic' nature checked the emergence of a conflict within the hero himself.

It is no doubt the consistent failure or refusal to explore the forces internal to the individual, and which, on a modern view, must have motivated his actions, that causes Romantic drama to appear so artificial. Here, if anywhere, a psychological exploration is called for and it is not made. The characters of Greek tragedy can be accepted at their face value and launched as simple and consistent entities into situations whose interest lies in the exploration of some general pattern of cause-and-effect. But since the Romantic mind challenged the validity of any such external pattern, its exploration, as we have said, offered no special interest. It was conserved as a conventional background, with all the implausibility, and in short theatricality, which that implied. The whole true interest now lay in the individual character, but such was the state of 'characterisation', or rather of the psychological assumptions on which characterisation could be based, that the Romantic dramatists were incapable of exploiting it. Freudianism, without much modification, could have supplied most of the basic assumptions which the Romantic ethos requires in order to ring true, and had it been possible for some kind of Freudianism to emerge in the Napoleonic era, what an extraordinarily rich and complex drama might have grown up around it. But as it was, science tailed behind the artists[18] of the early nineteenth

---

[18] If one speaks in terms of Two Cultures, this provides a reason why 'the Poet' occupied so high a place in the Romantic era—not only in his own esteem but in that of society, which unconsciously accepted Blake's image of the Artist. His claims to be a lawgiver, a prophet, a spiritual guide and even leader, were not unjustified in the absence of rival claims. Not only bourgeois materialism, but science itself, hit back at him through Positivism, to which the counter, now empty of social conviction, was *fin de siècle* aestheticism.

century, who were left to exercise a skill rarely equalled in the history of literature and the other arts upon material which, once the religious supernatural had been removed from it, hardly surpassed the level of the old wives' tale.

10

Imagination Dethrone d:
Ibsen, Chekhov

1

For the reasons just given, the divided personality, though a concept of paramount importance to the Romantic sensibility, appeared hardly at all in the drama of the time and only equivocally in the novel. It is quite possible that an exhaustive study of the European novelists who wrote in the first half of the century would reveal it as the underlying assumption of a large number of works of fiction, but it rarely comes to the surface in a defined form. The Romantic character, obsessed as he is with a sense of universal struggle, does not usually succeed in locating the enemy within himself.[1] Not until the second half of the century, when the driving impulse of Romanticism (the exaltation of Imagination) has faltered, is there a clear realisation of the seat of the malady. By then it is too late for it to emerge as a tragic recognition, or at any rate as undilutedly tragic. Mockingly, petulantly, or clinically the disillusioned heirs of the Romantics set about demolishing the Romantic hero, supercharged Man, in the same way as some of their predecessors had demolished the supercharged God; though whereas it had been possible to consign Nobodaddy to the junk-yard following the discovery of a new source of energy, the Hero was discarded more for his proved

[1] An exception is the theme of the Double or *Doppelgänger*, clear-cut if sometimes over-simplified, which appears recurrently in literature: from its earliest manifestation in Hoffmann's *Die Elixiere des Teufels* (1816) to the ultimate popularisation in R. L. Stevenson's *Strange Case of Dr Jekyll and Mr Hyde* (1886).

inadequacies than because there was a better development to replace him. Hence the literary phases of Realism and Naturalism, with their studied lack of a dynamic. And hence also the lingering respect felt in some quarters for the Hero, who, although faulty, had at least been something positive.

For a long time, however, this respect remained muted and the greatest writers of the later eighteen-hundreds were agreed on the failure of Imagination in Blake's sense to create a viable second world. Very generally, their bitterness towards the image of the Hero was in proportion to their early involvement with the Romantic ethos and the later their date the more objective their treatment of it. Flaubert, for example, after producing some wholly Romantic *juvenilia*, sweated out his wildest illusions in writing the *Education Sentimentale*,[2] and was then ready to make the cool and drab-looking statement of *Madame Bovary* (1856). His Emma Bovary is the daughter of a simple farmer who marries a dull and simple country doctor and is temperamentally unable to accept the mediocrity of her married life. She has love-affairs with two flashy but essentially ordinary young men, piles up unmeetable debts, and dies painfully after taking arsenic. The plot was suggested to Flaubert by an actual case.

Emma Bovary sees herself as a 'romantic' heroine, but nothing in her material or social environment supports her ideal or even responds to it. One night when she is sleeping with her lover Rodolphe she believes she hears footsteps—mistakenly, as it turns out:

'Someone's coming!' she said.
He blew out the light.
'Have you got your pistols?'
'What for?'
'To defend yourself, of course.'
'Against your husband? Oh, the poor devil!'
... Later, Rodolphe chewed over this question of pistols. If she had been speaking seriously, it was quite ridiculous, he thought, distasteful even. He had no reason to hate good old Charles, not being exactly tormented by jealousy.

Madame Bovary's dream is primarily one of escape from the limitations of provincial life. Her imagination—the word must be taken in Pascal's pejorative sense rather than in Blake's—has been

---

[2] The first version, completed when he was twenty-three. The published version, entirely re-shaped and rewritten, was composed after *Madame Bovary*.

stimulated by popular literature: the novelettes and historical romances smuggled into her convent school by a sewing-maid and, after her marriage, the fashion-magazines to which she subscribes. There has been one memorable real event, the night when she and her husband were invited to a ball at a neighbouring château and she tasted the wealth and elegance of the titled class.[3] These things alone give body to her Other World, which is sensual and social, with no trace of the true metaphysical. It is constructed round what Flaubert called 'the poetic need of luxury'. Paris, as portrayed in her women's magazines, is her lodestar, its fashions in clothes and furnishings, its social events, its manners.[4]

None of this was original, or even new. The woman besotted by the reading of romances was a familiar figure well before the Romantic era. Don Quixote's aberration stemmed from a similar source and was a subject, as we have said, for comic treatment by Cervantes, not, *pace* Unamuno, tragic treatment. But the novelty of *Madame Bovary* was that the heroine was not comic. Her single-mindedness, the sincerity of her practical attempts to translate her dream into actions, including adultery, the atrocious circumstances of her suicide, preclude comedy. A tragedy, then? It is impossible to apply the word to the story as a whole, though difficult to refuse it certain tragic features. It fails principally on the count of status. Emma Bovary is not, as Flaubert presents her, above our norm, though she is not much below it either. (This neutral position, neither inviting nor precluding admiration, sympathy, or condemnation is Flaubert's great achievement.[5]) Her Other World, however, is too directly derivative and commonplace. She stakes her happiness and ultimately her life on something which is represented as so ordinary that the reader cannot respect it. However far values are scaled down, there is still nothing that can be called a tragic duality. Quite certainly Flaubert did not intend one. What he did intend, and realised, in this symptomatic work was a demonstration of the impotence of Imagination to transform reality into the shoddiest of paradises. One can always add,

[3] Conceivably the germ of Anouilh's recurring theme of '*l'invitation au château*', worked out by him with a resistant heroine in place of a responsive one.
[4] Her second lover, Léon, persuades her to ride with him in a cab, in which the seduction takes place. His clinching argument, which overrides her hesitation, is: 'That's what they do in Paris.'
[5] Re-reading the novel once again, I incline to think that the character of Emma in itself does have sufficient moral stature to be tragic. But her possible field of action does not. In one sense, that is her tragedy.

'in this particular case', since Emma Bovary was poorly endowed with Blake's 'poetic genius'. But the fact remains that Flaubert deliberately chose a case weighted with possibilities of failure, in which he was typical of a generation reacting against the excessive claims which the Romantics had made for sensibility.

2

His near-contemporary, Ibsen, follows a comparable line of development. His early historical dramas reflect the Romantic conception of the heroic. *Brand* (1866) comes as a radical questioning of the idealistic dream. *Peer Gynt*, written in 1867, eleven years after the publication of *Madame Bovary*, explodes Imagination with a verve and openness quite different from the Frenchman's painstaking negation of it. If any single work had to be chosen to exemplify the unmasking of the Romantic hero and all he stood for, it would be hard to improve on this one.

One can begin with some almost irrelevant comparisons, in order to clear them out of the way. Ibsen's Peer Gynt is the child of a farmer, as was Emma Bovary. He has been left with one parent, his mother—his father having died when he was young; with Madame Bovary it was the opposite. He is given roots in the local soil and bears the name and some of the qualities of a character in Norwegian folk-lore. He represents, in fact, certain national characteristics depicted no less consciously than the features with which Flaubert endowed the inhabitants of Yonville, though Ibsen's view of his countrymen's failings issues in fantasy and satire far more exuberant than anything in Flaubert's deadpan treatment. Still, the localisation is palpable in both works and can be ascribed to similar preoccupations in the minds of their authors. At this date, however, the particular is of less interest than the general and for the purpose of this analysis can be practically ignored.

As a young man Peer Gynt already has the reputation of a boaster and romancer. While his mother struggles with the work of the farm, he escapes on long expeditions into the hills and returns with fantastic accounts of his hunting exploits. After one such absence he goes to a wedding at a neighbouring farm, where he abducts and seduces the bride and immediately deserts her. It was an act of bravado, which does not efface from his mind the image of another girl, the pure and modest Solveig, whom he has met for the first time at the wedding. Hunted by the whole parish, he escapes again to the hills. He sleeps with three strapping cow-girls and falls in with the sub-human mountain trolls, whose king offers him his daughter and half his kingdom on condition that he sheds some of his human habits. The ultimate demand is that he should have his eyes scratched out in order to see things as the trolls do. Peer balks at this and tries to get away, but the Troll King declares that he has seduced his daughter—a repulsive creature to human eyes—and will have to marry her:

PEER GYNT: Do you dare accuse me of——?

TROLL KING: Can you deny that she was the object of all your desire?

PEER GYNT: But no more than that. What the deuce does that matter?

TROLL KING: You human beings are always the same.
You are always ready to talk of your souls,
But heed nothing really save what is tangible.
You think desires are things that don't matter?
Wait. Your own eyes will prove to you shortly—
My Peer, ere the year's out you'll be a father.[6]

The ringing of church bells in the valley saves Peer from being torn to pieces by the outraged trolls. Outcast equally from the human community, he builds a hut in the forest where Solveig comes to join him. But at the last moment he turns away from her, feeling that she is too pure for him. His mother dies and he sets out on his travels abroad.

These occupy the greater part of his life. He grows rich by such activities as slave-trading, loses his money but acquires more, and bobs up irrepressibly in various scenes and circumstances with his self-confidence unpunctured. His guiding principle, conscious or not, is the motto of the trolls: 'To thyself be *enough*'—in contradistinction to the human motto, 'To thyself be *true*'—and this sustains him through all his vicissitudes. It enables his imagination to transform every reality, however unfavourable or humiliating, into an illusion which helps to build up a lovingly elaborated conception of the self—the Gyntian Self, as he begins proudly to call it. Ibsen's most pointed comment on this occurs in the scene in the madhouse in Cairo, which Peer Gynt is taken to visit. The lunatics, as the Director

[6] *Peer Gynt*, Act II, Sc. 6, trans. R. Farquharson Sharp (Everyman Edn, Dent).

of the Asylum remarks admiringly, are *themselves* through and through:

> It's here that men are most themselves—
> Themselves and nothing but themselves—
> Sailing with outspread sails of self,
> Each shuts himself in a cask of self,
> The cask stopped with a bung of self
> And seasoned in a well of self.
> None has a tear for other's woes
> Or cares what any other thinks.
> We are ourselves in thought and voice—
> Ourselves up to the very limit.
> And consequently, if we want
> An Emperor, it's very clear
> That you're the man.[7]

Their conviction of the absolute sufficiency of the self leads two of them to commit suicide, in order to become more faithfully and permanently themselves.[8] In a different context this could be represented as an heroic triumph of idealism, an example of Imagination inspiring the will to transcend the limits of the natural. But in Ibsen's play, these are lunatics.

Growing old, Peer Gynt returns to Norway. He begins to feel misgivings about the nature and destiny of the self he has created. They are confirmed when he meets a symbolic character, the Button Moulder, who says that he has orders to melt down his soul and return it to the common stock. Peer Gynt, it appears, does not possess a marked enough individuality, as saint or sinner, to be worth preserving intact. Given a short respite, he searches desperately for a witness to his identity, but fails to find one. At the last moment he is saved by Solveig, the woman he left half a lifetime before, who is still waiting for him lovingly and confidently in the mountain hut. To his question: 'Where has my true self been all these years?' she has the ready answer: 'In my faith, in my hope and in my love.' She takes him in her arms and rocks him to sleep like a mother.

The philosophical interest of this ending lies in Ibsen's adoption of two divergent ideologies. Most of the last act rests on Christian

---

[7] *Peer Gynt*, Act IV, Sc. 13, translation cited.
[8] An anticipation of Mallarmé's seriously meant:
    Tel qu'en Lui-même enfin l'éternité le change . . .

assumptions which are pre-Romantic and pre-Blakian and re-
markably close to Pascal's; the only difference is that Pascal nowhere
subscribed explicitly to the idea of annihilation (the Button
Moulder's casting-ladle) but apparently thought in straight terms of
salvation or damnation. However, for both Ibsen and Pascal the
soul, whether destructible or indestructible, is God-created and
distinct from the *self*, whose exaltation by imagination is illusory
and can only lead to a disastrous blindness to reality and a consequent severance from life. The 'self-centred concentration' of which
Peer Gynt boasts and which reaches its extreme point in the Cairo
madhouse is the same thing as Pascal's *amour-propre*. The remedy
is also the same. Just as the *moi*, the object of *amour-propre*, must be
suppressed,[9] so Ibsen's Button Moulder declares that: 'To be oneself
is to slay oneself.' And the dialogue continues:

BUTTON MOULDER: But perhaps as that explanation
                    Is thrown away on you, let's say:
                    To follow out, in everything,
                    What the Master's intention was.
PEER GYNT: But suppose a man was never told
                    What the Master's intention was?
BUTTON MOULDER: Insight should tell him.
PEER GYNT: But our insight
                    So often is at fault, and then
                    We're thrown out of our stride completely.
BUTTON MOULDER: Quite so, Peer Gynt. And lack of insight
                    Gives to our friend of the cloven hoof
                    His strongest weapon, let me tell you.
PEER GYNT: It's all an extremely subtle problem . . .[10]

The words translated here as 'insight' correspond partly to
Pascal's 'heart', intuition, or instinct, though without the warmth-
Caritas meaning which 'heart' also contains. Moreover, since 'insight'
can be 'at fault' (literally, 'misfire'), it has evidently become contaminated by Imagination in the post-Romantic mind. Two related
Norwegian words are involved: *ane* (to suspect, guess, feel instinctively) and *Anelse* (premonition, suspicion, irrational feeling).

The main lines of this, however, are recognisably Pascalian and
derived from orthodox Christian theology. The new and disparate
feature, typically Romantic, is the proposition of salvation through

---

[9] See above, p. 154.
[10] *Peer Gynt*, Act V, Sc. 9, translation cited.

human love—in particular the love of a woman transcending itself
to become divine. So, it seems ultimately, was Goethe's Faust
saved.[11] So were some of the nineteenth-century Don Juans. But it
must be observed that, although it provides Ibsen with a moving
and 'happy' ending to the play, he puts it forward as a provisional
solution only. While Solveig rocks Peer Gynt in her arms, 'singing
softly' according to the stage directions, the Button Moulder speaks
a last word from behind the hut:

BUTTON MOULDER: At the last crossroads I shall meet you, Peer.
　　　　　　　　Then we'll see—whether—I say no more.

Solveig's singing grows louder as the curtain falls:

　　　　　　　　I will rock you to sleep and guard you!
　　　　　　　　Sleep *and dream*, my dearest boy![12]

So the question remains open. Will the Woman ('Mother and
wife') succeed in saving him through the combined force of her
human love and her power of intercession with God, or will she not?

Apart from the intercessory factor—a metaphysical concept which
may well be intended as another human illusion (in Ibsen, though
hardly in Goethe)—it is clear that only one thing has changed. Peer
Gynt's image of himself, now exposed as false, has merely been
replaced by Solveig's image of him. This seems, on the evidence of
the play, to be equally false and no more than a rationalisation of *her*
subjective Other World. Pascal would have rejected it out of hand,
refusing to concede that salvation can be found through another
human being. But one may perhaps credit Ibsen with a less austere
theology, or at least extend his idea of charity to include doubt on
the point.

[11] See the whole of the last two scenes of *Faust*, Part II. The concluding
lines of the work are:
CHORUS MYSTICUS:　　All things corruptible
　　　　　　　　　　Are but a parable;
　　　　　　　　　　Earth's insufficiency
　　　　　　　　　　Here finds fulfilment;
　　　　　　　　　　Here the ineffable
　　　　　　　　　　Wins life through love;
　　　　　　　　　　Eternal Womanhood
　　　　　　　　　　Leads us above.
　　　　　　　　　　(Trans. Philip Wayne, Penguin Books, 1959.)
[12] *Peer Gynt*, Act V, Sc. 11, translation cited.

Whatever may be thought of the ending, the main theme of *Peer Gynt* is unmistakably the demolition of the Romantic Hero. His acts of defiance (directed against Society rather than against God, whom he conceives as being on his side, as part of his all-embracing egoism) are empty gestures which earn him only a straw crown from the lunatics. Imagination which, unlike Madame Bovary, he possesses in abundance, brings not self-realisation but self-dispersion. Instead of raising him to a divine level, it assimilates him to the sub-human trolls. His Ideal World, which he has constructed around himself with such persistence, crumbles at the touch of reality. It was not even worth the expense of the words and gestures which went into the making of it. Peer Gynt is of course not a tragic figure. It is impossible that he should be, because, in terms of the nineteenth-century tragic conflict, the second branch of the dichotomy is shown up as a chimera. There is no real conflict and the general notion of one is depreciated in Ibsen's fantasy. We are thus back to Before Blake, but with a sobering memory of all that has happened in the interim. How many deluded human aspirations have ended on the scrap-heap. How useless they all were and how more nearly ludicrous than pathetic.

3

Once *Peer Gynt* is accepted as the key to Ibsen's ideological position which we believe it to be, there is unlikely to be much place for the imaginative hero in the 'serious' plays which he went on to write. And since this type of hero has been exploded, and with him the illusory world to which he aspired, it is also unlikely that the conception of man's tragic duality will figure centrally in any of Ibsen's dramas. A narrower dramatist, dominated by cynicism, could indeed have continued to produce plays in which the unmasking of illusion is the main point, but they would then have been comic—either satirical comedy or the comedy of the absurd—and, although this streak is possessed by Ibsen, it is always subordinate to a deeper and more comprehensive view of human nature. He is never—one has only to state the fact for it to become self-evident—the nineteenth-century Molière which concentration upon disillusionment would have tended to make him. He recognises the existence in the human psyche of the element Imagination, whose period name, with its slightly different connotations, is now frankly Idealism. He recognises its force and by no means always condemns it. In fact it is difficult, and really irrelevant, to say whether he condemns or admires it. Neither 'believing in' Idealism, like a Victor Hugo, nor capable, like a Cervantes or a Molière, of dismissing it as a redundant accretion on man, he accepts its presence and goes on to explore its effects. It is in this exploratory process that the main interest of his drama lies—putting aside for the moment the nature and degree of its tragic content. It is not in any conflict between the real and the ideal or the finite and the infinite, although such a conflict can be found in various forms in most of Ibsen's plays. But it is now subsidiary to the examination of the characters who are affected by it. Ibsen's attitude to Imagination bears a close similarity to Racine's attitude to sexual passion before the desirability of taking up a moral standpoint has been borne in upon him.

Ibsen rarely poses a plain dilemma. Sometimes he shows a character placed in circumstances which he feels to be intolerable and who is forced into destroying himself rather than endure them. It is then self-destruction in the full meaning of the term, not a way of escape to a higher or even a different sphere. It is the same kind of act that a character in Greek tragedy might have performed in writing *finis* to a life recognised as pointless. Just as Flaubert's Madame Bovary was driven to suicide by the relentless logic of events, so Ibsen's Hedda Gabler shoots herself because there is no other way out. She shares Madame Bovary's nauseating boredom with her husband and his milieu. They are, if anything, more deadening to her than Charles Bovary and his milieu were to Emma, and much more articulate and insinuating. They threaten to invade her personality because they are so inexhaustibly simple and well-meaning—qualities tinged with horror for a woman who is neither. Her physical attraction and finer taste are based, unlike Emma Bovary's, on real social superiority. Full weight is given to her up-bringing as a general's daughter. One might write that she is 'exiled' by lack of money and the circumstances of her marriage from the circle in which she was bred. If this were stressed, her Other World would be a social one like Emma Bovary's, not however imagined but already experienced, and her feeling for it would be plain nostalgia. But it is not presented in that way. Her upbringing is merely recalled to explain the formation of her character and, incidentally, her possession of the pair of pistols which are necessary to the plot.

Amore viable Other World appears with the arrival of Eilert Lövborg, the talented and unstable man-of-letters with whom Hedda had flirted in her youth. In her eyes he represents a type of romance, associated not with love but with freedom extraverted as boldness—in social behaviour, in language, in thinking, all the things which her husband lacks. He has just published a successful book and brings with him the completed manuscript of another, bolder still in conception, which should make his name as an original thinker. But he loses the manuscript at the end of a drunken party, comes to Hedda obsessed with shame at this wanton loss of his work and hopes, accepts the loaded pistol which she gives him, and leaves after hearing her exhortation to use it 'beautifully'. If he does so, one might continue, his romantic image will be preserved in Hedda's mind and the reality of her Other World confirmed, though vicariously.

Disillusionment follows quickly. News comes that Lövborg has been found fatally shot, but not 'beautifully'. The wound is not in the temple or the chest but in the stomach and it appears that the gun was discharged in a scuffle in the bedroom of a courtesan to whom Lövborg had betaken himself. The Other World has collapsed and Hedda Gabler's last resource is to take the second pistol and blow out her own brains with it.

All these events are in Ibsen's play, but anyone who is familiar with it will at once protest that to summarise it in such terms is to distort it. Too much has been left out, and notably the character of Mrs Elvsted, the woman who has inspired Lövborg in his work and of whose influence Hedda is bitterly jealous; the character of Judge Brack, who desires to set up a *ménage à trois* with Hedda and her foolish husband, with himself as the dominant partner; and the fact that it was Hedda herself who deliberately destroyed the manuscript which Lövborg believed he had lost. These factors, on which the play largely turns, radically modify the Two-World dichotomy, though without obliterating it entirely. In its place there moves into the foreground Hedda Gabler's obsessive thirst for power, the true mainspring of the drama.

Her ambition is to exercise power over or through others. It motivates her suggestion—quickly discarded as unrealistic—that her ineffectual husband should enter politics. It explains her hatred of the mild Mrs Elvsted, who has succeeded in reclaiming the dissipated Lövborg and enabled him to write his two books after *she* had let him slip out of her grasp; it explains her burning of the manuscript as an act of revenge on the two of them; it explains her cry of exultation when she momentarily believes that Lövborg has killed himself 'beautifully' in obedience to her command and her frustrated disgust when she learns the true version. On top of that comes the revelation that she is now at the mercy of Judge Brack who knows that it was she who gave the revolver to Lövborg and can blackmail her with the threat of scandal. The realisation that, far from exercising her will over others, she is now 'a slave' herself determines her suicide, which is similar in causation and motive to that of any captive queen in ancient tragedy.

Although there are tragic features in *Hedda Gabler* which put it in a different class from *Madame Bovary*, they are so mixed with other elements, principally melodramatic, that it is difficult to describe the play as a whole as 'a tragedy'. The implications of this admixture over the whole range of Ibsen's drama must be returned to later. Meanwhile, some approaches to the question can be cleared by considering two plays which approximate more closely to the traditional idea of tragedy. *Ghosts*, written in 1881, eleven years before *Hedda Gabler*, is the story of a young painter who returns to his provincial Norwegian home from Paris, where, he believes, he has unknowingly contracted the venereal disease which is threatening his health and reason and making him incapable of creative work. His father died young and the family estate is in the capable hands of his mother, Mrs Alving. With her as her personal maid is an attractive young girl, Regina Engstrand—the daughter, it is supposed, of a local carpenter. Drawn to Regina by her healthy sexuality, Oswald Alving wishes to take her away with him. The 'joy of life' which he sees in her is an antidote not only to the rainsoaked atmosphere of his home, but above all to the enervating self-reproach which he experiences. For such is his idealised image of his father, fostered throughout his life by Mrs Alving, that he cannot believe that his disease is inherited and concludes that it must have been caused by some act of his own.

The truth, which Mrs Alving finally reveals, is different. Her husband was a dissipated brute who undoubtedly transmitted the disease to his son. Regina is his daughter by a former maid in the house, and thus is Oswald's half-sister. This is a situation based as firmly as the *Oedipus* and *Phèdre* on physical realities. But Ibsen complicates it by attempting to go further. Mrs Alving is an 'enlightened' woman, who would even permit the marriage of Oswald and Regina if it brought them happiness. What she blames herself for is her cowardly hushing-up of the real situation in obedience to outdated conventions. It would have been better to have been frank from the outset. More than that, she manages to discover in her own joyless propriety as a young wife an excuse for her husband's dissolute behaviour. He was frustrated in that second-rate town and 'I brought no holiday spirit into his home either.'

But, while she states a powerful case for the progressive outlook, the fact remains that Oswald is suffering, not only from a sense of guilt which might be removed by plain speaking, but from a syphilitic condition transmitted by a parent who, we learn, was already infected before his marriage. Oswald has been warned by a doctor in Paris that this condition may at any moment affect the brain.

This physical fact provides the formidable climax. Left alone in the house with his mother (Regina has immediately abandoned them on learning the true circumstances of her birth) Oswald shows her the lethal dose of morphia which he has obtained in case he should go mad and exacts her promise to give it to him when that happens. There follows the dramatically stunning curtain-fall, with Oswald sunk in sudden imbecility in his armchair and his mother standing before him in an agony of indecision and terror.

Several reasons have been given for this powerful play's relative lack of impact on modern audiences. In its own day, and for some time after, it was too 'daring' to be allowed public performance in several countries, including England. This daringness now appears somewhat melodramatic and hence artificial, although the plot follows an impeccable chain of necessity and the only fault one can find with it is that the events appear over-compressed in time. The propagandist intention is also perhaps too conspicuous. As we have hinted, the two strands, physical and psychological, do not knit well together. A hereditary curse in the form of disease is one thing. The influence of what Mrs Alving calls 'ghosts'—false images of the dead, dead beliefs and taboos, all conspiring to drag the living back into the past—is another. Natural though it may seem to associate them, they remain disparate in this particular play. One could either have a simple tragedy of the blood on the classic pattern, or a more modern tragedy of influences, in which the moral weight of the past crushes the present. Ibsen was perhaps too ambitious in wishing to combine both.

4

In *Rosmersholm* (1886) Ibsen might be thought to have learnt his lesson. Here the influence of the past is exploited differently and it is now confined to the psychological. The central character, Rebecca West, is a woman of thirty who is keeping house for John Rosmer, a scholarly man who has been a priest but has left the Church on conscientious grounds. Quietly encouraged by Rebecca, he has developed a new and future-looking attitude which in local politics can be equated with liberalism and brings him into conflict with the reactionaries. It also runs against the traditions of his family, embodied in the house in which he lives, where the records and portraits of the Rosmers of Rosmersholm are a constant reminder of the claims of 'duty'. This family of clergymen, civil servants and soldiers has long played a leading part in the neighbourhood and even has its own legend in the form of a local belief in the White Horses of Rosmersholm, apparitions which are seen when a death is imminent in the house.

Such is the outward setting, but the presence of the dead is also felt in a more intimate way. The play is dominated by the memory of Beata, Rosmer's invalid wife who had committed suicide a year previously by throwing herself into the millstream which runs through the garden. It was as companion to Beata that Rebecca first entered the household and when the pressure of circumstance leads to a scrutiny of her motives it becomes clear that she was morally responsible for Beata's death. It was she who insinuated that Beata was a drag on her husband and ultimately that he had fallen in love with her and must be left free to marry her. At the time this was an anticipation. Rosmer did not consciously love Rebecca during his wife's lifetime nor had he yet gone over to the 'progressive' ideas he was later to hold. Rebecca's justification was that she divined the trend of his mind and felt passionately that the man she admired could only find happiness and fulfilment by breaking free from the sterile influences around him. She saw the situation as a battle between 'joy' and the negative austerity of Rosmersholm. But then she herself was an interested party, loving Rosmer. And she had acted, with a premeditation which had driven Beata into the millstream. In the probing of conscience which reveals these things and in which the irresolute Rosmer is also deeply involved, the dead Beata's state of mind assumes crucial importance. Was she half insane and obsessed by sick fancies, as her husband believed? Or had she quite lucidly, impelled by an icy courage which neither of the survivors could match, gone to her death to clear the way for the others? It is this second interpretation which Rosmer and Rebecca come to accept, and finally Rebecca, converted from 'joy' to the 'nobility' of the Rosmer's creed of self-sacrifice, decides to fling herself into the millstream like Beata. Rosmer, with his faith in himself and her restored by her decision, goes with her. They will die together, authentically 'man and wife' at last.

While the ending at least of *Ghosts* was unreservedly tragic, there must be some doubt about *Rosmersholm*. The postulates of the play are impeccable, the psychological exploration undertaken by the characters can only be described as tragic, but the climax is ambiguous. For the school who hold that a true tragedy can end in serenity and reconciliation with a metaphysical law there is no difficulty. But if one requires a tragedy to result in spiritual disaster for the protagonists, there must be some hesitation here. Rebecca believes that she is finally victorious over Beata and all that she represented, though she only becomes so by adopting the Rosmersholm—Beata's—creed of 'anti-joy'. She carries Rosmer with her, completely acquired to herself, and she goes into the water 'gladly', not despairingly.[13] Though the psychology of the whole of this final phase tends to the 'heroic', there is hardly a place here for some exultant flourish of trumpets. But equally obviously, in the minds of the two protagonists, the final comment of the Housekeeper (in the rôle of Chorus) would be unjustified. This simple conventional soul, watching the drama through the window, screams hysterically:

> God forgive the sinful creatures! If they're not putting their arms round each other! Ah! Over the bridge—both of them! Out into the millrace! Help! Help! ... The dead mistress has taken them.

[13] Rosmer's mood is less certain. It seems fairest to conclude that, like Peer Gynt, he has abdicated responsibility and placed his soul in the hands of the Woman:

REBECCA: Do you know, beyond doubt, that this way is best for you?
ROSMER: I know it is the only way.
REBECCA: Suppose you were deceiving yourself? Suppose it was only a delusion? One of these white horses of Rosmersholm?
ROSMER: It might be. For we can never escape them—we of this House.
REBECCA: Then stay, John!
ROSMER: The husband must go with his wife, as the wife with her husband.
(*Rosmersholm*, Act IV, trans. U. Ellis-Fermor, Penguin Books, 1958.)

5

One can safely say that Hedda Gabler 'destroyed herself' as a consequence of actions which she had set in motion and which developed beyond her control; though if one is not entirely convinced of the necessity of those actions or, to adopt the Aristotelian criterion, of their 'high importance', one might not call her end tragic. Oswald Alving in *Ghosts* is undoubtedly destroyed body and soul, through no fault of his own, and the real hero of the play, Mrs Alving, stands before us as spiritually destroyed as a human being can be, though we do not witness the actual consummation. But to claim that either Rebecca or John Rosmer is destroyed would imply an external moral law which Ibsen explicitly writes out of his play. 'There is no judge over us,' says Rosmer, expressing himself like an exemplary existentialist hero. 'And therefore we must see to it that we judge ourselves.'

Before describing the equivocal ending of *Rosmersholm* as a withdrawal from the tragic, it would be well to consider another play in which a comparable ambiguity is used, though to different effect. *The Master Builder* is one of the most interesting of Ibsen's plays, besides being the most immediately modern in the issues it raises. Halvard Solness is, in today's language, a building contractor, self-made and successful, who designs his own houses with the help of a small staff who supply the architectural qualifications which he himself lacks. There are three of them—Knut Brovik, an ex-architect, now old and ill, in whose office the pushing Solness once worked; Brovik's son Ragnar, a talented draughtsman who would like to set up on his own account; and Ragnar's fiancée Kaja, a delicate girl who works as a book-keeper. Solness dominates this necessary backroom personnel by his force of personality, refusing to recognise Ragnar's ability or to allow him to take commissions for fear that he should leave, and complacently encouraging Kaja's timid adoration of himself as another way of binding her and her fiancé to him. He also has a temperamental disposition to pet young girls without becoming seriously involved with them. His half-conscious exploitation of others extends in a subtler form to his wife Aline, an anxiety-ridden woman and a semi-invalid (such as Beata became) who is oppressed by his vitality and has taken refuge in a rigid and cheerless conception of 'duty'. In the past her own family home, in which they both lived, has been burnt down in a fire, enabling

Solness, as though providentially, to divide the site into building-lots and launch himself as a master builder. As another consequence of the fire their twin infant sons died—not in the disaster itself but because Aline conceived it as her duty to breast-feed them after the shock had made her incapable of doing so. They have had no more children.

For all his apparent confidence, Solness has one obsessive fear—of being overtaken and eclipsed by the younger generation. This fear supplies his deeper motive for denying Ragnar's talent and keeping him and Kaja in subservience to himself. If these two break away, others will come storming in too. The middle-aged Master Builder will be crowded out of the picture.

Just when he is confessing his misgivings to the family doctor, a young woman appears out of the blue. She is Hilde Wangel, the daughter of the doctor of the mountain village of Lysanger where Solness once built a church. He has no recollection of her, but she seems to know him well. She quickly brings the past back into focus.

She recalls that when the church at Lysanger was finished, Solness had honoured an old custom by going up the ladders and hanging a wreath on the weathercock which topped the spire. The inhabitants massed below gazed up and cheered, among them a group of school-girls in their white dresses, all carrying flags to mark the occasion.

HILDE: It was so wonderfully exciting to stand down below and look up at you. Suppose he were to overbalance! He—the Master Builder himself!

SOLNESS: Yes, yes, yes, that could quite well have happened, too. For one of those little devils in white—she carried on and screamed up at me so—

HILDE (*her eyes dancing with delight*): 'Hurrah for Mr Solness, the Master Builder!' Yes!

SOLNESS: And flapped and waved her flag so that I—that I was nearly giddy with the sight of it.

HILDE (*more quietly, seriously*): That little devil—that was *me*.

SOLNESS (*fixing his eyes steadily on her*): I'm sure of that now. It must have been you.[14]

After a celebration dinner Solness had been invited to Dr Wangel's house. There, Hilde reminds him, he was alone with her for a few

[14] *The Master Builder*, Act I, trans. U. Ellis-Fermor (Penguin Books, 1958).

minutes. He caught hold of the twelve-year-old girl and kissed her 'many, many times'. He called her his princess and said (playfully as he now half-protests) that in ten years he would come and fetch her and give her a kingdom. The ten years are now up. In hiking clothes, carrying only a knapsack, and with no money in her pocket, Hilde Wangel has left home and come to hold him to his promise.

Her arrival coincides with a crisis in Solness's life. He has reached the masculine turn of age in the, after all, basically physical sense that his forward drive is faltering and he is beginning to go round the curve which will reconnect him with his childhood. One obvious sign of his struggle against this ineluctable process is his morbid fear of the ascendant younger generation. Another, less superficially evident, is in his relations with his wife Aline. He feels instinctively that she is already 'dead', in that she is entirely obsessed by the past, and he resents this drag on his own now questionable vitality. Believing that she was originally broken by the death of their children after the fire, he is bound to her especially tightly by his uneasy conscience, although in fact he did nothing to cause the fire. But he had desired it and, like other successful men who are over-conscious of 'luck', he has come to believe that he has special powers to command the lucky break. So the fire came because he willed it, giving him his chance as a builder, but at the same time destroying the children and Aline's old home—the basis of her life.

The couple live together in a hopeless atmosphere of mutual resentment, suspicion, guilt and solicitousness. Each knows or suspects that the other is ill, each suspects that the other is going mad, or rather—as a worse refinement—suspects that the other believes that *he* is going mad. As an attempt at renewal, Solness has built a brave new house with a tower across the road, into which they will shortly move. It is the artist's offering of his skill and labour to an utterly uninterested partner. For his wife tells him that the new house, with its three empty nurseries as in their present home, will not make one iota of difference to their 'desolate' life. They have really reached an impasse, beautifully rendered by Ibsen, with a psychological realism hardly approached by any earlier European dramatist and which makes Strindberg's domestic hells seem crude in comparison. It is a development beyond the relationship of Rosmer and Beata half sketched-in in *Rosmersholm*. The attempted break-out, through the agency of another woman, is however not dissimilar.

Hilde skilfully grills Mrs Solness. She leads her to talk of her two dead children and makes the spine-chilling discovery that it is not their disappearance which has created the void in her life, but the loss of her family possessions and, most of all, of the 'nine beautiful dolls' which she had 'gone on living with' even after her marriage. One need not look very far to see that these objects symbolised her childhood and the independent personality which she possessed before she was dominated by her husband. Hilde receives the revelation with a mixture of horror and pity. She is confident that she can capture the Master Builder, but at first she decides to go away and leave him to his wife. Then her sanguine youthfulness, her sense of life and 'joy', her 'idealism' and her animal love of 'excitement' reassert themselves and she decides to stay with Solness and help him to build their 'castle in the air'. Solness, at this juncture in his life, is helpless before her. The promise of her love and her contagious energy drive him on to attempt 'the impossible', represented in this case by the challenge of climbing the scaffolding of the new house and hanging the traditional wreath on top of the tower. Solness is constitutionally afraid of heights. What he did at the church at Lysanger was done in a rare moment of exaltation—and he was ten years younger then. But the image of him standing 'free and high up' has remained with Hilde and she wants to see it again before she gives herself to him. He goes up, to the incredulous horror of his wife, who knows his weakness. From the top he waves his hat to the crowd below. Hilde snatches up a white shawl—it is Mrs Solness's—and waves it frantically back, crying: 'Hurrah for the Master Builder!' Other spectators take up the cry and wave handkerchiefs. Solness, seeing them, loses his balance and plunges down to his death.

The play ends with two comments. That of Ragnar, the young draughtsman, is: 'Terrible business. So he couldn't manage it.' That of Hilde, still wild with ecstasy, still waving the shawl, still at heart the same diabolically dangerous nymphet who had screamed at her hero under the tower at Lysanger ten years before, is: 'But he got right to the top. And I heard harps in the air. *My—my* Master Builder!'

Solness's skull is smashed and his comment is missing. We are therefore denied the data on which to decide whether this ending should properly be called tragic or heroic. If Solness's last thought at the moment when he fell was one of despair and Ibsen had somehow contrived to give it to us, there would be the traditional tragic disaster befalling the tragic hero, and no uncertainty. In the absence of comment from Solness we are as much entitled to assume defeat for him as triumph (he reached the top but could not stay there, like Oedipus, like Macbeth—see Fortune's Directory) and the familiar tragic pattern is complete. A crime—no—a sin—no, an example of *hamartia* in the pseudo-Aristotelian sense of a characteristic flaw,[15] which had led a slightly drunk and over-excited Solness to embrace a little girl, has had consequences ten years later which have worked his destruction. In this, some sort of retribution can be descried. Concurrently, his two basic fears—his fear of youth and his fear of heights—have both been realised (the first ironically) and have come together to overwhelm him. It is as neat as *Ghosts* ought to have been, psychologically quite as rich as *Rosmersholm*, and with rather more verisimilitude.

But one remains unconvinced that the whole play can be summed up in such terms. If it could, the part of Hilde Wangel (not to mention that of Mrs Solness) would be purely functional. She would simply be the agent of retribution necessary to bring about the hero's downfall. But she is a credible and well-studied character pursuing a 'dream' which has been maturing in her for ten years and which she realises in action by getting Solness to the top of the scaffolding. When he falls, her dream does not collapse. On the contrary, *her* Solness has validated it more triumphantly and permanently than he could ever have done by tamely climbing down and sleeping with her. One might add, though this is not stressed in the text, that Aline Solness's 'dream'—her anxiety-state, equivalent to an unlocalised apprehension of impending disaster—is realised equally by the same event.

In these circumstances it becomes less important to know the final state of Solness's mind. Indeed it is better not to know it, for *The Master Builder*, like other plays of Ibsen's, seems after all to be something other than the drama of a conventional tragic hero. Solness's function is more nearly that of a prism in which two images of human nature in general, as well as of his particular character, are reflected. These images are projected by external characters (Hilde Wangel and Mrs Solness) whose divergent views of both him and the human condition compose the ideological pattern of the play. Admittedly they influence him also, in the same

[15] Devotees of *hubris* could fit this in also here.

way as John Rosmer was influenced by both the Rosmersholm (or Beata's) view and Rebecca's. They are different, contrasting, and indeed conflicting in the sense that no man could satisfy both of them in his actual life. But they are not represented as the cause of a duality conflict, a tearing-apart, *within Solness himself*. Whatever conflict there is in him is between his now flagging vitality and confidence and the impulse to transcend them renewed by the proximity of a young woman. As has been said, this is fundamentally a physical struggle set up by the inevitable process of ageing. Normally and traditionally, this process has always invited comic treatment. With very skilful handling it can be made pathetic. Perhaps the only tragedy in which it is exploited beyond pathos is *King Lear*, but there the circumstances and development are so different that no comparison with *The Master Builder* is possible. One must conclude that in Ibsen's drama the disparity between age and youth is not realised with sufficient intensity by Solness or pinpointed with sufficient concentration by the dramatist to provide a field for a clash between two worlds.

6

It seems important to make a distinction between the two forms which the duality factor takes in Ibsen's drama. One is the contrast between psychological reality and 'idealism' seen as a fraud or a delusion. Such is the idealism of Gregers Werle in *The Wild Duck*, of the father in *Little Eyolf*, and no doubt of Lövborg in *Hedda Gabler* and of Ulrik Brendel in *Rosmersholm*. Each of these characters harbours mistaken or unrealisable images which bring misfortune to themselves and those whom they influence. Theirs is broadly the Peer Gyntian imagination which Ibsen the anti-Romantic still deflates from time to time. Elsewhere, however, the dichotomy is between the young, the new, the free, the daring (symbolised by Paris in *Ghosts*, by America in *Pillars of Society*) on one hand, and the old, the narrow, the canny and the conventional on the other: in short, between the promise of the expanding future and the influence of the restrictive past. This is the progressive Ibsen, impatient of provincialism in mind and manners but never unaware of its tremendous subterranean strength. It manifests itself in social reaction (*Pillars of Society*, *An Enemy of the People*), but also has a much wider and deeper significance.

If the urge to break free of the past is called idealism, then Ibsen himself cannot be acquitted of it. But this sort of idealism is not the Romantic longing for the 'infinite' or the 'impossible'. In essence it is the natural impatience of the sanguine and the youthful-minded when confronted with their opposites. In action it pursues objects which are perfectly attainable in a finite sphere. Not perhaps for every character. Because of his inherited disease Oswald Alving can never lead the free, creative life which he has tasted in Paris. But others can, and there is no general bar. Erhart, in *John Gabriel Borkman*, escapes towards his individual happiness, leaving the dead and the half-dead to bury themselves. Lona Hessel, in *Pillars of Society*, brings the freedom and openness of the New World to her hypocritical brother-in-law and it frees him. When reaction is explicitly ascribed to a community, revolt against it may be condemned by some of the characters as 'idealistic', but it is not shown as futile. On occasion it succeeds, through the reforming efforts of certain sincere and clear-sighted individuals of the contrary persuasion.

All this has a bearing on the Romantic assumptions, no less than on other assumptions which figure in the sociological analysis of tragedy. Society for Ibsen is not monolithic. It is not conceived as some anonymous or unanimist force against which the individual must struggle in order to affirm himself.[16] It is a collection of people holding certain views and convictions and is amenable or reformable through its component members. Among other consequences, it cannot therefore be a substitute for God who, being absolute, is beyond reform. Neither is there a metaphysical God in Ibsen's works, at least after *Peer Gynt*. There are fugitive references to the supernatural—the God of churches and the ministering spirits of the Master Builder, the earth spirits of John Gabriel Borkman, even the white horses of Rosmersholm—but all these are represented as the subjective emanations of individual characters and not the manifestations of some cosmic force. There is no supernatural power in Ibsen, while the community, though it can sometimes be formidable, possesses no particular mystique. The whole power, to use Blake's language, resides in the human breast. The whole interest of the

---

[16] The Great Boyg (*Peer Gynt*, Act II, Sc. 7) is the only force in Ibsen's plays which at all corresponds to this description. But whatever symbolism is attached to the slimy, shapeless mass of the Boyg, which cannot be fought, penetrated, or discerned in outline, it is certainly not Society.

plays consists in the exploration of what lies *there*, but—and this seems to be the chief difference—with no desire to give it a transcendent significance.

Is this a tragic exploration? If one insists that tragedy should transcend nature, presumably it is not. But that condition, as we have pointed out, is not indispensable. Does it bear on questions which are too trivial to be given tragic status? The fact that it deals with the domestic and the familiar as these figured in contemporary life cannot be allowed to disqualify it on any reasonable view. In that context the issues are by no means trivial. In fact on the modern stage they and the characters involved in them sometimes appear a little larger than life. Why should there be any hesitation in describing Ibsen as a tragic dramatist and his plays as tragedies of the only type which could authentically express the spirit of his time?

The present writer accepts them as such—some of them—and subscribes to the view that any general account of tragic drama must include Ibsen alongside the major names from Aeschylus onwards. There is only one serious qualification to be made. It bears neither on the quasi-colloquial nature of the prose dialogue[17] nor on the melodramatic strokes which often occur,[18] but on the difficulty of entirely squaring Ibsen's plays with any definition of the tragic, including that put forward in this book. We suggested (p. 20 above) that 'a tragedy is a final and impressive disaster due to an unforeseen or unrealised failure involving people who command respect and sympathy'. The questionable terms are of course *disaster* and *failure*. We have already discussed the ambiguity of the climactic event in certain plays. In *Hedda Gabler* and *Ghosts* it seems wholly disastrous; in *Rosmersholm* and *The Master Builder* it may not be. Again, similar dramatic elements are used to yield different results. *Pillars of Society* contains several of the same general postulates as *The Master Builder*, yet ends on an openly hopeful note and is never a tragedy. Events which can be called finally disastrous for certain characters, such as the children in *The Wild Duck* and *Little Eyolf*, are not so for other

[17] One can safely dismiss Aristotle's 'language enhanced by distinct and varying beauties' (see above, p. 28) as an artistic but not basic condition. Or, if thought necessary, one could easily make the case that Ibsen's verbal skill does in fact satisfy the requirement.

[18] Since the nineteenth century was the great age of melodrama, Ibsen would be unrepresentative if he were free of it. Beyond that, the melodramatic elements are always subservient to the general design, as in Sophocles, as in Shakespeare, and are never introduced to remedy faulty plotting.

characters of at least equal importance. These somehow patch their lives up, or appear likely to do so.

The doubtful scope of the disaster affects the notion of failure. One can generally find a failure—her marriage to Tesman for Hedda Gabler, the father's 'fault' for the Alvings, or alternately the mother's concealment of it, Rebecca's passion in *Rosmersholm*, Solness' tendency to exploit others, and so on. But it becomes a somewhat academic exercise if one is either uncertain whether the consequences really were 'tragic' or unconvinced that the failure, when defined, is a particularly significant factor in the play.

The effect of holding that 'all deities reside in the human breast' and so of siting all power within the human psyche, while also rejecting the mystique of a collective power vested in the community, is to destroy the notion of an external authority, and with it that of any general law or sanction. Each man, as Rosmer said, judges himself—or else he submits consciously to the judgment of other individuals.

In this predominantly 'psychological' drama, in which the characters are engaged in examinations of their actions and motives which the situation invented by the playwright (the 'plot' in the simplest sense) has made it vital for them to try to understand, the only moral values consistently invoked are 'truth' and 'freedom'. It is all very well to say that we know what is meant by these, and even broadly what Ibsen meant by them, yet even in the context of his plays they are not presented as norms. 'Freedom' for Hedda Gabler is something quite different from the 'freedom' of Lona Hessel. While it is true that the posulated existence of a fixed moral law based upon absolutes and merely awaiting discovery would be untragic, it is also true that the denial of any such law almost removes the possibility of a tragic recognition, or makes it relative and personal in each separate case. Ibsen tends to avoid the recognition altogether, particularly in those cases in which, if we harbour moral preoccupations, we most feel its necessity. The only significant verdict would be that which the character pronounces upon himself, but we are left to guess what it is.

In the world which Ibsen's characters inhabit, this omission is not wanton but realistic. Who, working without external terms of reference, will condemn himself absolutely? Who will be absolutely sure of his own rightness? We thus have an undoubtedly tragic exploration, bearing on matters of spiritual life and death, which does not lead to the tragic discovery to which earlier dramatists had accustomed us. In that case Ibsen would be incompletely tragic by universal standards, though as tragic as was possible in the context of nineteenth-century realism.

Less favourable judgments can be passed on him. From a Marxist point of view, he is a bourgeois individualist. (Perhaps one day this will be accepted as a precise critical definition and not as a term of abuse.) As a dramatic innovator, he has inspired an inordinate number of those psychological or moral problem plays typical of the West European stage in the early twentieth century. Pirandello descends in part from him, though his concept of the fragmented personality was not Ibsen's. Some of his titles—*Così è, se vi pare* (*That's how it is, if you think so*), or *Ciascuno a suo modo* (*Each in his own way*)—would serve perfectly to head parodies of Ibsen's dramas. Much later, Sartre boldly exploited the well-proved technique in such plays as *Huis-Clos* and *Les Mains Sales*, in which past events are scrutinised in the light of the characters' motives and their motives are scrutinised by other characters until a truth of some kind emerges.

At its lowest, particularly in the first decade of this century, this relativity, which for Ibsen was based on serious psychological observation, was developed as a dramatic trick to provide audiences with talking-points. Instead of stunning them into silence, which is surely the effect of great drama, the theatre set puzzles to which intelligent people were invited to find the answers. A whole mass of dead plays revolving round now discarded problems of social or personal morality, or based on outdated notions of psychology, clutter the secondhand bookshops with small hope of resurrection even on the radio.

One cannot condemn all this out of hand. Much of it is spurious, but here and there, even in the most contrived plays, is an issue, a character, or an insight which deserves to be taken seriously. All critics have experienced the same real difficulty in deciding what happened to dramatic tragedy in the present century. Merely to say that it died is unsatisfactory. No doubt it did die as a single body, in the form of the works of any one dramatist or even any one complete play, but the tragic elements were still alive. They can be discerned in a great number of 'serious' dramas, more adulterated than in Ibsen, but still capable and worthy of evoking the kind of response which we have agreed to call tragic. To detect them one must obviously sacrifice Aristotle's requirement of (artistic) unity, but that was

213

already done by the Elizabethans, and there is no reason why their example should not still hold good.

7

The tragic in comedy: Chekhov

In considering Ibsen and his successors, we conclude that the tragic can be present in 'drama' and even melodrama. We must go on to inquire whether it can be found in comedy, which might be another of the forms or disguises which it takes. The obvious test-case is Chekhov.

Chekhov was absorbed, and in his three great mature plays succeeded, in perfecting a new dramatic idiom. The result was a late and perhaps the finest achievement of realism, inspired by the same intentions (however different the effect) as Flaubert's, Maupassant's and, in part, Ibsen's; all of whom sought to render contemporary characters and their preoccupations on the same scale as 'life'. Chekhov accomplished this not only by the conversationally 'natural' dialogue, but by the whole treatment of emotion. Besides expressing their feelings with restraint, mis-stating them, or throwing them away, his characters are sometimes denied the opportunity of 'realising' them at all. The action—to borrow a term from conventional drama for want of a better—turns away from the developing situation just at the point where the traditional dramatic craftsman would be shaping to exploit it, and in place of a confrontation we are given a diversion. The only previous example of a comparable technique, if it may so be called, which comes readily to mind is in the last act of *Macbeth*:

SEYTON: The Queen, my lord, is dead.
MACBETH: She should have died hereafter.

And even here the preoccupied Macbeth allows himself a few lines of general moralising by way of a requiem for his great partner in crime.

Chekhov conceived his later plays as comedies—not just 'high' but 'funny' comedies. He described even *The Seagull* as 'a comedy' while working on it. After finishing *Three Sisters* he wrote in a mood of apparent disappointment that the play had turned out to be 'dreary, long, and awkward . . . [with] a spirit more gloomy than gloom itself, as the saying goes'. His last play, *The Cherry Orchard*, was conceived as a light comedy, 'definitely funny, very funny—at least in intention'.[19] When complete, he wrote: 'It has turned out, not a drama but a comedy, in parts, indeed, a farce, and I am afraid I shall catch it from Vladimir Ivanich.'[20]

These surprising statements have never been accepted by producers or critics at quite their face value. But they are quoted here in support of the view that, if a classification has to be made, *Uncle Vanya*, *Three Sisters*, and *The Cherry Orchard* should be considered as comedies, though not necessarily of the laughable kind. The Chekhovian atmosphere, the unique Chekhovian lightness, need not be re-discussed, except insofar as it affects themes generally thought proper to tragedy. Among these are: the final extinction of a well-loved way of life, unrequited love, definitive parting of lovers, definitive frustration of hope.

It would be possible for a playwright to burlesque such themes, or to give them the sharper treatment of angry mockery, in either case reacting consciously against their tragic potentialities. This is not Chekhov's way, in spite of his declared intention to be 'funny'. Instead, he scales them down to what he considered to be life size, with an effect which can be instantly perceived but is much more difficult to analyse.

The confession of her passion by Phaedra, first to the Nurse (Euripides and Racine), then to Hippolytus himself (Racine only), is given full dramatic weight, as befits an essential part of the tragic machine which it accelerates towards the catastrophe. But when Chekhov's Sonia in *Uncle Vanya* makes some timid attempts to reveal to the doctor Astrov the love which is eating away her whole life, they are not even noticed by him. And when the matter is put plainly to him by Sonia's stepmother Yeliena (performing the same function as the Nurse in Euripides' *Hippolytus*), he still preserves his indifference:

YELIENA: . . . I want to put you through a little interrogation, and
    I feel rather embarrassed, I don't know how to begin.
ASTROV: An interrogation?

[19] The last two quotations (from Chekhov's letters) are taken from Elisaveta Fen's excellent introduction to her translation of the plays (Penguin Books, 1959). Passages from the plays quoted in this chapter are from the same translation.
[20] Nemorivich-Danchenko, co-founder with Stanislavsky of the Moscow Art Theatre. The quotation is from a letter of 15 September 1903 to Madame Stanislavsky, in L. S. Friedland (ed.), *Letters on Literature by Anton Chekhov* (Geoffrey Bles, 1924).

YELIENA: Yes, an interrogation, but ... a fairly innocent one. Let's sit down. (*They sit down.*) It concerns a certain young person. We'll talk frankly, like friends, without beating about the bush. We'll talk it over and forget everything we said. Agreed?

ASTROV: Agreed.

YELIENA: The matter concerns my stepdaughter, Sonia. Tell me, do you like her?

ASTROV: Yes, I respect her.

YELIENA: Do you like her as a woman?

ASTROV (*after a brief pause*): No.

YELIENA: One thing more—and that'll be the end. Have you noticed anything?

ASTROV: Nothing.

YELIENA (*taking him by the hand*): You don't love her, I see it from your eyes ... She is suffering ... Understand that, and ... stop coming here.

ASTROV (*rises*): My time is past ... Besides, I've got too much to do ... (*Shrugging his shoulders.*) When could I find time? (*He is embarrassed.*)

YELIENA: Ough! What an unpleasant conversation! I feel as though I've been carrying a ton weight about. Anyway, we've finished now, thank heaven! Let's forget it, as if we hadn't talked at all ... and go away.[21]

The situation is of course different from that in Euripides and Racine. Hippolytus had every reason to feel outraged by a declaration of love from one particular quarter, Astrov has none. Phaedra is 'guilty', Sonia is not. But one thing at least is the same: the happiness of both women is staked and lost in the confession scene. The treatment of this important factor could hardly be more different.[22]

A second parallel is perhaps even more telling. Masha, in *Three Sisters*, has fallen in love with the quiet and philosophical Colonel Vershinin, who returns her love. Both are married to partners with whom they are unhappy, but it never occurs to either of them to make a positive move towards happiness, perhaps because of human feeling towards their present partners, perhaps through acquiescence

[21] *Uncle Vanya*, Act III, trans. Elisaveta Fen, *op. cit.*

[22] At the time *Ivanov* was written Chekhov told his friends:
Let the things that happen on the stage be as complex and yet as simple as they are in life. For instance, people are having a meal at the table, just having a meal, but at the same time their happiness is being created, or their lives are being smashed up. (Elisaveta Fen, *op. cit.*, p. 19.)

in a social situation which they feel to be unchangeable. But while acquiescing, Masha feels an irresistible urge to confess, to unburden herself somehow in words. She is with Olga and Irena in their shared bedroom:

MASHA: My dear sisters, I've got something to confess to you. I must get some relief. I feel the need of it in my heart. I'll confess it to you two alone, and then never again, never to anybody! I'll tell you in a minute. (*In a low voice.*) It's a secret, but you'll have to know everything. I can't keep silent any more. (*A pause.*) I'm in love, in love . . . I love that man . . . You saw him here just now . . . Well, what's the good? . . . I love Vershinin . . .

OLGA (*goes behind her screen*): Don't say it. I don't want to hear it.

MASHA: Well, what's to be done? (*Holding her head.*) I thought he was queer at first, then I started to pity him . . . then I began to love him . . . love everything about him—his voice, his misfortunes, his two little girls . . .

OLGA: Nevertheless, I don't want to hear it. You can say any nonsense you like, I'm not listening.

MASHA: Oh, you're stupid, Olga! If I love him, well—that's my fate! That's my destiny . . . He loves me, too. It's all rather frightening isn't it? Not a good thing, is it? . . .[23]

In spite of the different circumstances, the main elements are the same as in Phèdre's confession to Oenone. At first Phèdre cannot bring herself to speak out and it is the Nurse who provokes the psychologically necessary unburdening. To that extent the roles of Oenone and Masha's sisters diverge, but Oenone's exclamation of horror parallel Olga's: 'I don't want to hear it.'

There is the same hesitation to utter the loved one's name:

OENONE: You are in love?
PHÈDRE: Love's furies rage in me.
OENONE: For whom?
PHÈDRE: Prepare to hear the crowning woe.
I love . . . I tremble, shudder at the name.
I love . . .
OENONE: Whom?
PHÈDRE: You know that prince whom I myself
So long oppressed, son of the Amazon?

[23] *Three Sisters*, Act III, translation cited.

217

OENONE: Hippolytus!
PHÈDRE: *You* have pronounced his name.[24]

Racine followed Euripides in reproducing this attempted transference of the guilt of revelation from Phèdre to the Nurse, with
undoubted dramatic effectiveness. But it may be thought that Masha's
simple, unprompted: 'I'm in love. I love that man ... You saw him
here just now ... Well, what's the good? I love *Vershinin*,' has a
truer ring. Finally, the gist of what Phèdre has to say in her next great
tirade, and indeed in the rest of the tragedy, might well be summed up
in Masha's: 'That's my destiny ... It's all rather frightening, isn't it?
Not a good thing, is it?'

But how inadequate such language would be to express the reactions of Racine's queen as the passionate creature writhes in torment
before gods and men, lashed on by Venus towards the precipice,
surrounded by a hostile universe of the dead and the living, with her
own terrible husband at the end of the road.

Masha's husband Koolyghin is far from terrible. He is a simple,
unexciting soul of the same human category as Hedda Gabler's
Tesman, but with more sympathy for his wife. When Vershinin's
regiment is moved from the town and Masha has said her last good-
bye to him, she breaks into sobs which she cannot control when her
husband happens to come in. It does not much matter, since Koolyghin is aware of the situation. With touching clumsiness he tries to
cover his embarrassment and reassure his wife:

KOOLYGHIN: Never mind, let her cry, let her ... My dear Masha,
my dear, sweet Masha ... You're my wife, and I'm happy in
spite of everything ... I'm not complaining, I've no reproach
to make—not a single one ... Olga here is my witness ...
We'll start our life over again in the same old way, and you
won't hear a word from me ... not a hint ...
MASHA (*suppressing her sobs*): 'A green oak grows by a curving
shore, And round that oak hangs a golden chain... A
golden chain round that oak.' ... Oh, I'm going mad ... By
a curving shore ... a green oak ...
OLGA: Calm yourself, Masha, calm yourself ... Give her some
water.
MASHA: I'm not crying any more ...
KOOLYGHIN: She's not crying any more ... she's a good girl.[25]

[24] *Phèdre*, Act I, Sc. 3, trans. John Cairncross, in *Racine: Phaedra and
Other Plays* (Penguin Books, 1963).
[25] *Three Sisters*, Act IV, translation cited.

But she does cry again and in a further effort to comfort her Koolyghin takes out a false beard which he has confiscated from one of his boys (he is a schoolmaster) and puts it on in the hope of making her laugh.

The mind reels at the thought of the adjustments necessary before Thésée could be shown making some similar gesture to console the desolate Phèdre. It would only be practicable in the form of burlesque amounting to anti-tragedy. And in this one particular it could just conceivably be argued that Chekhov has achieved a stroke of 'funny' comedy which makes any search for the tragic unreal. But, even if that were conceded, none of the rest is by any stretch of interpretation laughable. It is moving, and more immediately so, it may be thought, than almost anything in the acknowledged masters of tragedy.

Part of the immediacy is in the language, which registers directly, particularly on a modern audience, because of its 'naturalness'. But this language merely contributes to render an angle of vision which is absolutely level from author to characters and from audience to characters. The effect of seeing the characters from neither above or below, which incidentally precludes the passing of value judgments upon them, is to strengthen enormously the line of sympathy between them and the spectator. Sympathy, as we have seen, is necessary to provoke the tragic reaction, but in itself it is not enough unless it is accompanied by some form of admiration or respect. This is a demand which Chekhov's characters do not make. They do not even admire each other. Unlike Ibsen's characters, they form no heightened images of other people, even—an extraordinary feature—when they are in love with them.[26] Likeable, even lovable, as some of these characters certainly are, they remain 'ordinary' in the sense discussed earlier in this book.[27] And they are not raised to tragic stature—as they still could be in spite of the familiarity of the dialogue—by the nature of the events in which they are engaged. They are not seen,

[26] These considerations, like the rest of this analysis, apply fully only to *Uncle Vanya*, *Three Sisters*, and *The Cherry Orchard*. In *The Seagull*, an earlier play, there is some idealisation of Trigorin by Nina and of Nina by Trepliov. The frustrated Trepliov shoots himself, meeting what might reasonably be represented as a tragic death. But in the three mature plays, any tendency to form an idealised image (of the Professor by Uncle Vanya, of Andrey by his sisters, of Natasha by Andrey) is reversed in the course of the play; and the reversal does not come as a climax—in which case it might have constituted a 'recognition'.
[27] See above, p. 18.

and do not see themselves, as participants in serious bids for happiness or power. They know that they are unhappy and look back nostalgically to the past (the Three Sisters to their childhood in Moscow, Ranyevskaia to her childhood home with its cherry orchard) or to the future beyond their actual lives (the better Russia of Astrov, Vershinin, and Trofimov, the spiritual rest beyond the grave of Sonia), but none of these Other Worlds is so ardently desired as to set up a tragic dichotomy. They fail, yes, though it would be truer to say that, with a few exceptions, they already have a sense of failure when the plays open and simply resign themselves to it as the action proceeds. They have some of the fatalism of the characters of *Candide*, who counted disasters as too common to be taken seriously. Their sense of proportion is too developed for them to experience the shock of a tragic fall in disappointments which are regarded as the normal lot of humanity. These disappointments, as already suggested, occur mainly in love and marriage when they can be localised at all. Love is a promising tragic theme when experienced passionately, but when it is played cool it is questionably so. One must look at the dénouement before one can decide, and one finds that, after Trepliov's death in *The Seagull*, there are no conclusive disasters. One cannot say that any lives are irrevocably destroyed.[28] The characters seem geared to go on living somehow, and it is quite possible to imagine them experiencing phases of mild happiness in the future. 'Futility' is a word often used to describe their existences. It is perhaps too strong. 'Waste' is nearer the mark. But to speak of 'tragic waste' would imply that there was an apparently realisable alternative. Could they have hoped to achieve it by living their lives differently? An answer can only be given in qualified or neutral terms. Everything went a little wrong, but nothing resoundingly so. Nor could it be said that the world was conspicuously hostile. The

[28] There are two other deaths, actual or foreshadowed, in the last three plays. Toozenbach (*Three Sisters*), who is killed in a duel off-stage, is a somewhat minor character whose fate could never reach tragic proportions in itself. As for its effects, Irena has already made it clear that she does not love him and his sudden death on the eve of their marriage does not ruin her life. She was to have gone away with him in search of a new life. She decides to go away just the same, but alone, and devote herself to working for other people. The manservant Firs, whose last appearance in the deserted house provides the poignant ending of *The Cherry Orchard*, embodies the passing of an old way of life. It peters out in a pathetic senile muttering. If Firs were Lear or Liubov Andryeevna's home were Troy, all this would be differently conceived and would make a different impact.

sociologist can easily show that Czarist Russia was out-of-joint for the upper middle classes—though how much more so for the proletariat! But Chekhov's plays, read without the application of hindsight, do not necessarily give that social impression. One can just as well read into them the climate of an Edwardian afternoon, tinged with a not entirely disagreeable melancholy and spiced with bitter-sweet love-affairs which at least have the merit of relieving the tedium.

The inhabitants of the Chekhovian world are governed psychologically by Blake's law of the Philosophical and the Experimental.[29] Subject to what he called the Ratio between reason and sensation, they are 'unable to do other than repeat the same dull round over and over again'. They cannot break out by means of the Poetic Genius, or Imagination, which they do not possess to a sufficient degree for it to become an instrument of either salvation or destruction.[30] A realist writer, reacting against this essential quality of Romanticism, could not have endowed his characters with it. Alternately, the Pascalian escape through the Divine Order is never in question. Religion only figures as a conventional or a consolatory factor, lacking drive. Not only is there no way out, but the will to find one is enfeebled. The zest for either conflict or discovery is diminished to below the tragic level.

It would be tedious to say more in support of the view that Chekhov's great plays are comedies, or any way not tragedies. Anyone who reads them or sees sufficiently sensitive productions of them can reach similar conclusions without consciously troubling about dramatic categories. But if categories are required, there is a rational basis, which we have tried to indicate, for classing Chekhov's genius as comic. In perfecting realistic comedy he also proved that integral realism need not be drab, while whether it is ultimately 'pessimistic' depends on a point of view. It surrounds the human condition with certain limits which are too quickly reached and explored for there to be a scope for tragic curiosity, exercised in either expectation or apprehension. The *plus ultra* of both metaphysics and depth psychology is not there. It is still possible to praise Flaubert, and still more

[29] See above, p. 175.
[30] This is the significance of Masha's repetition of the lines of verse which haunt her: 'A green oak grows by a curving shore, etc.' (see p. 218 above). This instinctive attempt at a break-out through poetry is followed by the comment: 'Oh, I'm going mad,' and then by the willed attempt to control herself. Madness would be another kind of break-out, almost inevitably tragic, but she is determined to stay in the 'real' world.

Ibsen, for their 'power of suggestion'. To Chekhov, after *The Seagull* (in which the symbolism—the invitation to seek ulterior meanings—is half-hearted and ineffective) the phrase is inapplicable. His world becomes non-tragic because it is recognisably self-contained.[31]

These considerations do not, of course, rule out the possibility of a tragedy of 'ordinary' lives in contemporary settings. They do not affect the tragic potentialities of 'a man like ourselves' in any general sense. It is simply the particular author's line of vision which determines the implications of the material.

---

[31] All this, and particularly the inability to do otherwise than 'repeat the same dull round over and over again', would seem to apply with still greater force to Beckett's *Waiting for Godot*, considered in Chapter 12 below. But what saves that play from being classed unequivocally as a comedy is the hint of grace and the possible intervention of Godot who, whatever he represents, is outside the world of the characters on the stage.

IV

Twentieth-century Positions

11

Claudel: 'Partage de Midi'

1

What happened to the Tragic Muse in the twentieth century? Not her least memorable adventure was that she fell into the hands of philosophers. While this might seem to be a return to a very ancient position, there was a wide difference between the Aristotelian approach and that of more modern philosophy and near-philosophy. The former, if tending to be dry and pedantic, had the merit of working within well-defined limits, but the latter recognised no boundaries short of the totality of the human condition, enlarged as this now was by the ambitious assumptions of Romanticism; for most recent commentators on tragedy, from Nietzsche onwards, have been so profoundly conditioned by the Romantic *Weltanschauung*, even when claiming to react against it, that a partial or analytic approach to tragedy, as to any other subject with a high seriousness content, has ceased to be usual. Aristotle's stipulation that 'we should not try to get all sorts of pleasure from tragedy, but the particular tragic pleasure'[1] has been made to look far too restrictive, even if one stretches 'pleasure' to include pain, and the Tragic Muse has been forced into psychological and metaphysical situations which have gravely compromised her integrity.

These theoretical speculations on tragedy contrast with the relatively simple and definite concept of the untutored average mind, discussed in the first chapter of this book. They are also considerably bolder and less precise than the practice of modern dramatists, who should be regarded as skilled workers at grips with the problems of

[1] *Poetics*, Ch. 14.

225

expressing in artistic form an image of the human condition recognisable by a reasonably high proportion of their contemporaries. Hence a certain restraint, bred of professional experience of what can be effectively communicated and what cannot. No modern writer has been able to renew the vast achievement of Goethe's *Faust*, which just succeeded in bestriding the two domains—thanks to the particular genius of its author and the special conditions of its period. The writer we are about to consider perhaps came nearest to it in his most ambitious work, *Le Soulier de Satin*, though this cannot be claimed as a triumph of communication or, in the same degree as *Faust*, as a centrally positioned expression of the spirit of an age.

Numerous other twentieth-century writers might be investigated in a search for tragic features and the fact that we leave so many unmentioned should not be thought to imply that they have no tragic significance. This book is not intended as an exhaustive study of the tragic literature of any one period. It may prove more illuminating, in this and the following chapter, to consider two single plays which exemplify two violently contrasted types of drama. Neither is a pure tragedy, but both yield some answers to the questions we are asking about modern conceptions of the tragic.

2

Paul Claudel's play, *Partage de Midi* (*The Divide of Noon*) is concerned primarily with the two themes of religious vocation and passionate human love. If it centred on a conflict between them it could be plainly described as an application of the nineteenth-century idea of a tragic duality to a pre-Romantic situation in which the carnal order is opposed to the divine in its full supernatural sense. If, on the other hand, it contained an ultimate summation of sensual and divine love there would be a resolution of the Romantic conflict in the concept of Woman as the Redeemer and a direct development of the theme of *Faust*, Part II, and of all the lesser versions of transcendent Donjuanism. Both these things are in *Partage de Midi*, but it is not clear that either of them dominates. If it were the first, leaving the conflict unresolved, it would be a clear case of tragedy. If the second, culminating in a mystical reconciliation, it would not, narrowly speaking, be tragic. Or it might possibly qualify as one of the very few true tragedies which end 'happily', though only after a metamorphosis of the protagonists.

Claudel aims at this reconciliation, while making it, in the original version of his play, as difficult as possible and ending with an element of ambiguity which, in spite of his Catholic abhorrence of Ibsen and all he stood for, reminds one of that dramatist. The ambiguity is inherent in the imperfectly coordinated images of themselves, each other, and the cosmos entertained by the two principal characters.

Partage de Midi was first published in 1906 in a limited edition intended for private circulation.[2] It was based on a personal experience of the author, then serving as a consular official in China. The original version can be summarised thus:

Act I. The four characters of the play form a group on board a liner, steaming slowly across the Indian Ocean on its outward journey from Marseilles. The principal character, Mesa, is a Frenchman returning from a period of leave to China, where he holds an influential 'advisory' post. Ysé, the only woman of the quartet, is a 'foreigner', conceivably Polish, vivacious and unsatisfied. She is travelling with her children and her husband, De Ciz. The latter is an ingratiating opportunist who is taking his family to China in the hope of picking up a lucrative living there. The fourth member of the group is Amalric, a tough, blunt adventurer of a different mould, also going east in search of a quick fortune. He has known Ysé in the past and would like to become her lover. The period is evidently the eighteen-nineties, in a late but blatant stage of individualistic colonial adventurism.

Mesa, an administrator rather than a businessman, has been passing through a deep religious crisis. He has heard 'the call of God', but when he tried to respond to it by offering himself, he was met by absolute silence and blankness. He is returning hopelessly to China to take up the old life again, 'with no other expectation than God, who will not have me'. Now his path crosses Ysé's and both feel, with trepidation, that there is something fateful about the meeting.

[2] Edition of the *Bibliothèque de l'Orient*, limited to 150 copies. Principal later editions of this version: (1) *Mercure de France* edition, with new preface by Claudel, 1948, (2) Gallimard edition, 1949, (3) In *Pléiade* edition: Paul Claudel, *Théâtre*, Vol. I, 1947.

Claudel's own final version ('*nouvelle version pour la scène*') was published separately in 1949 (Gallimard). The *Oeuvres Complètes de Paul Claudel*, Vol. XI (Gallimard, 1957) contains both the original and final versions and also the intermediate acting version used by J.-L. Barrault in 1948. Containing also discarded variants and relevant correspondence, it is the edition in which to study the development of the play in Claudel's mind. Page references in this chapter are to this edition.

Act II. The characters have reached China. Amalric has gone off on his own business and does not appear in this act. The scene is the Happy Valley cemetery at Hongkong, where, among the English and Chinese tombs and under a grey sky full of boding, Mesa has arranged a meeting with Ysé. He sees himself as a gambler about to stake his soul. When Ysé comes, the two experience a physically passionate recognition of each other, into which also enters—to use language appropriate to the dialogue—the feeling that they are soul-mates. Ysé's husband is cunningly sent off by Mesa on a mission which could result in his death.

Act III. The scene is the interior of a house in another Chinese port. A local massacre of the Europeans is in progress and the windows are barricaded. Inside are Ysé and Amalric. In the interval Ysé's husband has disappeared—he proves later to have died—and after living with Mesa for a time she has left him for Amalric, who combines practical strength with a disarmingly direct human affection. The couple's situation is hopeless. While, in the next room, the child which Ysé has borne to Mesa cries fretfully, Amalric expertly sets up a time-bomb. The mob will not attack them until the next day and before that they will have blown themselves to pieces with all their household possessions.

While Amalric is out of the room, Mesa reappears. He bitterly reproaches Ysé for deserting him and leaving his letters unanswered. Amalric returns and the two men fight. Mesa is seriously injured and knocked unconscious. In his pocket they find the Chinese safe-conduct which he has used to reach them. They can use it to escape themselves. 'Fetch the child,' says Amalric. But the child, already very ill, has died. It is impossible to take the inert Mesa with them. They place his body on a sofa, to be blown up when the bomb explodes, and go out guiltily to find the boat which brought him to them.

Mesa recovers consciousness. In a long and moving meditation (the *Cantique de Mesa*) he interrogates God, who has sent the Woman to teach him what a terrible thing love is—the agony of total desire—and finally to betray him. He compares his suffering with that of Christ on the cross. But enough is enough. He recognises his sinfulness and his nothingness. Now let his soul leave his broken body and be taken back by the Father.

At this point Ysé returns. She has slipped away from Amalric and come back to die with Mesa when the bomb explodes. 'Love' has triumphed after all. Broadly, it is sensual love transformed into spiritual love, but not conceived as a comfortable union in some romantic afterglow. There is at least a hint of purgatory to be faced and Claudel makes it clear that if there is to be a marriage of souls it will not in any way be an extension of a marriage of bodies. The tone and intention of the climax can best be conveyed by quotation from the closing 'duet' between the two protagonists.

YSÉ: And now look at my face while there is still time,
And see me standing at my full height like a great olive-tree in the beams of the earthly moon which lights the night,
And stamp your mind with this mortal face, for the time of our dissolution draws near and you will never see me again with the eyes of the body.
I hear you and do not hear you, for already my ears fail me. Do not be silent, my belovèd, you are there!
Only give me the note, that I may flow out, and hear myself with my own golden sound for ears
Beginning, welling up like a pure song and a true voice answering your voice, better than brass and the ass's skin of the drum.
I have been the flesh which yields beneath you and like a horse between your knees, like a beast which is driven on not by reason,
Like a horse going wherever you turn its head, like a horse bolting, faster and farther than you intend.
See her now at full stretch, Mesa, the woman full of beauty extended in the greatest beauty of all!
... Follow me, delay no more!
Great God! Here I am, laughing, rolling, unrooted, with my back on the very sustenance of light as though on a wing beneath the wave!
O Mesa, this is the divide of midnight, and I am here, ready to be set free.
Giving you for the last time the sign of my long hair unleashed in the wind of Death!

MESA: Farewell, I have seen you for the last time!
By what long, difficult roads,
Far distant yet always bearing upon each other,
Are we to lead our labouring souls?
Remember, Ysé, remember the sign!
And mine is not hair vainly tossed in the storm, the little handkerchief waved for a moment,

229

> But with all veils cast aside, myself, the strong and fiery
> flame, the great male in the glory of God,
> Man in the splendour of August, the Spirit victorious in
> the transfiguration of Noon![3]

The audacious rhetoric of this climax can hardly be described as
other than triumphant, regardless of the tragic passages and implications of earlier parts of the play. Somehow sensuality and spiritual
aspiration have been reconciled, though not on the simple Don
Juanesque pattern, nor even on that of Goethe's *Faust*. Mesa and
Ysé go forward into death still remaining essentially separate. The
female principle in Ysé and the exultant male principle in Mesa
remain unreduced by each other, and they set out on their last
journey along 'distant' roads, each following their own. Yet they will
'always bear upon each other', and the possibility of some ultimate
union of a mystic kind does not appear to be excluded. This was
about as far as Claudel, the would-be orthodox Catholic, could go,
remembering, as he almost certainly would, the text that, 'In the
resurrection they neither marry nor are given in marriage, but are as
the angels of God in heaven.'[4]

One can but admire this highly ambitious attempt to relate the
whole Romantic conception of the man–woman relationship, frankly
rooted in carnality, to a religious conception of the destiny of the soul
which hitherto had appeared directly opposed to it. The conclusion,
so far as it can be abstracted from a play with certain partially
contradictory features, is that love, originating in a natural or human
form, is capable, with time and suffering, of liberating the individual
spirit, now better equipped to establish contact with a supernatural
force.[5] The original human love will then be discarded as only a
memory, but may possibly reappear in some other form which is left
undefined. In the story of Tristan and Yseult, which *Partage de Midi*
partly recalls,[6] and the stories of other non-Christian lovers, as

[3] End of Act III. *Oeuvres Complètes*, Vol. XI, pp. 105–6.
[4] *Matthew*, xxii. 30.
[5] As will be readily appreciated, this is a reversal of the effect of 'love'
as shown in *Madame Bovary*. In that work the exaltation of the senses,
projected into near-mysticism by imagination, led to ultimate degradation,
physically emphasised. Claudel returns to the older Romantic belief in
successful transcendence, varied or renewed by genuine Christian and
neoplatonic elements.
[6] In Act I the lovers meet on a ship and realise that they are 'fated' to
each other. Amalric brings up a tray of drinks from the bar to be shared
out among the characters. After seeing a production of his play, Claudel

Antony and Cleopatra, Romeo and Juliet, there is no post-climactic indefinition. The situation is self-contained as a humanly complete emotional experience, which can be poeticised after to round it off artistically.[7] Rosmer and Rebecca (Ibsen's *Rosmersholm*) left behind them a question dependent on their personal reactions at the point of death—unknowable and therefore technically unanswerable—but purely human. Claudel links his question to a conception of a physical-cum-metaphysical universe and suggests a bridge between those two aspects of it by his mention of fire and 'transfiguration'. Only by some such process, which destroys the body yet leaves its essence intact, can the same consciousness experience both aspects. It is the old problem and, inevitably, more or less the old answer. If it cannot be reduced to a logical statement about human relationships in a divine context, that is little to the point. The author undoubtedly felt that some such statement *ought to be possible*, that somewhere there must be that convergence of the finite and the infinite which a century of Romanticism and anti-Romanticism had failed to find. In holding this conviction he was certainly not unique. *Partage de Midi* expresses a reasonably widespread human attitude or aspiration, whether or not one believes that it reaches a viable conclusion. Its subject is therefore a legitimate subject for a play of high importance. It belongs, moreover, to the domain of tragedy as we have characterised it, in that it undertakes an exploration of two kinds of power which may influence human existence. These are Love-Passion, to adopt the irreplaceable French term, and the concept of divine grace. More reflective and experienced theologians

[7] As in one embellishment of the Tristan legend in which a rose-tree springs from the tomb of Tristan and plunges into the neighbouring tomb of Yseult. An example of the poetry of 'nature'.

recognised a reminiscence of the love-potion of the Tristan legend: '. . . the distribution of glasses in which no doubt are mixed a few drops of the legendary elixir'. (Note to J.-L. Barrault, *Oeuvres Complètes*, Vol. XI, p. 324.)

It is also hard not to see in the unusual name of Ysé a reminiscence of Yseult, though Claudel gave a quite different explanation of it in a radio interview in 1951: 'To tell the truth, how do names suggest themselves to us? It's always hard to say. The first origin is obscure. What can be said is that each of the characters represents in short an idea of middleness. Ysé, in Greek, is equality, *isos, isé*, it means 'equal'. Mesa, that's half. Amalric, phonetically, you have the cut into two. It's the name of an umbrella shop on the Boulevard Magenta, A-mal-ric: (*evidently changing his mind*) it's divided into three. And finally, De Ciz, it's a clean cut.' (P. Claudel and J. Amrouche, *Mémoires Improvisés*, Ch. 25, Gallimard 1954.)

than Claudel have wisely regarded the second as inscrutable, but he was ready to attempt its exploration. If this does not end in disaster, the work as a whole may not qualify as a tragedy. But a convinced Christian, faced with those particular issues and not prepared to brand Passion as a sin, could hardly get nearer, and the degree of ambiguity in the ending does at least attenuate the impression that a squarely 'happy' solution has been found.

3

The original version of *Partage de Midi*, in its limited edition of 1906, redolent of a freshly experienced psychological crisis of Claudel's and also, to a considerable extent, of the literary climate of the time (Symbolism), lay almost disregarded for forty years. In 1948 the actor-producer Jean-Louis Barrault, having succeeded in staging Claudel's *Soulier de Satin* a few years previously, now wished to act *Partage de Midi*, virtually for the first time. Claudel was at first reluctant to agree. The personal crisis which had inspired it was a thing of the past, while the ethos of the play seemed at variance with the more orthodox religious views he had come to adopt. But he referred to his religious directors and was encouraged to go forward. He began work on the old text in consultation with Barrault and with the aim of evolving something both suitable for the Parisian stage and expressive of his actual moral outlook.

In this reassessment there was much that was personal on the author's part, much also on that of Barrault. The latter held strongly original views on the requirements of the theatre and in particular of his own company, which included the passion-typed actress Edwige Feuillère, who was cast as Ysé. But from this situation, highly interesting in itself, at least something general can be learnt about the transformation of near-tragic drama between the nineteen-hundreds and the late nineteen-forties. One can think of no other case of an eminent dramatist revising a forty-year-old work to suit a new conception of dramatic idiom and moral purpose. Claudel was of course given to rewriting. The four successive versions of the play which became *L'Annonce faite à Marie* provide the outstanding example. But in that case the revision was fairly continuous, while for *Partage de Midi* there had been a long interval of complete neglect.

What principally troubled Claudel was the character of Mesa, a projection of his own younger personality, but now seen as bordering on the 'romantic hero', a figure he had come to detest. Mesa is no longer 'the strong and fiery flame, the great male in the glory of God' of 1906, but 'a nasty little *bourgeois*, very egoistic, very insular, very self-centred'.[8]

This self-centredness, already recognised in the first version but not explicitly condemned, is now frankly moved from the category of virtues and demi-virtues to the category of vices. In this respect, the octogenarian author has aligned himself with the old Christian thinkers such as Pascal. But he still has Love-Passion and Woman on his hands, and if these were discarded nothing would be left of the play or of the personal experience in which it originated. To conserve them, he develops the rôle of Ysé and gives her, as Woman, a new function which might almost be said to be his own invention.

The story remains the same. The first two acts undergo no essential change. The language of the dialogue becomes more familiar in places, but the original 'poetic' idiom is retained at moments of high tension. It is on the last part of Act III, from the point at which Amalric and Ysé steal out, leaving the injured Mesa alone with the bomb, that Claudel's main revision bears. Ideologically there is now a parting of the ways, which was reflected in the pre-production discussions between Claudel and Barrault, continued after production in numerous afterthoughts. The present writer, commissioned a few years later to make an English translation for sound radio, was also brought face to face in practice with the difficulties involved. His solution was a combination of the two texts, more or less along the lines which Barrault finally took. But strictly a compromise is not legitimate. An audience capable of enough detachment to reflect in the theatre would be bound to reject it. It must be one ending or the other.

Claudel complicated matters by substituting for the magnificent poetry of the original a language which he himself described as 'silly, simple, artless, almost childish, almost vulgar!'[9] One of his motives may have been to make his lesson quite comprehensible on what he conceived to be the level of the audiences at the Théâtre Marigny.

---

[8] '*Après tout un sale petit bourgeois, très égoïste, très sevré, très concentré sur lui-même.*' Letter to J.-L. Barrault, 8 October 1948, in *Oeuvres Complètes*, Vol. XI, p. 316.

[9] '*Tout cela dans ce nouveau Acte III, on a essayé de le faire comprendre sans grands mots, dans un langage bête, simple, naïf, presque enfantin, presque grossier!*' Letter to J.-L. Barrault, Good Friday, 1954, in *Oeuvres Complètes*, Vol. XI, pp. 327–8.

Another was certainly connected with his effort of de-heroisation. If Mesa and his situation were no longer heroic, the rhetoric which had originally surrounded them must also be deflated. But the new idiom was disastrous, descending at places, in the mouth of Ysé, to the level of baby-talk. The colloquial familiarity of some of the exchanges between the lovers no doubt owed something to that studied Parisian coyness (the consciously anti-Grand Manner) which so often pulls one up in Cocteau, Giraudoux and Anouilh. But what has been fashionable coyness in those experienced entertainers, working with one finger on their public's pulse, became something different in the remote and never fashionable Claudel. He had never had a light touch and his lifelong tendency to move straight from the sublime to the bathetic became exaggerated to the point of embarrassment. The same applied to the once splendid *Cantique de Mesa*, which in the original version began:

> Here I lie on my funeral bed,
> And all around, on left and right, I see the encircling forest of candles.
> Not twinkling tapers, but mighty stars, like tall virgins flaming
> Before the face of God, as in the holy pictures Mary appears keeping her own counsel.
> And I, man, the mind-endowed,[10]
> Lie here on the Earth, ready to die, as though on a solemn bier,
> At the deepest point of the universe and the inmost heart of this seethe of stars and the swarm and the worship of God.
> I see the innumerable clergy of the night with its bishops and its patriarchs,
> Above my head the Polestar and at my side the Gulf and the Equator of the teeming beasts of space
> Which is called the Milky Way, stretched like a strong girdle.
> Hail now, my sisters! Not one of you, shining ones.
> Lodges the spirit,[11] but alone in the centre of all, the Earth
> Has germinated its man, and you, like a million white sheep
> Turn your faces towards it, this Shepherd and Messiah of the worlds!
> Hail, stars! Here I lie alone. No priest surrounded by the pious community
> Will bring me the last sacrament.
> But already the gates of Heaven

[10] *Et moi, l'homme, l'Intelligent.*

[11] Alternately, 'the mind': *l'esprit.* This gave Pascal his Second Order. See above, p. 156 *et seq.*

Burst open, and the army of all the Saints, carrying candles in their
    hands,
Come forward to meet me, surrounding the terrible Lamb.[12]

In the stage production Barrault retained this *Cantique* in a somewhat modified form. Claudel continued tinkering with it, until in his
final version it becomes a kind of dialogue between Mesa, now
speaking in very ordinary prose, and something which he calls 'the
Stellar Kettle' and explains as 'the noise of the stars'. The Kettle,
which is equally the voice of the firmament and the voice of God,
hums and buzzes wordlessly on various notes in reply to Mesa's
questions and complaints.

It is clear that the poetry of the original version would carry
conviction only if written and spoken with conviction, but that it
would be unsustainable if doubt crept in. That was what had happened. Claudel made the point himself in his radio interviews of
1951–2:

> CLAUDEL: There were things I really would have liked to keep in,
> but they were incompatible with my idea of the final form of
> the play. You have to be courageous in art and not hesitate to
> make sacrifices, even painful ones. But I couldn't ask Barrault
> to make the same sacrifices. There were things which he liked
> enormously—for example, the beginning of the *Cantique de
> Mesa*, images like 'the clergy of the night', etcetera.
> INTERVIEWER: Yes, magnificent images incidentally . . .
> CLAUDEL: I couldn't bear them any longer. They didn't square with
> the idea which I had of Mesa. So I simply cut them out. I can
> understand that that may have been too much for Barrault.
> INTERVIEWER: I should think so . . .[13]

4

So Claudel finally turned his back on the concept of the lonely human
hero, who was ultimately the Romantic hero, stationed on an anthro-
pocentric earth in a terracentric universe, and whom he himself had
enthroned in his defiant funeral chant. In the final version the Stellar
Kettle does utter two articulate words: *'Les autres'*, *the others*, which
now appear explicitly in the play for the first time. In introducing this
element in these terms, one cannot help feeling that Claudel may have

[12] *Partage de Midi*, Act III, *Oeuvres Complètes*, *XI*, pp. 91–2.
[13] P. Claudel and J. Amrouche, *Mémoires Improvisés*, Ch. 25.

been influenced, however unconsciously, however much against his will, by the existentialism of J.-P. Sartre, who stresses the importance of the Other as a control upon the Self and whose play *Huis-Clos* (1944) contained the soon famous sentence: '*L'enfer, c'est les Autres.*'[14] For Claudel, however, the Other was not hell, but a line to heaven. He developed the idea in the radio interview quoted above:

> If you know the last version, you will have seen the stress I place on *the other*. Well, Mesa such as he was until the time of *Partage de Midi* was on balance a rather disagreeable character, very selfish, very preoccupied with himself, very hard, very withdrawn, who absolutely had to be transformed, given the impression of *the other*, of something different to himself—something to teach him what humanity is, in a word.

The means of doing this was Ysé, who now grows in stature in comparison with Mesa, scolds him for his pettiness, and mothers him towards death. But she is not merely the Mother, or the soul-mate of transcended sex, but the instrument of torture which extracts his soul by tearing it from its *amour-propre*. This, we think, is an entirely original conception of the rôle of Woman and one which allows (better than in the first version) both Woman and Passionate Love to be fitted into a scheme of traditional Christian values. Since Claudel is Christian, his instrument of torture is the Cross, and this Ysé claims to be for Mesa. It would probably be more logical to see Love-Passion as the Cross, on which the man and woman are both crucified. Ysé for her part has suffered terribly on account of Mesa—not only because of her unsatisfiable desire to reach his soul through his body, which is the counterpart of his desire, but through remorse at the death of her children and her betrayals of other men into which her passion has forced her. The theme of the tortured woman recurs through Claudel's work, from the crucified Princess in his first play, *Tete d'Or*, to Doña Prouhèze of the *Soulier de Satin*,[15] and it would be quite normal for Ysé to fall into this line. But in that case the woman would be no more than an equal sufferer with the man, whereas in the last version of *Partage de Midi* she is represented as his superior. Hence, it seems, her assimilation to the Cross, or the instrument of salvation, a function which Claudel finally preferred to assign

[14] 'Hell is other people.' *Huis-Clos*, Sc. 5, near end.
[15] This play contains the same theme as *Partage de Midi*, but in less concentrated form. It also contains the Cross *motif*, though this again is less explicitly stressed than in *Partage de Midi*, final version.

to the personified concept Woman rather than to the generalised concept Passion.

But this distinction makes little real difference to Claudel's explanation of the human condition. In either case he has succeeded in reconciling sexual appetite at its most intense with the idea of a divine ordering of life; in short, the natural order with the supernatural order. He has outlined, with a minimum of mysticism, a theory in which Sex, Suffering, Redemption, and God all co-exist in a coherent system. In the light of all the previous attempts to solve this riddle, it seems an enormous achievement. Why, then, does it not make a much greater impact?

Mention has already been made of the banality of the new dialogue which Claudel wrote. It stemmed from the justifiable wish to relate the theme to some kind of contemporary reality, but in practice it fell below a level at which it could be taken seriously. Whether Claudel could have aimed slightly higher, while still avoiding the remoteness now associated with fully 'poetic' drama, is a hypothetical question. But it seems highly improbable that the theme of *Partage de Midi* could ever be rendered in unaffectedly 'natural' dialogue of the Chekhovian type; or indeed that any dramatic idiom in existence around 1950 was capable of carrying it home to the intimate sensibility of an audience. The inference is that the theme in its new form was not communicable, which is another way of saying that it could not be made to appear significant. Ideologically, the second *Partage de Midi* must be considered as the rearguard action of a splendid but vanished cause. The production of Barrault and his company, helped by a hybrid text, may have obscured the fact momentarily, but could not permanently conceal the development of an altered image of humanity.

The explanation is not precisely in the substitution of humanism for religion, though that can enter into it and was taken up by François Mauriac in his commentary of the production.[16] Mauriac, the Catholic novelist, whose work is full of conflicts between passion and faith, was exceedingly well qualified to see what Claudel was doing. He wrote in part as follows:

> I wondered what that coughing audience made of the old triangular drama, husband, wife, lover, in which there suddenly

[16] In *Le Figaro*, 20 December 1948. Quoted in Claudel's *Oeuvres Complètes*, Vol. XI, p. 310–11.

intervenes a fourth protagonist: He whose death Nietzsche has announced, that God who is necessarily outmoded to-day since M. Sartre doesn't need him to explain the world. I would have liked to know if some spectators dimly realised that in *Partage de Midi* the human drama at last find its true dimension. Ever since my early days, when I read this play and came to love it, greater master-pieces, even *Tristan*, have seemed limited in comparison. Even *Phèdre*; in that God is present, but he is the God of the theologians, the implacable God, not the one to whom the dying Mesa dares to cry: 'If you have loved each one of us as I loved this woman...'

Yes, what were the thoughts of the non-Christians in the audience, who nurse illusions on the 'consolations' of religion? Did they understand the martyrdom of Mesa; that God who suddenly withdraws—and the desert, and the soul delivered up not to the beasts, but to another soul; for Ysé is a soul also: the hell of another—it will be seen in what sense I understand this.

And Mauriac continues, in a paragraph to which we must return a little later.

> The astonishing thing is that those non-Christians are incarnated on the stage in the person of Amalric. There again Paul Claudel has had the luck to light upon Pierre Brasseur [the actor], who re-presents perfectly the normal man whom all this business about God bores stiff, possessed by a kind of physical lyricism, believing in nothing but the body which he holds in his arms, or the business he is doing, and who gorges and gluts himself to the limit of his appetite.

While one can respect Mauriac's position and admire his robust defence of religion, one can see with hindsight that his reading of *Partage de Midi*, or rather, of its significance for the audience, was partly erroneous. Whether they believed in God, and what sense, was a little beside the point if they had ceased to believe in *Amour-Passion*. If *this* was dead as an absolute concept, what could it matter if the two were interrelated or not? Compulsive love with transcendent implications was still viable in 1906, as a late hangover from Romanticism, but what was it in 1948? One is inclined to write that it was out, but the question is more complicated than that and deserves a certain examination.

The character of Amalric is underestimated by Mauriac. He is, it is true, a materialist and is limited to the things of nature. In the play, he is a perfect foil for Mesa. He is consistent in both versions and is

given practically the same lines to speak. Claudel's characterisation of
him is done with skill and certainly not contempt—this is reserved for
the evasive De Ciz. Capable when excited of 'physical lyricism', he
can also speak very crudely and pointedly:

YSÈ   (*to Mesa*): A woman is a bigger burden than you think!
        A woman all to oneself, the whole time, the one woman
        you need—
        Not just any woman!
        She gives herself to you, and what does she get in
        return? Does the man give himself?

AMALRIC: All that is too subtle for me. Hell, if a man must spend
        his whole time
        Worrying himself sick about his woman, wondering if
        he has really given the right dose of affection
        Which Mary or Margery deserves, taking the tempera-
        ture of his heart, what a fuss!
        All this sentiment—it's a kind of private hoard which
        women have, like those boxes they keep bits of thread
        and ribbons in and odd buttons and corset-bones.
        And the disgusting part is that they're always being ill.
        The main thing is that she's there, isn't she? You have
        to make the best you can of it. We should miss her if
        she wasn't. It's nice to have her now and again.
        What do you say, Mesa my boy? Am I right or wrong?[17]

Amalric's insensitivity is more obvious in his words than his acts.
Spiritually limited though he may be, he loves Ysé and goes after her
until he gets her. He snaps her up when she runs away from Mesa in
despair and gives his protective affection to her and the child she has
conceived. He appears at his best at the beginning of the last act, when
the mob howls in the distance and he calmly and efficiently sets up his
explosive device.

YSÈ: . . . Is it true we're going to die, Amalric?
AMALRIC: I don't see anything else for it.
YSÈ: Going to die. How odd that sounds. Isn't there a chance
        —just a little one?
AMALRIC: None. We're in a trap.
        So far they've been rather half-hearted about us. They
        don't dislike me, really. I don't dislike them. They're
        not bad people, you know.

[17] *Partage de Midi*, Act I. *Oeuvres Complètes*, Vol. XI, pp. 44–5 (old
version), 232–3 (new version).

But now that the others have gone, it's our turn. There's
no getting away from it. It's the usual thing.

YSÈ: But they won't get us alive? . . . You won't let them get
me alive?

Listen!

What are they shouting? Do you hear them? What is it?

AMALRIC: It's nothing. You needn't dig your nails into me.

They're just finishing off yesterday's business. The
missionaries, probably. What's left of them.

YSÈ: They're not coming here?

AMALRIC: I tell you there's nothing to be afraid of. We made it too
hot for them the last time.

And tomorrow—tomorrow it will be too late. No one
in!

Flitted, the *yang kouitze*, flown away![18]

Amalric is the man of action who accepts the inevitable as 'the
usual thing' ('*C'est régulier*'). He does what has to be done without
question and with no more self-interest than he conceives as a normal
part of his virility. He loves and reassures Ysé, but cannot satisfy her.
Like Mesa, she is looking for something *beyond*:

AMALRIC: Did he really love you?

YSÈ: In a way you never will. And I loved him in a way I
don't love you. To you I am bound by duty, for I'm
an honourable woman and I know what I've been
doing.

But with him it was despair and desire, like a sudden
storm, and a kind of hatred, and a contraction of the
flesh and a convulsion in the depth of my entrails like
tearing a child out of me.

You mastered me, but you don't know what a woman is
like who hasn't been mastered . . .

It went on like that for a whole year and I felt that he
was caught,

But I didn't possess him and something in him remained
foreign,

Impossible . . .

How can he say that I was to blame? He didn't give
himself, so I—went away.

I have my life, too!

I had a right to live, to see this everyday sun, to live, to
live as I used to—

[18] *Partage de Midi*, Act III. *Oeuvres Complètes*, Vol. XI, pp. 265–7.

The same life as everyone else—and to escape from that
love which was like death.
And now this has happened. I don't mind, I accept it all.
AMALRIC: I love you, Ysé.
YSÈ: I know you do.[19]

Immediately after this dialogue Mesa returns, and the whole
question is thrown open again.

5

If one looks first at the play as a drama of the 'eternal triangle' made
up of one woman and two lovers,[20] one has to admit that one's
sympathies can easily stray in the wrong direction. While the direct
effect of playing down Mesa in the final version was to augment
Ysé, a secondary effect, which can hardly have been intended, was to
point up Amalric. He is a better man as a man and (this is a love-
story) a better male as a male. His character, moreover, is also conceived in the heroic convention. If the story were injected—naturally,
it is a big supposition—with the 'virile' ethos of a Hemingway story,
he would be a hero unequivocally. In order to put Mesa above him
and give Mesa a stronger attraction for Ysé than Amalric possesses,
there must be transcendence. Mesa must be able to rise (even when
unheroic) to a sphere which Amalric can never attain. In Mauriac's
terms (which agree with Claudel's) God must intervene in the
triangle and the human drama will then find its true dimension, which
is the divine dimension.

One instinctively feels that this is both unfair and unreal, that this
is not its true dimension, and that 'God' has no business in this
particular place.

Such a statement cannot be other than subjective, though in
making it the present writer believes that it is widely representative of
modern opinion, not by any means confined to 'non-Christians'. It is
of course a flat, dogmatic contradiction of the Claudelian conviction

[19] *Partage de Midi*, Act III. *Oeuvres Complètes*, Vol. XI, pp. 274–5.
[20] See Mauriac's comment, p. 237 above. Mauriac wrote, 'husband, wife,
lover', in which he was only echoing Claudel's own programme note
(quoted in *Oeuvres Complètes*, Vol. XI, p. 307). This also speaks of the
theme of adultery. But the legal husband, De Ciz, is a nonentity in the
play, who disappears from the action and, virtually, from the argument.
The only significant human triangle consists of Mesa–Ysé–Amalric.

of the opposite, which seems equally dogmatic.[21] It is not put forward with a polemical intention, sterile and indeed ludicrous as that would be, but as contributory evidence of a change in ideology which seems to be confirmed at least in modern literature and drama.

A reasoned critical justification of this would be fastidious and no doubt superfluous. We will therefore put the case as it appears to us briefly and plainly. Whatever may have been the feeling a few decades ago, and might just conceivably be a few decades hence, at the present time it is impossible to regard Love-Passion as a serious potential factor in the soul's relationship with God. The terms are difficult enough to accept in isolation. In combination they become quite unassimilable.

6

But there is something else in *Partage de Midi* which is virtually timeless. It is the theme of unfulfillable love—though here 'love' is a blurred and hardly accurate term. In part the theme is quite familiar, e.g., in *Phèdre*, in which one member of the couple violently desires the other, who remains indifferent. One could extend this situation, without changing it basically, to an actual physical union of the couple, even with physical satisfaction, but which left one of them still unsatisfied and the other still unresponsive. The desire for total

---

[21] But one should never underrate Claudel's psychological insight. He states the contrary position before rejecting it:

YSÉ: Tell me, Amalric, tell me the truth. You're quite sure, aren't you, that there really is no God?

AMALRIC: Why should there be? If there was one, I should have told you.

YSÉ: All right. Let's stop talking about it.
And:

YSÉ: . . . And yet there are times, you know, when it is like feeling that someone is watching you, continually, and you can't get away, and whatever you do—
For instance, if we laugh, or you kiss me, *he* sees us. He is watching us at this moment.
Oh God, is this really worthy of you? Need you be so solemn and serious with a woman?
Patience, patience, just a little longer and we shan't be there . . .

AMALRIC: That sounds like Mesa's jargon. These are absurd dreams.
Let your dear old God watch us as much as he likes, that's his business.
I say that he doesn't concern us.

(Act III (last version). *Oeuvres Complètes*, Vol. XI, pp. 272-3.)

possession, total knowledge, or total identification would not be fulfilled.[22] The remarkable novelty of *Partage de Midi* is that both lovers respond to each other with intense physical passion, yet both experience frustration. They cannot really get through to each other. They cannot, as they put it, reach the soul through the body. No doubt, on a normal view, they are expecting too much of a human relationship. Claudel says as much in his religious idiom: 'It is dangerous to demand God from one of his creatures.'[23]

But this kind of situation, though 'abnormal', is sufficiently common and recognisable to be a fit subject for a tragic exploration at any period in which a suitable idiom can be found to express it. One would incline to transfer it today to a purely psychological plane and the result could well be a drama which went right home to contemporary sensibilities. Mesa and Ysé are both suffering from an erotically motivated psychosis (which at once excludes the 'normal' Amalric from their field). Whether one uses the psychologist's language or the priest's, the thing is the same and it is still there. And though the diagnosis is simple, the cure or resolution is obscure. We think that Claudel had the material for a tragedy and that he saw its implications—he seems, indeed, to have experienced them personally —but that he marred the work by making it end, somehow, in heaven. One has only to study his many re-wordings and reformulations of the last Act to realise how uncertain he himself was, and how nearly he must have come to the recognition that he had written three-quarters of a magnificent drama which was uncompletable. Unless, that is, he had been able to accept a final disaster and so make it a tragedy in the full sense.

[22] It was evidently to this kind of desire that M. Goldmann attributed Pascal's tragic sense. See above, p. 70. But Pascal unhesitatingly by-passed humanity.

[23] Programme note for 1948 production. Quoted *Oeuvres Complètes*, Vol. XI, p. 308.

12

Beckett: 'Waiting for Godot'

At first sight, Mr Beckett took the easy way in his *Waiting for Godot*, first produced in France in January 1953, in England in August 1955.[1] He dispenses with Woman and quite definitely with *Amour-Passion*. Man is whittled down to essentials and perhaps beyond them. God is a question-mark to which we shall have to return, but it can be said at once, to borrow the title of one of Beckett's earlier works, that if existent he seems a source of more pricks than kicks. As to Nature, she is represented by a single tree, bare in the first act and sprouting a few leaves in the second, as though to show that in the vegetable kingdom at least some life still stirs.

Before this tree, the sole scenery, two tramps, Vladimir and Estragon, converse and perform various restricted movements while awaiting the arrival of a certain Mr Godot, with whom they have an appointment in this vaguely desolate place. They are on the stage for the entire two acts of a play which runs for about one and a half hours. Diversions are provided by the entrance in both acts of Pozzo, a seedy landowner accompanied by his slave Lucky, and by two appearances of a messenger boy, or boys, who tell them each time that Godot will not come this evening, 'but surely to-morrow'. They consider hanging themselves, but their only rope is the piece of cord which holds up Estragon's trousers and it is not strong enough. At the final curtain they stand facing the audience and uttering the words: 'Let's go,' but in fact they remain motionless.

To strip down action, situation, emotion and characterisation as

---

[1] The quotations in this chapter are from the English version by the author (Faber and Faber, 1956).

far as this is, for a dramatist, the equivalent of clearing out a houseful of old lumber, leaving the way open for a fresh start. But this freedom from inherited complications is only superficial and, even if real, it would not make the playwright's task easier. Racine's remark that the hardest thing of all is to make something out of nothing applies forcibly here—even if Nothing, with its formidable new connotations, is no longer the artistically barren field it once seemed.

Waiting for Godot, however, is scenically and emotionally bare only in comparison with the lushness of earlier drama, of which Claudel's was an outstanding example. The stripping-down process can go much further, as Beckett himself went on to prove in *Endgame* and *Happy Days*. What must be nearly the ultimate is reached in his novel *How it is*, whose crippled 'characters' crawl painfully along face downwards in the mud and communicate by jabs with a tin-opener. Compared to any of these, Vladimir and Estragon are highly articulate entities possessed of an almost quivering sensitivity. They are bound together by the sub-type of love variously known as fraternity, comradeship, or solidarity. It shows in Vladimir's maternal, or nurse-like, solicitude for Estragon, in Estragon's dependence on Vladimir. The nurse-child relationship is emphasised by Estragon's resentment of it, by the several attempts he makes to break free. But at the approach of the Others, mysterious and hostile, he runs back for protection, which Vladimir readily gives. This fraternity, though largely a defensive feeling sustained by the terror of loneliness, has not, in this play, become mechanical. It rests on a real psychological need and is more than the product of habituation.

Pity is also experienced spontaneously. When Pozzo first appears, driving before him the miserable Lucky, laden with baggage and with a rope round his neck, they are full of compassion for the pale, exhausted creature. They are even indignant against his master. It is true that, after Lucky has kicked one of them and Pozzo has explained how sorely tried he is by his servant's tiresome behaviour, the direction of their sympathies changes abruptly. But they have shown themselves capable of pity and indignation, even if they are not quite sure where to apply them. They are still more capable of unhappiness, while maintaining that happiness does not exist or that they themselves have never experienced it. So conscious are they of their suffering that they continually protest against it. Estragon is particularly vocal:

VLADIMIR: Your turn.
Estragon does a balancing exercise, staggers.

ESTRAGON: Do you think God sees me?
VLADIMIR: You must close your eyes.
    Estragon closes his eyes, staggers worse.
ESTRAGON (*stopping, brandishing his fists, at the top of his voice*):
    God have pity on me!
VLADIMIR (*vexed*): And me?
ESTRAGON (*as before*): On me! On me! Pity! On me!

In short, these imperfectly heartless hobos, contemporaries as they
may have been of the Beat Generation, have progressed only a certain
way beyond the Romantics in the direction of total nihilism. To go
the whole way, *Weltschmerz* should not be *experienced*, but ignored,
or at most parodied. Their parody lacks conviction. Unlike Hamm
and Clov in *Endgame*, they still retain enough remnants of hope to be
tormented by despair. And in place of hope as a dynamic they have
expectancy. This is the main motif of the play, spelt out in the title,
which in an earlier version was simply: '*Waiting*'.

The two tramps are in a place and mental state in which nothing
happens and time stands still. Their main preoccupation is to 'pass
the time' as well as possible until night comes and they can go. They
realise the futility of their exercises and that they are merely filling up
the hours with pointless activity. In this sense, their 'waiting' is
mechanical; it is the same thing as not moving. In another sense, it is
an obligation. They have to remain where they are, though they resent
doing so and would like to leave. This might be called a moral obligation, since it involves the possibilities of punishment and reward. If
Godot comes, as he has given them to understand that he may, a new
factor may be introduced into their existence, whereas if they leave
they will certainly miss him. Their waiting, therefore, however
cynical they may be about it, contains a certain element of hope.

2

It hardly matters whether, or in what sense, Godot stands for 'God'.
But it is hard to attach him to any other concept. He is the external
figure who can bring a change to their immobility. For Vladimir and
Estragon he certainly exists. Their uncertainty bears on his attitude
towards them:

VLADIMIR: Let's wait and see what he says . . .
ESTRAGON: What exactly did we ask him to do for us? . . .
VLADIMIR: Oh, nothing very definite.
ESTRAGON: A kind of prayer.

VLADIMIR: Precisely.
ESTRAGON: A vague supplication.
VLADIMIR: Precisely.
ESTRAGON: And what did he reply?
VLADIMIR: That he'd see.
ESTRAGON: That he couldn't promise anything.
VLADIMIR: That he'd have to think it over.
ESTRAGON: In the quiet of his home.
VLADIMIR: Consult his family.
ESTRAGON: His friends.
VLADIMIR: His agents.
ESTRAGON: His correspondents.
VLADIMIR: His books.
ESTRAGON: His bank account.
VLADIMIR: Before taking a decision.

To compare the impredictability of Godot's response to the mysteries of grace has not seemed far-fetched to several critics. The idea of grace—the possibility of salvation—is prominent in the play, from the moment when Vladimir is puzzled over the different accounts given in the four Gospels of the fate of the two thieves crucified with Christ. According to one evangelist, one of the two was saved, the other damned. As he remarks, 'It's a reasonable percentage.' A religious, indeed theological motif runs through this near-static farce, and it is not surprising that critics should have established comparisons between Beckett and Pascal. Pascal's wager—the rational necessity of betting on the mercy of God, since in view of the finite stake the infinite jackpot is so tremendous that the odds are irresistible—is the first analogy that comes to mind. More generally, the Pascalian picture of the misery of man abandoned to himself is Beckett's picture in *Godot*, and one has only to develop Anouilh's reported description of the play as 'a music-hall sketch of the *Pensées* performed by the Fratellini clowns'[2] to perceive the similarity of their views on the human condition. But there are some differences. Pascal's God was, or included, the Supreme Good. There was no doubt at all that union with him would mean total happiness and solve every problem. There was little doubt either of his good will towards men. Waiting for him was very likely to be rewarded. Godot, on the other hand, inspires much less confidence. Apart from his

[2] See Edith Kern, 'Drama Stripped for Inaction', in *Yale French Studies*, No. 14 (1954), quoted N. A. Scott, *Samuel Beckett* (Bowes and Bowes, 1965).

refusal to make a definite promise to do anything, there is also doubt about the nature of his offer if he should make one. Will it be advantageous and, if not, are the tramps free to 'take it or leave it', as Vladimir suggests? They feel uneasily that they may not be, for the dialogue quoted on the previous page continues:

ESTRAGON: And we?... Where do we come in?
VLADIMIR: Come in? On our hands and knees.
ESTRAGON: As bad as that?
VLADIMIR: Your worship wishes to assert his prerogatives?
ESTRAGON: We've no rights any more?
VLADIMIR: You'd make me laugh, if it wasn't prohibited.
ESTRAGON: We've lost our rights?
VLADIMIR: We waived them.
> *Silence. They remain motionless, arms dangling, heads bowed, sagging at the knees.*
ESTRAGON (*feebly*): We're not tied? (*Pause.*) We're not—
VLADIMIR (*raising his hand*): Listen!
> *They listen, grotesquely rigid.*
ESTRAGON: I hear nothing.
VLADIMIR: Hssst! (*They listen, huddled together.*) Nor I.
> *Sighs of relief. They relax and separate.*
ESTRAGON: You gave me a fright.
VLADIMIR: I thought it was he.
ESTRAGON: Who?
VLADIMIR: Godot.
ESTRAGON: Pah! The wind in the reeds.
VLADIMIR: I could have sworn I heard shouts.
ESTRAGON: And why would he shout?
VLADIMIR: At his horse.

Whoever Godot may be, he is a powerful and possibly hostile person. He has some hold over the tramps which prevents them from cutting their appointment with him. They *must* wait, on purely compulsive grounds:

ESTRAGON: And if we dropped him? (*Pause.*) If we dropped him.
VLADIMIR: He'd punish us.

If he comes, this may bring a change to their present vacuous state, although, as already remarked, they are not sure that it will be a change for the better. The last few lines of the play suggest salvation:

VLADIMIR: We'll hang ourselves tomorrow. (*Pause.*) Unless Godot comes.

ESTRAGON: And if he comes?
VLADIMIR: We'll be saved.

But, in view of all that has gone before, this can hardly be accepted as a firm conclusion. Vladimir's tendency is to look on the bright side, mainly because he cannot quite accept the alternative. His remark is hardly inspired by the kind of conviction which Pascal called 'faith'.[3]

To attach this to the Pascalian-Blakian ideological progression: the God within the psyche has failed; the idea that the humanity to which Vladimir and Estragon belong possesses an 'energy' capable of moving mountains is almost too laughable to be mentioned. But if there is no driving force inside them there may, or should, be one outside. The trouble is their lack of faith in its relevance to them. Godot holds their future—if they have any future—in his hands, but he does not seem very interested in them. Godot bears a sinister resemblance to Nobodaddy, less, seemingly, his impotence. He may in fact be Nobodaddy—for them, if not for some other department of the universe—and this is the shadow which haunts the play religion-wise. Beckett's characters grope to construct an acceptable image of Godot/God. One of them appears in Lucky's celebrated 'think-piece' in Act I:

> Given the existence as uttered forth in the public works of Puncher and Wattmann of a personal God quaquaquaqua with a white beard quaquaquaqua outside time without extension Who from the heights of divine apathia divine athambia divine aphasia loves us dearly with some exceptions for reasons unknown but time will tell . . .

If Godot is like this there is not much left to hope for, and it must be admitted that the description given by the second messenger-boy (he minds the sheep, while his brother minds the goats) who brings word that Godot cannot come that evening is not reassuring. What if he is the old Jehovah-Daddy all over again?

VLADIMIR: What does he do, Mr Godot? (*Silence.*) Do you hear me?
BOY: Yes, sir.
VLADIMIR: Well?
BOY: He does nothing, sir.
                    Silence.
VLADIMIR (*softly*): Has he a beard, Mr Godot?

[3] Vladimir's attitude is discussed more fully below (pp. 258-60), as is the fuller context of the lines just quoted.

249

BOY: Yes, sir.
VLADIMIR: Fair or . . . (*he hesitates*) . . . or black?
BOY: I think it's white, sir.

Silence.

VLADIMIR: Christ have mercy on us!

Vladimir's exclamation of horror stems from the obvious truth that a twentieth-century mentality can derive little comfort from the image of an Old Testament-type God. The kind of salvation which a white-bearded Godot is likely to offer will hardly satisfy even Vladimir and Estragon, impoverished though they are. From the religious point of view, strongly implicit in the play, *Waiting for Godot* might well have been subtitled 'Nobodaddy's Revenge'.

3

On both of the entrances of Pozzo, Estragon believes for a moment that Godot has arrived. The mistake is soon realised, but not before a familiar idea has been insinuated: that God and Society, while not the same thing, can be easily confused with each other. Society's two complementary sides are represented by Pozzo and Lucky, who together make it up. They are totally interdependent. Without Lucky, Pozzo cannot move forward, sit down to eat, or get up. Lucky cannot move either, except in response to Pozzo's shouted orders and whip-cracks. Together they compose a functioning organisation from which the two tramps are excluded, or have contracted out. Vladimir and Estragon lack any such organisational framework and cannot 'function' as isolated individuals either. Their 'exercises', whether physical or verbal, are strictly non-functional, being unrelated to any necessity or purpose, however limited. True, they serve to pass the time, but 'it would have passed in any case'.

Society, however, is in little better shape than the outsiders. Its functioning is largely mechanical and the only defined purpose of Pozzo and Lucky's laborious journey is to reach the market where Lucky will be sold. The objective result of this would be to break their society up, but Pozzo does not see so far and airily boasts that he is not short of slaves. He only sees that Lucky has grown sour and tiresome, so that he has no more pleasure in his company.

It is easy, if one wishes, to interpret this as a caricature of 'feudalism' in decline. In English productions Pozzo has been presented as the traditional Irish squireen, dressed in a blanket-coat and a brown billycock. He thunders awesomely in the manner of Colonel Blimp and at the same time is a slave to formality. In his punctiliousness and his whiplike use of sarcasm he possesses the two most resented qualities of an old governing class. He can unbend towards the two tramps with a condescension which reeks of superiority and which gradually gives way to his overwhelming need of an audience to talk to. 'Yes, gentlemen, I cannot go for long without the society of my likes . . . Even when the likeness is an imperfect one.' He suggests the capitalism of the third or fourth generation, at a point where it has merged irreparably into the squirarchy. But although Pozzo wears the outward image of the country gentleman, it would be absurd to read Brechtian implications into *Godot*. This is not an attack on senile capitalism, but a more general image of society as a whole—and even conceivably a lament for it. It corresponds indifferently to any division into haves and have-nots, top-dogs and bottom-dogs. Pozzo owns and commands, Lucky produces and obeys. He is equally the beast of burden (the 'worker') and the artist and intellectual. In the past he has taught Pozzo all he knows of 'beauty, grace, truth of the first water'—a wonderfully revealing catalogue. He can still manage a tottering dance to entertain them all. He can still, at a word of command and jerk of the rope, be made to think—so long as he is wearing his hat. And, like the professional intellectual in any organised society, his 'thinking' leads by its own momentum to conclusions so discomforting and so near the bone that the others jump on him and try to shut his mouth. This is the effect of Lucky's breathlessly spoken and chaotic tirade of which we quoted the opening lines on p. 249 above. It ends in a seeming incoherence which is nevertheless dismally and intolerably clear:

LUCKY: . . . what is more for reasons unknown in spite of the tennis on on the beard the flames the teams the stones so blue so calm alas alas on on the skull the skull the skull the skull in Connemara in spite of the tennis the labours abandoned left unfinished graver still abode of stones in a word I resume alas alas abandoned unfinished the skull the skull in Connemara in spite of the tennis the skull alas the stones Cunard (*Mêlée, final vociferations*.) tennis . . . the stones . . . so calm . . . Cunard . . . unfinished . . .

POZZO: His hat!

Vladimir seizes Lucky's hat. Silence of Lucky. He falls. Silence. Panting of the victors.

ESTRAGON: Avenged!
> *Vladimir examines the hat, looks inside it.*
POZZO: Give me that! (*He snatches the hat from Vladimir, throws it on the ground, tramples on it.*) There's an end to his thinking!

Even while still 'thinking', Lucky was drawing near to the eternal immobility of bedrock ('the skull . . . the stones . . . so calm'). Deprived of his hat, the habitual, perhaps Pavlovian, stimulus, comparable at the least to an Editorship or a Chair, his thinking stops finally, 'unfinished'. When he and his master reappear in Act II, the physical run-down is fast catching up with the mental run-down. Lucky is now dumb and Pozzo blind. They fall flat on their faces and are unable to get up without help. Society, so far as they may be taken to represent it, is near to the point when it ceases to function altogether.

But Pozzo, though now stripped of arrogance, is still very articulate. It is he who first utters the memorable phrase, 'They (humanity) give birth astride of a grave,' to express the brevity of life:

POZZO: . . . one day he went dumb, one day I went blind, one day we'll go deaf, one day we were born, one day we'll die, the same day, the same second, is that not enough for you? (*calmer*) They give birth astride of a grave, the light gleams for an instant, then it's night once more. (*He jerks the rope*) On!

Lines such as these do something to qualify any over-precise parallel one might be tempted to draw between the Pozzo-Lucky combination and a two-tiered social order. Some of Pozzo's speeches go beyond what seems dramatically plausible in a decaying boss-figure. But, whatever language he uses (and one may suppose that it was Lucky who originally taught him to utter 'these beautiful things') his thoughts are always platitudes, so that on a wider view he can still be equated with a stagnant upper class. To his relative enjoyment of wealth and power would then be added the benefits—still relative to his capacity for using them—of a non-vocational education by social dependents. The characterisation would remain consistent.

If divested of social significance, the now enigmatic Pozzo could be summed up in the same comment as that made by Peer Gynt on the white-faced Stranger who kept pestering him for the gift of his corpse:

> Ah, it slipped out of him at last—
> He was a wretched moralist.[4]

[4] *Peer Gynt*, Act V, Sc. 2. Everyman translation.

But that in itself would seem an insufficient justification of the considerable rôle allotted to Pozzo in the play.

4

So far we have considered *Waiting for Godot* for the meanings it yields to the plain reader or the plain spectator at a performance. Presumably these are the principal meanings and it is on them that the play stands or falls if Beckett's intention—as must be assumed— was to communicate through drama with his contemporaries. Numerous critical studies of great ingenuity have, however, pushed the analysis further in various partial directions. Apart from the fringe-theses, which inevitably continue to multiply, the most important studies bear on one or more of four main points: Beckett's attitude to Christianity or, more generally, to religion; the concepts of Existence, of Nothingness, and of Time. Writing from a limited but, we hope, consistent point of view, we feel no necessity to go at great length into any of these questions for the purposes of the present study on tragedy and tragic drama. It should be enough to see them in the perspective of the play.

The religious theme in Godot centres upon the God–Godot–Grace syndrome,[5] already discussed above (pp. 246–50). Existence and Nothingness are complementary concepts, one the obverse of the other. Their exegesis by contemporary critics has been strongly conditioned by Existentialist theory and has consequently acquired a slightly distorted emphasis. Beckett's art and thought belong to quite a different line to Sartre's and one cannot see at what point phenomenology could ever have entered into his development. However, since both have apparently similar preoccupations which loom large in modern ideology, some confusion is not unacceptable. As for Time, this must enter into almost any theory of existence, but its provenance as a concept is quite clearly distinct. For both Beckett and those critics who have based aesthetic systems upon it, it derives either from Bergson or, more immediately, from Proust. Proustian studies have very naturally concentrated attention on the distinction—or better, the complex relationship—between chronometric time and

---

[5] Syndrome: 'A complex going together of the various symptoms of a disease.' (J. Drever, *A Dictionary of Psychology*, Penguin Books, revised edn, 1964.) 'Consciousness (*alias:* conscience) is a disease.' (Unamuno. See above, pp. 57–8.)

time experienced, and this subject has been a rich exegetical pasture-ground for a number of years. Beckett himself engaged in it in his study on Proust published in 1931, well before Existentialism had emerged in a defined form. Given consciousness, memory, and apprehension, the question of Time is not and cannot be new. Expressed as the contrast between (natural) time and eternity, with the desire either to escape permanently from the tyranny of the first into the second, or to capture 'eternal moments' from natural time[6] and preserve them from its ravages—usually by means of an apparently transcendent ecstasy, or sometimes more artificially by the use of drugs—it was a commonplace of Romantic and pre-Romantic thought. Such universally understood cliché-quotations as 'Time was abolished', '*O temps, suspends ton vol!*', 'One crowded hour of glorious life . . .' contain the whole of the basic concept, upon which every intellectual elaboration will be built. It is possible to be fascinated by these elaborations without experiencing intense enthusiasm. They are rationalisations of what everyone knows instinctively from infancy, as Pascal has already pointed out.[7]

In *Waiting for Godot* the two sorts of time figure prominently, not to say obtrusively. Vladimir and Estragon constantly complain of the slowness with which time passes and do their best to hurry it on with their futile diversions. Ironically, they have attained, or almost attained, a godlike timelessness, the impossible Romantic ideal. But instead of Paradise, the halt in endless bliss, it is a limbo or a purgatory. Somehow they have got stuck in a pocket of misery. 'Nothing happens, nobody comes, nobody goes, it's awful,' says Estragon. Outside them, natural time and its consequences flow on. Between the acts, the tree has grown five or six leaves. Between the acts, Pozzo has gone blind and Lucky dumb. 'They all change', as

[6] 'Clock time', of which it is usual to speak slightingly, is only an accurate means of marking natural time, which rules all natural reality. The only escape from it is through recourse to the supernatural, which is then called the Higher Reality, or through illusion, the Romantic or subjective reality. The second process is common in art, and perfectly legitimate. Most difficulties stem from the obscure distinction between this 'unnatural' time as a technical resource, e.g., compression, selective narrative, the flashback, and its psychological application to what is thought of as 'existence' but might more properly be called 'experience'.

[7] 'Knowledge of first principles, such as the existence of space, time, motion, numbers, is as sure as any knowledge which reasoning gives us. And it is on this knowledge supplied by the heart and instinct that reason must rely, founding all its arguments upon it.'

See above, p. 168 for the full context.

Estragon remarks, 'Only we can't.' It is with satisfaction that Vladimir in Act 2 recognises the wound on Estragon's leg made by Lucky's kick in Act 1 and observes that it is beginning to fester. Here is confirmation both of a remembered past event and of the fact that nature is taking its course even in them. With a little luck, one feels, they might even die naturally and be saved the effort of trying to hang themselves.[8]

All this is a variation on an old theme, an illustration of what can happen when the Romantic wish is granted and the fleeting moment really threatens to become eternal. But since Proust particularly it has been hardly possible to separate the question of time from the questions of existence and identity. Was the 'I' which existed in the past the same 'I' as now? Can it even be said to have existed, or is it a mere creation of the selective memory? Without continuity of experience, or at least of consciousness, the self becomes undefinable. Whether as actor or observer, it has at best a floating identity. It needs, to put it primly, a frame of reference, and the best frame so far discovered is the temporal one, the days and the years.

Unable to relate themselves to this, the two tramps wonder not only when and where they are, but who they are. The second act apparently takes place on the day immediately following the first act, but none of the outward things which identified them with 'yesterday' seem the same. The boots which Estragon left on the stage are, he says, different boots. Vladimir, brightly determined to find a rational explanation, concludes that some thief has come and substituted another pair, but a doubt subsists. On Pozzo's second appearance they are not certain that he is the same man, while he clearly does not remember them. The second messenger-boy, who looks exactly like the first, does not recognise them. Is he a different boy or is there something different about them? 'You're sure you saw me, eh?' cries Vladimir. 'You won't come and tell me tomorrow that you never saw me before?'

In these examples the haziness of the time factor merges into the concept of the Other, the Existentialist—but also pre-Existentialist— witness to the identity of the self and the other external point of reference which the self-contained Romantics believed they could do without. The most reliable Other is of course God conceived as an

---

[8] Though this idea is not explicit in *Godot*. It becomes more nearly so in *Endgame*:

CLOV (*of a rat he has left half-dead*): 'If I don't kill that rat he'll die.'

all-seeing absolute. Reduced to an elusive Godot and his ambiguous messengers, he is less satisfactory. As a human Pozzo, who can go blind from one day to the next—if it is the next—he is almost useless. Existentialism, with its categories of the *être-pour-soi* (the conscious self) and the *être-pour-autrui* (the self seen by others), defines this problem neatly without resolving it. It has not much relevance to Vladimir and Estragon's predicament, since their Others are as hazy as themselves. In this respect they are water reflecting water, of little help in any possible advance towards a definition. As for self-definition through meaningful acts, this resource of Existentialism is mocked almost to the limit of absurdity in the passage in which Vladimir persuades his companion to try on the pair of 'different' boots:

VLADIMIR: What about trying them?
ESTRAGON: I've tried everything.
VLADIMIR: I mean the boots.
ESTRAGON: Would that be a good thing?
VLADIMIR: It'd pass the time. (*Estragon hesitates.*) I assure you, it'd be an occupation.
ESTRAGON: A relaxation.
VLADIMIR: A recreation.
ESTRAGON: A relaxation.
VLADIMIR: Try.
ESTRAGON: You'll help me?
VLADIMIR: I will, of course.
ESTRAGON: We don't manage too badly, eh, Didi, between the two of us?
VLADIMIR: Yes, yes. Come on, we'll try the left first.
ESTRAGON: We always find something, eh, Didi, to give us the impression that we exist?
VLADIMIR (*impatiently*): Yes yes, we're magicians. But let us persevere in what we have resolved, before we forget.

Acts are meaningless, time does not flow consecutively, memory seems deceptive, existence in an 'impression', or perhaps a dream, happiness is acutely absent—though removed, the gap it has left still aches. This tooth-aching void supplies as good a metaphor as any other for the Nothing which the two tramps feel within and without them. They are on the point of becoming hollow men in a possibly hollow universe. This can be related to various philosophies of existence and essence, but as presented on the stage it really demands no other equipment in an audience than the bond of common perception.

5

Do audiences recognise Vladimir and Estragon as 'men like ourselves'? The public were disconcerted by the early productions, uncertain whether to look up, down, or straight ahead. The aura of *avant-garde*, which critics tend to interpose like a gauze curtain, helped to blur their vision. Gradually, as Beckett's dramatic idiom and ethos became more familiar, the play was able to make a direct impact unmuffled by novelty. In the London production of 1965, ordinary middlebrow audiences from Kensington and Chelsea responded spontaneously both to the gross farcical effects and to the moments of high seriousness which the play contains. The most striking of these occurs near the end when Vladimir, advancing to the front of the stage and fixing the void of the auditorium with eyes lit with a horrible kind of moribund gleam, soliloquises:

VLADIMIR: I don't know what to think any more.
ESTRAGON: My feet! (*He sits down, tries to take off his boots.*) Help me!
VLADIMIR: Was I sleeping, while the others suffered? Am I sleeping now? Tomorrow, when I wake, or think I do, what shall I say of today? That with Estragon, my friend, at this place, until the fall of night, I waited for Godot? That Pozzo passed, with his carrier, and talked to us? Probably, But in all that what truth will there be? (*Estragon having struggled with his boots in vain, is dozing off. Vladimir stares at him.*) He'll know nothing. He'll tell me about the blows he received and I'll give him a carrot. (*Pause.*) Astride of a grave and a difficult birth. Down in the hole, lingeringly, the gravedigger puts on the forceps. We have time to grow old. The air is full of our cries. (*He listens.*) But habit is a great deadener. (*He looks again at Estragon.*) At me too someone is looking, of me too someone is saying, He is sleeping, he knows nothing, let him sleep on. (*Pause.*) I can't go on! (*Pause.*) What have I said?

This speech is heard in dead silence, a silence compounded of sympathy and 'awe'. From a logical point of view, it is all wrong. Who is poor Vladimir to perceive all this and to express his recognition so articulately? Why does he appropriate Pozzo's grave-birth analogy and alter its basic significance by adding 'lingeringly' and

'We have time to grow old'? Does the man find that life is too short or too long? And who does he think is looking at him? Has he too turned out to be only a wretched moralist, with a theological bias in addition?

Again, this is a piece of fine writing in a play which deflates rhetoric—the kind of thing in a different idiom to which Marlowe and Shakespeare were addicted. Mr Beckett's excuse could be the same as theirs: that having got so far successfully, he has the right to let himself go, that at this point the audience will take anything from him, greedily, And this is sufficient immediate justification. Whether or not the speech is ideologically and characteristically in tone, it is unquestionably effective.

But Marlowe and Shakespeare were writing tragedy. One cannot say the same of Beckett in *Godot*. This play happens to be 'classed', even if tentatively. In the English edition of 1956 it is subtitled 'a tragi-comedy'. The present writer asked Mr Beckett if he would care to enlarge on this and got no answer, as he rather expected. In the absence of an authoritative lead, one is left with the tame but probably correct conclusion that *Waiting for Godot* is a tragi-comedy because it combines tragic and comic elements.[9] The former can be recognised at a reading or a performance and they evoke a reaction which is more complex than simple pity. The characters are hardly the 'little men' of the Charlie Chaplin tradition at whom one smiles while feeling sorry for them. They rejoin that human condition which we all take seriously because we recognise it as ours. Yet our response is not exactly fear, and even disquiet would seem too strong a term, for what worse thing could happen to them—and, by extension, us— than has happened already? If Godot does not come they will be left as they are, which at moments seems unbearable but is not absolutely so. And if they cracked, what difference would it make? Where could they escape to? One feels that if there were ten more acts they would still be going through the same motions, since there is no line of development open to them.

It is true that several are indicated. They are all summed up in almost the last lines of the play:

ESTRAGON: Didi.
VLADIMIR: Yes.
ESTRAGON: I can't go on like this.

[9] In the latest Parisian production to date (1966), however, it was simply styled 'a play'.

VLADIMIR: That's what you think.
ESTRAGON: If we parted? That might be better for us?
VLADIMIR: We'll hang ourselves tomorrow. (*Pause.*) Unless Godot comes.
ESTRAGON: And if he comes?
VLADIMIR: We'll be saved.

One can eliminate the improbables in this and be left with the single certainty. Our interpretation is that Godot will not come because Godot is the person one waits for: it is in that capacity that he exists. They will not hang themselves because they have already considered this twice and each time have found it impracticable. (Vladimir's remark is intended as consolatory, to give Estragon at least something to look forward to.) They will not separate because this again has been tried by Estragon and he has been driven back by unmaterialised fears of the Others or the unknown. We are left with Estragon's 'I can't go on like this' and Vladimir's: 'That's what you think,' which exactly echo the final sentences in Vladimir's grand soliloquy: 'I can't go on!' followed by the rebound: 'What have I said?'

The fellow-feeling which binds the characters to the audience is therefore a sensation of *impasse*. They are blocked in some desolate place and suffer because of it. Awareness of such a situation would not properly be tragic if exteriorised merely as an all-embracing pathos. It would be the situation of a herd of captives left to die slowly in a pit and would be in the highest degree lamentable, but tragic only in the medieval and Chaucerian sense.[10] To be fully tragic it must not be seen as definitively hopeless. This is where criticism of the play, like the play itself, balances on a knife-edge. If hope, or expectation, is entirely absent, it will not deserve even the partial qualification implied in 'tragi-comedy'. Not even the feeblest exploration of a possible change would be worth undertaking. The play nearly makes this point. It is, in fact, possible to interpret it as though it did, and in our conclusion that Godot will never come we may seem to have adopted that interpretation. In that case audiences which are moved sympathetically by *Godot* would be simply indulging in an act of self-pity. As a matter of observation—though this can only be a subjective impression—they seem not to be. What then? One can conclude that Godot will not come, one can say that objectively it does not matter in the slightest who or what Godot is, but one is still left with the spectacle of Vladimir who has not quite given up

[10] See above, p. 98, footnote.

and who is apparently prevented from giving up by some moral or natural imperative. It is in his attitude that the tragic uncertainty, however meagre, lies. Mr Beckett has necessarily not committed his character to anything very positive. Vladimir is not a figure on whom one could pin the Unconquerable Spirit of Man without feeling that the honour was (comically) incongruous. At most he deserves the Order of Perseverance, Third Class. The play is far from being a drama of Stoic endurance, yet there is some endurance in it. This, it seems to claim, is the human situation and the true human reaction (with no moral qualification of 'right' or 'wrong') is to put up with it. In that case there is some kind of virtue, not only in the tramps' physical and verbal exercises, but in their religious exercises too—the whole Grace syndrome. Like the rest, they help to pass the time.

If we accept this, we focus the whole of the tragic uncertainty/exploration on Vladimir, as already remarked. He is a weak focuspoint, though one would not call him uninteresting. The more obvious alternative is to focus it on Godot. Perhaps one should be left to take one's choice, but we think that the first—the theme of tenacious humanism sustained by ninety per cent of habit and ten per cent of hope—puts the play in a more satisfactory perspective. There is further support for this view in the opening dialogue of Act I:

VLADIMIR: It's too much for one man (*Pause. Cheerfully.*) On the other hand what's the good of losing heart now, that's what I say. We should have thought of it when the world was young, in the nineties.

ESTRAGON: Ah, stop blathering and help me off with this bloody thing. (*His boot.*)

VLADIMIR: Hand in hand from the top of the Eiffel Tower, among the first. We were respectable in those days. *Now it's too late. They wouldn't even let us up.*

Historically, this makes excellent sense. If Chekhov's generation were born too late for the Romantic illusion, Beckett's were born too late for disillusionment. The paradox, if it is one, seems nevertheless to rest on a sound psychological basis.

6

But *Godot* is more than half comic. The dialogue is funny and the overall tone of any production must reflect this. Let us suppose that Vladimir and Estragon, instead of merely testing the cord which holds up Estragon's trousers by pulling on it and nearly falling backwards, got as far as attaching it to the tree and round the neck of one of them. The cord would still break, the half-strangled tramp would still look grotesque, the bungled hanging would make a riotously funny scene. Within the atmosphere of *Godot* as it is, a more 'serious' development would be inconceivable. The attempted suicide would excite the same kind of laughter, by slightly more brutal means, as that actually aroused by the rest of the play. If the characters were strongly objectified, one could call this 'cruel' comedy; if strongly identified with the audience, 'bitter' comedy. In fact, the play is usually classed in the 'comedy of the absurd'.

This comparatively modern category assumes the meaninglessness or pointlessness to which we have already referred. It has particularly bleak implications. The old, light-hearted kind of absurdity was based on a feeling of security, or at least superiority. One could laugh unreservedly at the traditional antics of clowns, such as trying to fill a holed bucket with water, because one knew of a more effective way of doing the same thing. One would fetch a sound bucket. But in watching Vladimir and Estragon one does not readily think of better alternatives to their awkward actions. The 'absurdity' cannot be abolished by rectifications of detail. It embraces the whole situation in which they find themselves—the whole of life and personality—and one must, as spectator, either reject this situation *in toto* and walk out of the theatre, or consent to inclusion in it. In this case—assuming one stays and still laughs—one's laughter ought to have much in common with the anti-tragic guffaw discussed in relation to *Candide*.[11] And there are indeed several Rabelaisian moments in *Godot*, in spite of attenuations to satisfy the requirements of the Lord Chamberlain. Yet the contemporary laughter at the futility of everything is not exactly the same as the Voltairean—or better, perhaps, Swiftian— reaction to conditions of extreme horror. Horror, like disillusion- ment, appears to have lost its sting—thanks, to quote some of the various explanations given, to habituation, to irreligion, to mass conditioning in insensitivity, to television. The bogy which haunts the world of *Godot* is not horror in any sensational form, but limbo. And it is useless to react against a limbo, as Estragon is inclined to do. Once again, Vladimir appears to represent a sounder attitude. He dare not laugh, because it gives him a pain in his stomach, but he manages to smile, although, as he observes: 'It's not the same thing.'

[11] See above, pp. 135-6.

The 'absurd' element in *Godot* is nihilism sometimes smiling at itself, sometimes being protested against, but almost the whole time presented as the reality. If it is real, the best course is to accept it and not, as did the characters in *Candide*, attempt to make sense of it. Beckett suggests a state of things which is so appalling that it *must* be meaningless. If it had a meaning, it would be unbearably horrible. This is the anti-tragic side of his work, in which human existence is assimilated to the earthquake or the act of God discussed in Chapter 1 above. It is, in fact, another 'natural disaster', and perhaps the greatest of them all.

Whenever this notion dominates (it is not universal in *Godot*) the meaninglessness of meaninglessness must be respected. That is what Beckett's characters, with some difficulty, attempt to do. They silence Lucky, an inverted Pangloss. At least they have the right idea:

ESTRAGON: I'll go and get a carrot.
> *He does not move.*
VLADIMIR: This is becoming really insignificant.
ESTRAGON: Not enough.

In *Endgame*, the characters have progressed nearer to the ultimate objective:

HAMM: We're not beginning to ... to ... mean something?
CLOV: Mean something! You and I, mean something! (*Brief laugh.*) Ah, that's a good one!
HAMM: I wonder. Imagine if a rational being came back to earth, wouldn't he be liable to get ideas into his head if he observed us long enough? (*Voice of rational being.*) Ah, good, now I see what it is, now I understand what they're at! .... And without going as far as that, we ourselves ... (*with emotion*) ... we ourselves ... at certain moments ... (*vehemently*) To think perhaps it won't all have been for nothing!
CLOV (*anguished, scratching himself*): I have a flea!
HAMM: A flea! Are there still fleas?

If one laughs at this kind of dialogue, it is not the mocking laughter of superiority, neither is it the earthy laughter which has traditionally greeted things too huge to be taken seriously. It springs, no doubt, from the almost delighted shock with which audiences have always hailed exteriorisations of their own repressed thoughts and fantasies. On the music hall level, the comic exteriorisation is firmly based on such things as chamber-pots and sexual habits. At the

Godot level it is based on nihilism, a forbidden subject which becomes vastly funny when aired by a pair of plain-speaking lay-abouts. To invoke theory, this is what is conjectured to have been the comic *catharsis*, through laughter.

7

How representative is, or was, *Godot*? A critic recently wrote:

> Having the kind of absolute clarity of form that is possessed by such modern masterpieces as Kafka's *Das Schloss* and Faulkner's *As I lay dying*, Camus' *La Peste* and William Golding's *Lord of the Flies*, the play rapidly burned itself into the memories of audiences all over Europe and the Americas; and, by the end of the fifties, its décor and its images had become an undisposable [*sic*] part of the furniture of the contemporary imagination.[12]

This is the kind of claim which only a rigorously dedicated specialist could make. Even in what may be called Top Culture, it is easy to think of half-a-dozen influences which have done more to the contemporary imagination than Beckett's. In spite of the numerous studies published on him, for the most part in academic and specialised reviews, Samuel Beckett is not even yet a widely known writer, while only a minority of the serious theatre-going public can have seen his plays. This would not necessarily disqualify him as the mouthpiece of a contemporary mood, since a society does not need to know an author in order to be represented by him. The great majority of typical late Victorians had probably never heard of Ibsen, and most of those who had rejected with horror his interpretation of their age, which is now seen as imaginatively faithful. One can therefore question the literal truth of Professor Scott's statement without disputing its more general implications. These—to write very prudently —may or may not be exact. It is possible that time will tell. What can be said with a reasonable degree of confidence is that the words quoted are prophetic. Future ideological historians will hardly be able to dismiss Beckett as a fringe writer. They will almost certainly have to place him in a fairly central position. They will do this, according to all precedent, less because they will possess quantities of confirmatory sociological material than because of this individual author's artistic achievement. Unfairly perhaps, the artist is accepted

[12] Nathan A. Scott, *Samuel Beckett* (Bowes and Bowes, 1965).

as the voice of his period because of the excellence of his art. Having expressed something memorably, his representativeness is taken as read. The people one would really like to consult when recreating the past are the mute inglorious Miltons who lived it intuitively. But, since they have disappeared without trace, it is the Miltons who were neither mute nor inglorious who seem to hold the key. Yet through what hypersensitive and often neurotic distortions of what for less gifted contemporaries appeared a simple reality is one obliged to pursue the elusive approximation to the truth.

Realising this and accepting Beckett as one of our outstanding writers, what an opportunity we seem to have. Abandoning for the moment insistence on integral tragedy and taking *Godot* as the only type of tragic expression possible in the nineteen-fifties, could we not decide once for all from our own experience whether tragedy is a minority or a majority art, whether it is protest, subversion, or catharsis, whether it stems from weakness or strength? It should be easy, since we have lived through the period, but for the present writer at least it is not.

One thing is clear enough. Beckett's work represents, with minor variations, the whole frame of mind known as 'beat'. It is near-nihilism in reaction against—to adopt a still valuable nineteenth-century term—positivism. But which is the dominant trend, neo-*Weltschmerz* (making the necessary post-Romantic adjustments) or neo-positivism? Is the 'beat' attitude and the art which goes with it the expression of a sick minority, or is it the underlying ethos of Western society as a whole? On another score, is neo-positivism, undoubtedly vigorous in the short term, built on a sound basis of 'health', or merely on *hubris*? If the latter, the bubble may one day burst and the Vladimirs, already conditioned to near-despair but still just keeping afloat, would be seen as 'healthier' because of their greater survival-potential. A dramatic event such as a nuclear war would test this out but short of some spectacular catastrophe the answers must await the verdict of history.

Even that may not be conclusive. A section at least of modern Greek scholarship tends to regard Euripides as a 'sick' writer (as M. Goldmann regarded Racine) while others disagree. If Euripides was 'sick' it was because he was beginning to question an earlier view of the gods and the moral values they symbolised. But it might be more accurate to conclude that the old gods were 'sick' and that Euripides, in initiating a reassessment, was on the line which led to future health. To many of our contemporaries a readjustment to the values of Beckett's world would be a fate little preferable to death. But it is conceivable, without swallowing the whole of his ethos, that it contains some vital elements which will be incorporated in the prevailing future ideology and that in the course of time their relevance to this will become clear. If one cannot be certain that it will be clear, it is because 'history' means historians, just as posterity means one's own children or grandchildren. Are they likely to be more infallible or unanimous than comparable judges in the past?

Meanwhile, it seems at least highly probable that such a play as *Waiting for Godot* will be scrutinised and rescrutinised for ideological and sociological clues and will be valued as evidence of a mood of the fifties. For our present purposes, that is as far as we need go. Whether or not the mood was dominant, it was at least sufficiently widespread, in comparison with similar moods as reflected in the art of other periods, to be noteworthy. Its characteristics are to eliminate the heroic, to reduce 'tragic' curiosity considerably without suppressing it entirely, to lament the human condition indirectly, via irony and double-take, and—surprisingly enough in an age which was supposed to be sex-obsessed—to eschew the 'natural' passions almost completely and set up instead a kind of humanist asceticism which some critics have assimilated to Puritanism. If it is this, it is Puritanism without the support of divine sanctions, adopted with no ulterior motive whatsoever. One can understand this as an exercise or a penance in view of a reward, but to practise it for its own sake is a little revolutionary and is certainly the most radical challenge to the old gods that can be extracted from Beckett's work. After the sensualism of Claudel, the austerity of Beckett[13] comes like a blast of cold air. It would be odd if it came to be seen as characteristic of a whole generation.

[13] *Not* masochism, which is properly a form of sexual enjoyment.

265

13

Consequences

1

We are now in a better position to draw explicit conclusions on some of the issues raised in the course of this book. Contemporary criticism tends to discount the value of all general theories, including a theory of tragedy. One would be bound to agree if the theory were expected to be comprehensive, applicable aesthetically to all periods of drama, and at the same time consistently satisfactory from the moral and sociological points of view. It would be a lot to demand and one would have to be unrealistically sanguine, or arrogant, or both, to do so. But theories can still proceed by trial and error, as they have done hitherto. It should not be impossible to affirm certain principles on which a working hypothesis, if wanted, can be based.

We have a contemporary concept of tragedy and the tragic is 'life', which is definable in broad terms.[1] We have a number of established dramas commonly accepted as tragedies. We have a larger number of dramas and other literary works in which tragic features can be recognised in various degrees (this is the most debatable area). We also have Aristotle, a critic who was not afraid to make generalisations on well-considered grounds and who, though necessarily incomplete on certain points and questionable on others, traced out lines still capable of development. From all this something can be concluded which is neither too restrictive nor too vague.

A preliminary question, raised in the first chapter and left un-answered, is whether the tragic in 'life' is the same thing as the tragic in drama. We think that it is, if one confines oneself to fundamentals.

[1] See Chapter 1 above.

The archetypal tragic situation, in both fields, is that of the individual or the community going down a slope which leads to destruction. To this situation, working itself out in action, are attached three basic reactions: fear of the threatened disaster, the sense of error or failure at some point leading to the downward path and, primarily for the spectators, the feeling of sympathy or solidarity with the sufferers in the disaster. Although these reactions cannot affect the objective reality of the event, they have to be taken into account. They enter into it and determine its nature. Unless they are experienced, the bare event in itself will not qualify as tragic. It may become, as has been seen in earlier chapters, either comic, or obscene, or ridiculous (farcical), or absurd (meaningless).

There is thus a recognisable type of situation which, when regarded in a certain light, is universally accepted as tragic whether it occurs in life or in art mirroring life. Everything else which may attach to it is non-essential from the analytical point of view. It takes the form either of subsidiary lived reactions or of the variations and extensions of situation and/or reaction developed by the artist-dramatist. Regarded non-analytically, these variations and developments may well seem so organic to the tragic nucleus that any attempt at fragmentation becomes a falsification, and it is true that on grounds of psychological plausibility the ambiguous situation exciting mixed reactions appears 'truer' today than the starkly tragic situation—*Godot* 'truer' than the *Oedipus*. But the analytical approach, though it may be held to oversimplify the psychological reality, is something more than a convenient critical instrument. It also embodies a temperamental conception of both art and life, which is certainly no less common than the other conception of their indivisible complexity.

It therefore seems quite legitimate to attempt to separate the basically tragic elements as just described from the non-tragic and the less tragic and to apply such a criterion to—in particular—the work of art with a good prospect of reaching a 'true' understanding of it.

2

One factor whose importance we have stressed in examining dramatic tragedy is much less evident in 'life'. It is the sense of exploration directed at some kind of discovery about human nature and the powers which influence it. In a 'lived' tragedy the events themselves occupy practically the whole attention, which becomes completely absorbed in the shock of the final disaster. There is not much place for anything else except fear and sympathy-cum-pity. But it will be observed that an event which excited *only* those instinctive reactions would be classed as an accident or a plain disaster rather than as a tragedy. 'It just happened that way. What more is there to be said?' Before the event can be felt as tragic, there is certain to be some speculation on its causes, exercised at the least in the form of post-mortem curiosity. There is also likely to be a sense of wonderment before the catastrophe about what is happening and why, distinct from the feeling of apprehension. These reflective reactions may be rudimentary in a 'lived' tragedy and in themselves hardly constitute an 'exploration', but they provide the whole of the necessary basis on which the dramatist builds his exploration. This will be implicit rather than premeditated. If it were the latter, there would be a temptation to reach conclusions which would turn the work into a demonstration possessing some moral utility. This, as has been seen, is not a quality of the great tragic dramas. They cannot be used as 'a school of virtue'.[2]

The tragic mood is one of unsatisfied—and ultimately unsatisfiable—curiosity about the deepest issues which affect human well-being. At its most authentic it is distinct from the other two principal moods which determine both the lived reaction and the nature of the work of art. It avoids, as has just been said, didacticism aiming at firm conclusions. Equally, it avoids the 'absurd' and its variations, which are all characterised by the refusal to speculate and the acceptance of the human condition as radically inexplicable—this gives either despair or the nihilism beyond despair.[3] Tragedy, in practice, will rarely be quite pure. It is quite likely to be tinged with didacticism or nihilism, either of which a critic may stress according to his reading of a particular work. The interest then is to determine the importance of the uncommitted exploratory content. If it seems to be dominant, one is justified in claiming the work as tragic even though it may not be a rigorously perfect tragedy.

In the classic tragedies at least, the exploration bears on a stretch of existence between two points in natural time. The second point is death or some other kind of finality. The first point may be birth, or before birth, as in the *Oedipus*. It can also be much nearer to the end of the temporal sequence. In French classical tragedy, observance of

[2] *Pace* Racine. See above, p. 106, footnote.
[3] In theory, also the stoicism beyond despair. But one is not convinced.

the unity of time makes it appear to be very close to the end, but this appearance relates only to the dramatic action. The story, recalled verbally, extends as far back into the past as is necessary to motivate the few hours of action represented on the stage. Exactly the same principle applies to other drama whose action, as witnessed by the spectators, is less compressed in time. One goes back to the point at which the tragic event, or complex of events, was set in motion, but one need go no further in order to have a complete 'tragedy'. The tragedy of *Macbeth* 'begins' with the first meeting with the Witches, *Othello* with the hero's wooing of Desdemona, *Hamlet* and *Electra* with the murders of the fathers, *Phèdre* with her first sight of Hippolyte, *Rosmersholm* with the arrival of Rebecca at the Rosmers' house, *The Master Builder* with the completion of the church at Stavanger, and so on. These were the points, whether represented or recalled, at which elements with a general tragic potential combined in a situation which had plainly tragic consequences in action. One might object that it is too great a simplification to divide the tragic process into elements, situation, and action (or events), and very naturally the reflective mind probes the antecedents of the situation in the inevitable but sometimes over-subtle search for the *hamartia*. But it must be remembered that the alternative is predetermination (Macbeth was 'fated' to meet the Witches) and that predetermination conceived as a universal law is inimical to tragedy, which requires a degree of uncertainty. To exploit the metaphor used earlier, of the protagonist going down the slope to destruction, his position may be seen as desperate once he is on the slope. But it was not inevitable that he should find himself upon it; in other circumstances he might have avoided it altogether. In this instance, the slope represents the tragic event, the tragic situation is located at the point where the descent began. One will of course ask how the protagonist came to be in that situation, but the mere fact that one does ask is a denial of predetermination. If he *must* have come there or, on the wider view, if the potentially tragic elements in human life *must* always lead to ultimate catastrophe, there are no questions to be asked.

Two qualifications suggest themselves. One is that determinism is one of the possibilities which tragedy may explore, without necessarily concluding in its favour. The other is that the tragic hero is a special figure who is singled out for predetermination, without establishing a rule for mankind in general. This view has been very strongly held and is related to the concepts of the scapegoat and the sacrificial king, already discussed. All that one would say is that the doomed Corn King. like the Byronic 'man of destiny' is merely one image of the tragic hero, and that others are possible without destroying the conditions of a tragedy.

This, we believe, consists primarily on the events as they proceed from a particular situation. The events occur consecutively in natural time and are and must be embodied in what is called existence. In this sense, Aristotle's disregard of the deepest kind of characterisation and his insistence on action were fully justified. Existence is the subject, with the hazards which attend it, and essence is important only so far as it helps to throw light on existence. Being is thus subservient to doing, not *vice-versa*. (One knows, of course, that such distinctions are artificial, if drawn rigorously. But they are still of paramount importance in any conception of the human condition, dramatic or other.) It is when the hazards are predominantly internal or 'psychological' that the distinctions become less clear and the difficulties of interpretation increase. But even then they are shown and realised through action in a time continuum, without which their tragic potentialities must remain latent.[4] To explain a sequence of events a modern dramatist may well remount in action, by such devices as the flashback, to an earlier period in the protagonist's life, but he cannot make that period the climax. The climactic disaster which confirms the tragedy can only occur last in natural time. (See above, pp. 86–9, our discussion of the 'recognition' in *Hamlet*.)

3

The pattern of the tragic story is that of the journey rather than of the battle. It is the journey through life, or a part of life. As in stories of other kinds, there may be incidental battles. In the happy-ending story (as the *Odyssey*, *Pilgrim's Progress*) these are clearly episodic and usually represent obstacles which the hero must surmount in moving towards his desirable goal. In tragedy the goal—disaster—is undesirable and the battles are usually attempts to avoid moving

[4] If Beckett's *Godot* is interpreted as a play without action, one might say that the characters have reached the tragic situation, but that the event does not follow. This would explain why the play seems incompletely tragic. But the characteristic of the tramps' situation is that it cannot develop into events. One must either regard this as a novel formula for tragedy, or qualify the situation by a different word, e.g., horrible, pathetic, absurd.

towards it, to retain a foothold on the slope. But though they are lost battles, and fought with an opposite intention, they are still subservient to the theme of the onward march. In considering some classic examples we found that the acted part of the story—the tragedy proper—was not constructed round a conflict, and there seems no reason to revise this finding to suit later tragedies and tragic plays. They also are based on the concept of the journey, however long or short, which is certainly superior as an exploratory theme to the concept of the battle. The contrary view, apart from the Romantic theory of the agonising 'tragic' choice, owes its force to another theory, also of the nineteenth century, that drama entails conflict—in fact that 'dramatic' and 'conflicting' are inseparable terms. Unsound though this is historically, it has led to many retrospective misinterpretations of tragic dramas conceived on a different pattern, and some of the consequences still persist.[5]

Examining this question on a psychological level, we found that the notion of an internal fissure in human nature, resulting in a so-called tragic duality, did not appear to assume importance for the European mind until the Romantic era. To say that it was non-existent before would no doubt be an unjustified generalisation. The most dubious area and the richest field for investigation would be the age of the Reformation, in which orthodox Catholicism, emergent Protestantism, and the humanist revival of secular Stoicism were contending for the loyalties of communities and individuals. The stresses so set up were considerable, but on the evidence of literature,

---

[5] One consequence, today almost discredited, was the theory of the 'well-made' play, which in the detail of its construction proceeds by a series of engagements between the characters. This encourages scenes of combative dialogue, in which each tries to convince or defeat the other by force of telling repartee. Critics easily assumed that French classical tragedy, whose stage action is highly concentrated in obedience to the unities, was built on the same technique. Later and better analysis shows that Racine's characters and, to a lesser but appreciable degree, those of Corneille, do not 'argue it out' with each other. Each pursues his own interior monologue, as it might now be called, and is impervious to the monologue of the other. Each is exploring his own reactions in relation to the situation and is affected by the parallel monologue only so far as it provides a cue for a new line of self-exploration. It might be added that the Senecan device of *stichomythia*, the tit-for-tat dialogue composed of short sentences which seems an ideal vehicle for the verbal duel, was hardly used by Shakespeare in his great tragedies. The monologue and the 'indirect' dialogue (the reply, not to the immediate argument, but to the thought it sets up in the speaker's mind) are characteristic of these plays also.

271

including dramatic literature, they were not generally realised and in any case not seen as tragic material. The human personality was still regarded as one and indivisible, as it had been with the Greeks. It might go one way or another, to salvation or damnation, but it went *en bloc*. That at least is the overwhelming impression given by the characters of drama and the novel and, even if it were ascribed to over-simple characterisation, to an undeveloped sense of psychological analysis, this would hardly matter for the purposes of the argument. The whole contention is in the mind, and there is no need to broach the truly formidable question of whether the human psyche was in fact less complicated in earlier centuries, or whether it merely conceived itself as being so. For the practical purpose of establishing a generally accepted norm the two things are the same. In short, and subject to a very thorough analysis of West European attitudes in the sixteenth and seventeenth centuries which has not yet been undertaken from this point of view, it seems that awareness of the great 'tragic' dichotomy remains a Romantic innovation. A probable explanation of this has been suggested above in the chapter on Blake.[6] Although it is theoretically possible that a comparable two-way strain should have been set up in the sixteenth century by the Calvinist doctrine of inner grace, this doctrine does not seem to have exteriorised itself in the same way or to have yielded an altered image of humanity such as the nineteenth century undoubtedly produced.

The tragic exploration as we have seen it is always human-centred. No doubt this is ultimately true of all art, a human production. But attempts can be made to simulate a supernatural angle of vision (particularly in theologically influenced works, such as the Mystery Plays) which, in terms of artistic execution, does alter the stature and perspective of the human characters. In tragedy the divine element ceases to give the standard dimension and recedes into the half-known to become one of the forces among which the human protagonist moves in his journey towards disaster. *His* efforts, discoveries and ultimate failure constitute the tragic theme. This is certainly true of Ibsen, of Racine, of Shakespeare, and even of Greek tragedy. Dramatically, if not morally, the gods of the Greeks fill secondary rôles in the play enacted on the stage. If, for example, the *Hippolytus* of Euripides was intended to show a conflict between two goddesses, each championing a different principle, it would be perfectly practic-

[6] See particularly pp. 180–3 above.

able to allow them to dominate the stage and to use the human characters in a subsidiary capacity, as is done in the 'mythological' play and in some opera. The opposite course is in fact taken, because the point of the play is to show the effect of the supposedly divine contention upon the human protagonists.

In such cases, gods and goddesses represent powerful forces, external to man to a degree which is debatable, which influence the human situation. They possess some power in their own right, as, rather more questionably, do the gods of Racine's *Phèdre* and the Godot of Beckett. If conceived as frankly external, their dramatic function is identical with that of human powers. They act as tyrants, tormentors, enemies, or avengers, with precisely similar effects on the victims. Whether the hero is persecuted by Zeus or by Creon, by Olympus or by Society, his tragic experience is the same. It is when the gods 'enter into men' that there seems to be a difference, for the source of suffering becomes partly or wholly internal. But it should be remembered that a human force can do as much. The loyalty or the admiration felt for a human tyrant by his would-be assassin works inwardly upon the latter, the moral influence exerted by a social order sets up the same reactions as the influence of a divine imperative. The same feelings are involved in the betrayal of a Cæsar or a Jesus.

Nevertheless, it is more usual to regard the secular force as external and the spiritual force as internal or, from a modern standpoint, 'psychological'. In that case the god, like other spiritual powers right down the supernatural scale from the angel to the ghost to the earth spirits of Ibsen's *John Gabriel Borkman*, can be given two different names with no change in its tragic function. In that capacity, it does not matter whether the mysterious force at work in the individual is called a god or a psychosis. Whether Phèdre was brought to the brink of the slope by Venus, a supernatural entity, by the sexual aberrations of her ancestors, by her own personal erotic proclivities or even, on the shortest view, by the 'fault' of her husband in leaving her unhusbanded in the company of her stepson, the result is still a tragedy. We quote this in disproof of the widely held view that tragedy is 'numinous' by nature. The numinous quality is in the eye of the beholder. One would not dispute for a moment the importance of the kind of distinctions just indicated in the framing of a cosmology. The sources to which a society attributes its reactions have a deep influence not only upon its moral outlook but also upon its behaviour.

273

One can readily recognise this while maintaining that it has no essential bearing on the 'tragic' situation. The only bearing it might have would be one of status. In a spiritually-conditioned culture, it might well be that a situation attributable to purely material factors would appear too trivial to qualify. Every casual act of sex followed by an abortion is not normally regarded as a tragedy. Yet why not? Perhaps it should be. It is purely a matter of ideological perspective.

4

When considering the social significance of tragedy, a distinction must be drawn between 'gods' and 'God'. The former, in whatever sense they are understood, represent partial and sectional values or impulses. The latter is a total and absolute concept, which exists only in virtue of being universally taken for granted. Not only is it unquestionable, but it is such that the possibility of asking questions about it never occurs to the mind. In ages of faith, i.e., of unquestioning acceptance of a divine order, there is no room for a tragic exploration of the most fundamental issues affecting humanity. This still provides the most cogent reason why the European Middle Ages had no true notion of tragedy, which was whittled down to the bare theme of the sad decline from greatness. Monotheism is in any case less favourable to tragedy than a polytheistic religion, such as that of the Greeks, which contains in itself the germ of an analytical process which sets off one moral value against another and leads to qualitative comparisons. The concept of One God precludes this. In theatrical jargon its totality is bound, almost by definition, to steal the whole show. When God is introduced as 'a protagonist', even if only notionally—as happened according to M. Mauriac in *Partage de Midi*[7]—the tragedy falters and the keen line of exploration sputters out in a poetic euphoria, eventually recognised as such by the author himself.

As with gods, so God can descend (though riskily) from the theological and reign for a time in other spheres. The political régime or the social order, so long as they are accepted as unquestionable or 'natural', are really God for the no doubt deluded believer in them. Nature itself, when conceived as a principle whose workings cannot be scrutinised or changed, is God until it incurs the scientific examina-

[7] See above, pp. 237–8.

tion. Pascal's curious list of God-substitutes,[8] though seen as substitutes by the Christian believer, are not so for the individual who
conceives them as absolutes. If one amends or extends his list to cover
material ambition, physical enjoyment, money, and so on, one
merely emphasises its general truth. One also sees why his grand
design was doomed to failure. It is not possible to set up a dialectic
between two fundamental convictions, each resting upon a different
Order. Only a traumatic conversion, not a dialectic, could achieve
the reorientation he desired.

Tragedy, it would be easy to conclude, is the questioning of an
absolute hitherto taken for granted and it *therefore* embodies the
protest or challenge of a dissenting minority as discussed above in
Chapter 4.[9] In considering this persuasive theory one has to move
very warily indeed, and sift the available evidence with the utmost
circumspection. Complete precision, entailing the formation of moral
and aesthetic judgments and the assessment of the force of social
ideologies at certain dates, is impossible in such a field. One comes as
near to it as one can. As applied to the seventeenth century, the
theory appeared to be of dubious validity. On general grounds, too,
it seems to be near the mark but not quite on it. We think that the
exploratory spirit of tragedy is not, in itself, 'subversive'. It may,
looking back, be seen to have heralded an overthrow of established
values, but that was not its motivation. The exploration occurs
historically at a point at which God is conceived as open to scrutiny
—which is certainly the beginning of the end of absolutism—but
without an iconoclastic intention. It may, indeed, imply the opposite:
admiration, conviction of rightness—'to justify the ways of God to
men'. It is admittedly difficult to demarcate the stages in the sequence:
free inquiry, protest, rebellion. But we think that tragedy at its most
authentic belongs predominantly to the first stage, with no thought
of the further developments which are likely to follow. Nor, in
practice, is it inevitable that they should follow. After the first stage,
it is always possible for the situation to take a different turn. We do
not see tragedy as a minority challenge, so much as an examination
initiated from strength (even, if one likes, from *hubris*) from a
position *within* the Establishment. The eventual consequences may or
may not be revolutionary, but they are what comes *after* tragedy and
are not inherent in the impulse which created it.

[8] *Pensées*, La. 300, quoted above, p. 155.
[9] See particularly pp. 72–4.

This aspect of the tragic process in action can be illustrated by isolating one of the principal themes of *Hamlet*, the revenge theme. One postulates a social ethic which requires the killing of a father to be avenged by his son, and which is taken all the more for granted when the father is a King and his son the lawful successor. In some of Shakespeare's historical tragedies this ethic is incorporated without discussion or question. In *Hamlet* its presentation is different. It is shown working itself out, with all its disastrous consequences, among a certain group of people. But it is not condemned. The whole run of the play assumes that Hamlet *ought* to avenge his father and when he finally does so there is no question of his having acted wrongly—only tardily. One would never conclude, on the evidence of this one play, that Shakespeare was challenging an accepted moral principle. He was merely exploring what it might lead to in its human implications. From this demonstration others might go on to establish, if they wished, that the revenge principle was morally or socially pernicious and raise an explicit protest against it. All that Shakespeare does is to draw attention to it in a tragic situation. There is nothing in *Hamlet* to suggest that he himself, or any ideological trend he represented, was against it. Even if, to invoke a well-aired theory, 'Shakespeare' was Bacon, the tragic dramatist's uncommitted curiosity would not be compromised by Bacon's famous pronouncement that: 'Revenge is a kind of wild justice, which the more man's nature runs to, the more ought law to weed it out.'[10] For this is the voice of the moralist, whereas the tragic dramatist, whether he is the same man or another, speaks with a different voice owing to the nature of his art. He is not to be regarded as an apologist for a point of view.[11]

5

The greatest tragedies create a passionate interest in the consequences of a situation and a lesser, though indispensable, interest in its

[10] Francis Bacon, *Essays*: 'Of Revenge'. Bacon's condemnation bears principally on private revenges, of the *vendetta* type. At the end of the same essay he is inclined to excuse 'public' revenges—for the assassinations of rulers. Hamlet's revenge might be said to partake of both types.
[11] Tragedy is also distinct from the problem play. Corneille's *Le Cid* poses openly, and debates, the question of the vengeance obligation *versus* its consequences. It is not, except nominally, a tragedy. Various seventeenth-century Spanish plays pose similar problems in debates involving the 'point of honour'. These also fail to be tragedies. In Ibsen the tragic temperature drops whenever the 'problem' becomes too obtrusive.

causes. One must recognise that this is the order in which the tragic presents itself, not merely as a matter of dramatic technique, but because the tragic experience is only fully realised in action. By 'action' is meant not only the events of the plot, but the reactions of the protagonists on their way to destruction. The *Oedipus*, *Phèdre*, and *Lear* move us by the spectacle of what happens and the way it happens, not as illustrations of the operation of some moral principle. Our emotional response is more than the immediate response; it is the response which is most necessary before the work can be classed as tragic. In that case, it might be asked, if the effect is the true tragedy and the possible cause is a secondary factor, why bother about *hamartia*?

The answer emerges most clearly from a brief consideration of the idea of poetic justice, which is sometimes held to rule tragedy. Aristotle appeared to subscribe to this view when he remarked that 'decent people must not be shown passing from good fortune to misfortune, for that is . . . disgusting,' and 'vicious people must not be shown passing from misfortune to good fortune, for that is the most untragic situation possible . . .' But these statements do not imply a belief in an absolute principle of equity: they are part of Aristotle's recipe for achieving the 'tragic pleasure'. They derive from his assessment—not perhaps the most demanding one—of audience-reaction. This is obviously variable, according to the time and the place. The dramatist and the producer are always exercising judgments, even if largely unconscious, on the degree of cruelty, obscenity, horror, or pathos that their public will take. The oppression of the innocent, with the apparent injustice entailed, is in the same category. What is involved here is not a philosophic principle, but a dramatic, or even a theatrical, consideration.

Even in that form, how often it is flouted. In tragedy the good and innocent are constantly oppressed, with little hint of a metaphysical compensation. All the playwright concedes is some attenuation of the visible sufferings of the victim. Antigone, walled-up in the cave, hangs herself to finish it quickly, but is not seen. Cordelia is hanged, also off-stage; her limp body afterwards is not 'disgusting'. Ophelia is drowned, a 'muddy death', but given some elegiac quality in the description. Desdemona is smothered, but on the inner stage. Iphigenia is butchered on an off-stage altar—unless Diana saved her.

One thinks at once of such characters, virgins or young brides, because they are images of innocence. They are the nearest a dramatist can get, apart from children, to blamelessness personified. That does not save them. The undoubted mental agony of their deaths and, on a realistic view, the probable physical agony, is softened only for the eye of the audience. If one still insists on an idea of justice, how could their sufferings be explained?

It would be impossible to avoid the theory of retribution, which we have already found to be untenable. It would be necessary to manufacture a particular *hamartia* for each of these characters and, although with academic ingenuity it can no doubt be done, the overall results are so artificial as to bring any assumed 'law' into contempt. Antigone's defiance of the temporal power might, at a pinch, be held blameworthy, but Desdemona's only detectable crime was to lose her handkerchief. Unfair to virgins: such is tragedy, less as an incidental by-product than typically and recurrently. (More experienced-looking characters may be less conspicuously innocent in the flesh, but their sufferings sustain the same principle.) One is almost bound to conclude that the agonies of the innocent and the nearly innocent are an important component of tragedy even though they are not its main one.[12] They also, in the more limited sense with which Aristotle was concerned, enter into the 'tragic pleasure'.

Against this realistic and possibly pessimistic presentation of the human condition runs the profound conviction that 'unmerited' suffering is 'wrong'. Emotional, not rational, this is the God that never fails because the survival of humanity as a gregarious species depends on its not failing. Apparently disproved by events again and again, it constantly revives. Perverted at times almost beyond recognition, it is still worshipped in the guise of justification. Whether or not it is preferable to kill a man on a trumped-up charge than with no justification at all, it is always done that way. The dramatist, caught between the downward impetus of the tragic event and the seemingly instinctive force of a moral impulse, is obliged to leave a place somewhere for *hamartia*.

When this is done too literally, either by the dramatist or his exegetists, it appears contrived and trivial. But the silliest analyses of *hamartia* stem from a natural compulsion, of which they are simply myopic applications. The *hamartia* in *Othello* does not attach to the detail of Desdemona's handkerchief, but to a whole complex of circumstance and character which brought a certain group of people together in a certain way. Something went wrong—this is the in-

[12] Overstressed, they put the work in the 'horror' category.

stinctive reaction—but what it was escapes exact definition. Or alternatively, it can be defined in several different ways.

Tragedy thus satisfies our conception of the cruel reality, and even our perverse pleasure in seeing the innocent victimised, without totally frustrating our moral sense. The deep general conviction that there was a failure somewhere—that the disaster either need not or ought not to have occurred—is respected. But it remains general. The failure cannot be located in the transgression of an established law, since the laws of the tragic universe are uncodified. They are as much an object of exploration as everything else. They are, one might say, the prime object of exploration—which, however, they always elude. The tragic sense can thus include and even encourage moral curiosity, while leaving it continually unsatisfied. As for the idea of poetic justice, with the principle of compensation which it embodies, it is really too neat to apply to tragedy. But one sees why it persists: as an over-definite attempt to rationalise an instinctive thirst for equity which it is impossible to disregard.

The tragic sense of failure is a sign of basic optimism. Only a mentality which assumes that it is normal for things to go right will think of 'failure' when they go wrong. In a nihilistic or totally a-moral scheme no such thought will occur. With equal force, a scheme of total pessimism, accepting the domination of evil, has no room for it either. In this one can find a further general reason for relating the historical incidence of great tragic drama to the ideo-logical upcurves of societies. At such periods the urge to confront 'ought' with 'is' is particularly strong and there is sufficient dynamism to exteriorise it in boldly conceived art-forms.

6

The dilution of tragedy in the past hundred years or so must be accepted as a trend which is unlikely to be reversed, in Western culture at least. It can be ascribed in part to the growing size and diversification of societies which make comparison with small, unified cultures such as the Athenian, Elizabethan and Louis-Quatorzien somewhat misleading. The tragic idea of descent can persist, as can the tragic sense of failure. But to relate them to a subject of common interest and to convey them more or less pure to the ideologically fragmented societies of today is a task which drama can no longer perform without sacrificing plausibility. (The so-called monolithic societies, mainly communist, have so far been hostile to the tragic exploration. As regimentation decreases they may well enter a phase of great tragic art before becoming ideologically fragmented in their turn.) It seems that we must be content to find the tragic mixed with other elements, whether this occurs in a compact work such as *Waiting for Godot* or a work of Brechtian proportions which manages to elude, in some of its aspects, the directing hand of the author-moralist. To isolate the tragic in the complex of implications which modern psychological awareness both creates and finds in a work of art is a formidable assignment for the critic. But it is not an impossible one. Neither, as far as can be seen, need it be a sterile exercise, but rather a means of approach which still has something to contribute to the understanding of literature.

Index

Index

Hidden God, 165–6, 178–9; *see also* Goldmann, L.
Hoffmann, 189n.
Homer, 24, 26n., 113n.
Horace: *Ars Poetica*, 21
Horror, 32–4, 135, 261
Hubris, 80, 208n.
Hugo, Victor, 183

Ibsen, **192–213**, 214, 219, 222; *Brand*, 192; *Peer Gynt*, **192–7**, 210, 252; *Hedda Gabler*, **198–200**, 204, 209, 211, 218; *Ghosts*, **200–1**, 203, 204, 209; *Rosmersholm*, **202–4**, 206, 209, 211, 231; *The Master Builder*, **204–9**, 211; *Pillars of Society*, 209, 210, 211; *The Wild Duck*, 209, 211; *Little Eyolf*, 209, 211; *John Gabriel Borkman*, 210, 273
Idealism, 197–8, 209–10
Imagination, Pascal's conception of, 168–71; Blake's conception of, **172–6**, 177, 178, 180; 189–98, 221
Irony, 14–17; in *Oedipus*, 84–5; in *Macbeth*, 97; in *Phèdre*, 104–5

Jansenists, 67, 148–9, 166–7
Jehovah, 178–9, 249
Joan of Arc, 97n.
Johnson, Samuel, 63
Jung, C. G., 64n.

Kafka, 136
Karloff, Boris, 34n.
Keane, A. H., 64n.
Kern, Edith, 247n.
Keynes, Geoffrey (ed.): *Poetry and Prose of William Blake*, 173n.
Kierkegaard, 59
King in tragedy, 17, 49–52, 118, 123
Kitto, H. D. F.: *Form and Meaning in Drama*, ix, 90n.; *The Greeks*, 39–40
Kleist, Heinrich von, 59
Kyd, 95

Lamennais, 139–40, 146, 164
Lanson, G., 28n.
La Rochefoucauld, 158
Lawrence, D. H., 65n.
Lawton, H. W.: *Handbook of French Renaissance Dramatic Theory*, 48n.
Lenau, 58
León, Luis de, **142–7**, 150, 151
Leopardi, 58, 59
Love, transcendent, 185, 196, 226, 230–1, 236–7
Love-Caritas, 156, 157, 175
Love-Passion, 100, 102, 120–3, 151n., 198, 226, 231, 233, 236–7, 238, 240, 242–3, 244

McDougall, W., 63–4n.
Madariaga, S. de, 64n.
Maeterlinck, 62
Maistre, J. de, 186
Mallarmé, 194n.
Marlowe: *Dr Faustus*, 161, 184, 258
Marxist theory of tragedy; *see* Goldmann, L.
Maupassant, 214
Mauriac, François, 237–8, 241 and n.
Milton, 19
Miracle Plays, 48
Moi, the, 154; *see also Amour-propre*
Molière, 72, 185, 197, 198
Moore, Thomas, 62
Moorehead, Alan, 8n.
Moralities, 164
Musset, 183
Mystery Plays, 48

Naturalism, 190
Nature, 153–4, 155–6, 162–3, 174–5, 177
Nemorivich-Danchenko, 215n.
Neoplatonism, **141–7**, 163, 176–7; *see also* Plato
Nietzsche, 225, 238
Nobodaddy, **179**, 183, 185, 189, 249, 250
Nostalgia, 182

283

Index